ARGUMENT AS DIALOGUE
ACROSS DIFFERENCE

"I can think of no more timely, moral, and smart approach to literacy in and out of school than Jennifer Clifton's new book. Unless we humans learn to discuss critical issues with each other across differences in a joint journey, not to conversion, but to a better shared world there may soon be no livable world left for us."

James Paul Gee, *Mary Lou Fulton Presidential Professor of Literacy Studies and Regents' Professor, Arizona State University, USA*

"Jennifer Clifton's ideas should provoke teachers of argumentation—that is, all English, debate, and composition teachers—to re-think the nature of argument as well as their purposes and practices for teaching it. In thoughtful, but accessible prose that invites readers into dialogue, Clifton unpacks a theoretical and practice based stance that veers from the polarization so evident in contemporary society and instead offers innovative ways to engage wide-ranging perspectives within ever-changing and diverse contexts."

Bob Fecho, *Professor of English Education, Teachers College, Columbia University, USA*

"Clifton offers a theoretically rich and beautifully felt account of why we must teach argument as a means of positive social change in secondary through university classrooms. As Clifton notes, the stakes could not be higher, from police brutality and wage disparities, to marriage rights and access to clean water; how youth learn to argue together is fundamentally about crafting more equitable futures. Necessary reading for all of us who teach and study literacies, composition, and justice."

Django Paris, *Associate Professor, College of Education, Department of Teacher Education, Michigan State University, USA*

In the spirit of models of argument starting with inquiry, this book starts with a question: What might it mean to teach argument in ways that open up spaces for change—changes of mind, changes of practice and policy, changes in ways of talking and relating? The author explores teaching argument in ways that take into account the complexities and pluralities young people face as they attempt to enact local and global citizenship with others who may reasonably disagree. The focus is foremost on social action—the hard, hopeful work of finding productive ways forward in contexts where people need to work together across difference to get something worthwhile done.

Jennifer Clifton is Assistant Professor, Department of English (Rhetoric and Writing Studies), The University of Texas at El Paso, USA.

ARGUMENT AS DIALOGUE ACROSS DIFFERENCE

Engaging Youth in Public Literacies

Jennifer Clifton

Routledge
Taylor & Francis Group

NEW YORK AND LONDON

First published 2017
by Routledge
711 Third Avenue, New York, NY 10017

and by Routledge
2 Park Square, Milton Park, Abingdon, Oxon, OX14 4RN

Routledge is an imprint of the Taylor & Francis Group, an informa business

© 2017 Taylor & Francis

Library of Congress Cataloguing in Publication Data
Names: Clifton, Jennifer, author.
Title: Argument as dialogue across difference : engaging youth in public
  literacies / by Jennifer Clifton.
Description: New York, NY : Routledge, 2016. | Includes bibliographical
  references.
Identifiers: LCCN 2016028180 | ISBN 9781138665927 (hardback) |
  ISBN 9781138665934 (pbk.) | ISBN 9781315619590 (ebook)
Subjects: LCSH: Debates and debating—Study and teaching. |
  Rhetoric—Study and teaching. | Social interaction—Study and teaching.
Classification: LCC PE1431 .C59 2016 | DDC 808.53—dc23
LC record available at https://lccn.loc.gov/2016028180

ISBN: 978-1-138-66592-7 (hbk)
ISBN: 978-1-138-66593-4 (pbk)
ISBN: 978-1-315-61959-0 (ebk)

Typeset in Bembo
by Apex CoVantage, LLC

"Any decent society has to be built on trust and love and the intelligent use of information and feelings. Education involves being able to practice those things as you struggle to build a decent society that can be nonviolent."

— Myles Horton, *The Long Haul: An Autobiography*

CONTENTS

FIGURES

INTERLUDES: ENGAGING YOUTH IN PUBLIC LITERACIES

PREFACE

This book marks a long journey of trying to make sense of the ways we need each other and the ways we need to be able to call on and rely on one another in a limited world among imperfect people. Carolyn Miller (2010) notes that the problem isn't simply that some people are "dishonest rogues" and that we cannot reliably determine who the dishonest rogues are, but that a social situation where material resources, power, or knowledge are unevenly distributed may cast reasonable, mostly trustworthy people as adversaries. This book asks, Then *what?*

In response, this book proposes engaging youth in public literacies. It supports youth in both shared inquiry about the world "as it is" and shared invention of the world as it *ought to be* (Branch, 2007; Horton, 1961). It is exactly the contested and contingent nature of our everyday worlds that necessitates the development of expert *praxis* and practical rhetorical wisdom in public life. However, many writing textbooks and much of writing instruction about argument has traditionally focused on slow analytic reasoning (Bay, 2002; Knoblauch, 2011; Welch, 1987), which tends to impede situated expert performance, rather than focusing on "bodily involvement, speed, and an intimate knowledge of concrete cases" (Flyvbjerg, 2001, p. 15) necessary for the development of performative expertise (Dreyfus & Dreyfus, 1986).

Thus, engaging youth in public literacies entails coordinating *praxis* in public life—cultivating experience in uncertain terrain in which they must make decisions, take actions, and learn the effects of their actions. Engaging youth in public literacies puts students and teachers in a space to "grapple with the material realities of genre and access" (Atwill, 2010)—of the forums and tools available (to whom, for whom) and of what must be created and designed to enable the kind of political agency in pursuit of alternative futures that was once the primary aim of rhetorical instruction.

In the kinds of predicaments Miller (2010) describes, it is not clear what we should do. We must *determine* the best ends as well as the best means to pursue. And yet the very nature of an uncertain practical situation is that it is a situation that is not—perhaps cannot be—fully known. Often, what we've previously known—ends, means, resources, strategies—is now insufficient. We "must first decide—by practical deliberation—what *kind* of situation we are encountering, what is at stake, and how we might best respond. Having deliberated, we might then proceed" (Kemmis, 2012, p. 151). In public life, deliberation itself—argument as dialogue across difference—is also an uncertain situation, one in which it is not often clear what to do. This book commends well-supported experiences of uncertain terrain as youth learn to foster inclusive dialogue across difference, embrace a rhetorical pragmatism, and become agile performers in contemporary public life.

Quoting Hans-George Gadamer, Joseph Dunne (1993) notes: We never really graduate from the school of experience to a university of higher knowledge. "The perfect form of what we call 'experienced' does not consist in the fact that someone already knows everything and knows better than anyone else . . . the dialectic of experience has its own fulfillment not in definitive knowledge, but in that openness to experience that is encouraged by experience itself" (p. 131).

Youth learn that their words and actions have consequence in public life as they experience them having consequence, shaping the understanding of others, calling near and distant strangers and kin to consider together and to build together a world as it *ought to be.*

References

Atwill, J. M. (2010). *Rhetoric reclaimed: Aristotle and the liberal arts tradition.* Ithaca, NY: Cornell University Press.

Bay, J. L. (2002). The limits of argument: A response to Sean Williams. *Journal of Advanced Composition, 22,* 684–697.

Branch, K. (2007). *Eyes on the ought to be: What we teach when we teach about literacy.* Cresskill: Hampton Press.

Dunne, J. (1993). *Back to the rough ground: "Phronēsis" and "technē" in modern philosophy and Aristotle.* Notre Dame, IN: University of Notre Dame Press.

Horton, M. (1961). Myles Horton's talk at experimental citizenship school workshop, February 19–21. Highlander Archives, Box 40, folder 4, n.p. Monteagle, TN: Highlander Folk School.

Kemmis, S. (2012). Phronesis, experience, and the primacy of praxis. In E. A. Kinsella & A. Pitman (Eds.), *Phronesis as professional knowledge: Practical wisdom in the professions* (pp. 147–162). Rotterdam, Netherlands: Sense Publishers.

Knoblauch, A. A. (2011). A textbook argument: Definitions of argument in leading composition textbooks. *College Communication and Composition, 63*(2), 244–268.

Miller, C. (2010). Should we name the tools? Concealing and revealing the art of rhetoric. In Ackerman & D. J. Coogan (Eds.), *The public work of rhetoric: Citizen-scholars and civic engagement* (pp. 56–75). Columbia, SC: University of South Carolina Press.

Welch, K. E. (1987). Ideology and freshman textbook production: The place of theory in writing pedagogy. *College Composition and Communication, 38*(3), 269–282.

ACKNOWLEDGMENTS

I am deeply grateful to the decades of work Wayne Peck, Joyce Baskins, Linda Flower, Elenore Long, Lorraine Higgins, and others did with youth like Mark Howard at the Community House. You are my Scattered Church. Your work infuses my thinking in this book in ways that citations don't adequately account for.

Deep thanks to the young people I taught and coached, laughed, loved, and learned with in the classroom and on the basketball court; to my friends and colleagues at Cartersville Middle School and Calhoun Middle School in Georgia. My time with you was foundational and has shaped much of what I've been up to since.

I've learned so much with and from youth and teachers in Phoenix, AZ; Columbia, MO; and El Paso, TX. Thanks for being so generous with your time and energy. Many other pre-service, new, and veteran 6–12 teachers as well as FYC teachers across the country have helped shape and test these ideas and practices: Thank you! I am particularly grateful to Steve Scott and eighth graders in mid-Missouri who care deeply about the worlds they inhabit. Working with Julie Sheerman and her dual-credit seniors has been a delight and enormously helpful for thinking about public literacies in rural towns.

I want to thank Naomi Silverman at Routledge for letting me write what we both knew might be a timely and much needed but potentially contested book. Thanks to David Bloome for seeing the promise of this book and for turning me on to the work of the team at Ohio State University. David, this book is a different book, the book I wanted to write, because of your review of the prospectus. Thank you! Thanks, too, to Katherine Tsamparlis, Autumn Spalding, Danielle Fontaine and their teams for their adept and careful handling of so many moving parts. "Reviewer 2": This election cycle and your review that equated conflict in public life with a small "Fox News fringe" let me know just how much this work is needed.

Thanks to Bob Fecho who read early, messy drafts. Any place you see a "framing paragraph" that lets you know what's coming next, you can thank Bob. Thanks to Rachel Pinnow for reading early drafts of what would eventually become this book. I am incredibly grateful to Sidouane Patcha Lum who read and edited early drafts and helped with citations; I'm not sure you knew what you were getting into, but your work saved me time and energy I desperately needed—thank you.

Thanks to the Missouri Writing Project Network folks, especially Katie Kline at UMKC and the justice-oriented teachers of the UMSL project. Whether you knew it or not, your enthusiasm for these ideas was, and continues to be, such a gift.

Thanks to the University of Missouri's Campus Writing Program, and Amy Lannin in particular, for internal funding that allowed me to pursue and test these ideas with youth and teachers. I am grateful to Selena Van Horn, Kathryn Fishman Weaver, Justin Sigoloff, Irene Wan, Colleen Cleary, and Laura Darolia for thinking together with me about methods and public deliberation in a Photovoice class, sponsored by the Missouri Writing Project and the Campus Writing Program at MU. Selena and Laura, thanks for teaching me that second graders are paying attention and that public literacies are for them, too. Thanks to a whole host of folks at MU who worked with me for two years to pursue an NSF grant based on this work. You are the dream team.

I owe a debt of gratitude to Beth Daniell and Mary Lou Odom, who knew I was a rhet-comp person before I did. I am grateful to Carol Harrell for her solidarity and shepherding in and out of graduate school. The faculty at Kennesaw State are some of the finest there are: you all have embodied a soulful nurturing that marks the best of public education and public institutions.

Shirley Rose's stance as a WPA at ASU was foundational. In her words, "our ideas have to matter." Shirley, these ideas would not have come to fruition in the same way without being able to test them with students in my First Year Composition courses. Thank you for protecting those courses and TA training as sites of the messy but important work of knowledge-building for me and for students. Rebecca Dingo and Donna Strickland, your presence at MU and at a distance was and is great comfort. Donna, I will never forget your shout out—"YES!!"—at my job talk. Everyone needs to experience a moment like that. Thanks to Helen Foster, a dear friend, drinking buddy, and solid ally. Thanks to Kevin Brooks, who knows the stochastic nature of this work better than most. Thanks to Tap, Samra, Saher, Dahlila, Roda, and William: Because slung as we are between the *is* and the *ought to be,* despair is not an option; this work is for and with you. Finally, thanks to Elenore Long, Django Paris, Jim Gee, and Doris Warriner: Your ideas and your friendship are all over this book.

INTRODUCTION

"This isn't a problem in our community. We are all friends, we all get along at this school." These are the words one girl spoke and others echoed in a Phoenix-area high school English class on the Day of Remembrance in fall 2010, as young people at this school and across the nation wore purple shirts and gathered at flagpoles to remember 15 gay youth who killed themselves in response to the ways they were being treated in schools.

For Nate Boswell,[1] a gay student teacher, this day was especially important. He explained, "[S]tatistics of it are interesting to me because September is the beginning of a school year, . . . and these kids [were] already being bullied to the point where they took their own lives. It was really upsetting."

That there was a public Day of Remembrance that students participated in seems to mark a shared issue of concern. And yet, Nate remembers:

> [I]n the morning . . . when the bell rang for class, there were just a bunch of people in the hallway like, "Oh, it's gay pride; it's gay pride," . . . and that's not what the purple was there for at all. It wasn't gay pride in any way. It was a remembrance for these kids that were being bullied in many ways—cyber-bulling and face-to-face in the schools—because of their sexuality, because they didn't fit into these molds that people expect boys and girls to fit into. . . . Some students were wearing purple and didn't even know why.

What was an important issue for some of the students and teachers at the high school was misunderstood by others, even some of the students who participated locally in this event of national importance. Even more disconcerting to Nate and to students in the class who experienced day-to-day taunting and violence from their peers was the realization that not everyone agreed that the suicides or bullying were issues of public concern or that these were local issues, affecting people they knew.

This situation—with its competing logics and conflicting understandings and experiences—is not out of the ordinary either for our schools or for what public sphere's theorist Nancy Fraser (1989) terms "actually existing democracy" (p. 56). Even in the most democratic moments of day-to-day life where people "have a voice" and offer their vote—by casting a ballot in a voting booth, by wearing a purple shirt, by "like-ing" something on the internet—the "life-world disturbances" (Habermas, 1996, p. 173) motivating them to go public are often isolated from public dialogue. And yet, those life-world disturbances are the very things they hope garner not only more public attention but also public deliberation and public action. Momentary performances of solidarity at a flagpole or of protest at a rally may garner more public attention, but without contexts and tools to support dialogue across difference, those most removed from the concern being raised may not have a sense of what it is they are being called to attend to. What some see as a point of stasis—the central issue of a dispute—may not circulate in ways that do justice to the experiences of those most closely connected to the life-world disturbance being named. In order to do justice to those experiences, we—and the young people we teach—need tools for engaging conflicts in ways that are capable of calling people with divergent interests to the table.

It is through deliberation together that we "clarif[y] problems, risks, and possibilities we face as humans and societies" (Flyvbjerg, 2011, p. 4), frame (and then re-frame) issues of shared concern, and weigh possible courses of action. But if the confusion over the Day of Remembrance is any indication, greater visibility and broader circulation alone are not enough to call people into productive dialogue across difference.

Typically, when students engage in debate in a classroom, they take an adversarial approach and argue along binary lines: the problem is this or it's that. But this binary thinking that maintains a predetermined point of stasis, a point of impasse, refuses to be open to other ways of seeing or constructing a "point at which discourse *ought* to begin" (Foster, 2005) and often oversimplifies, generalizes, and perhaps even distorts the many related and interweaving concerns that may need to be co-constructed, discovered, and addressed. In this adversarial and binary approach, as debaters encounter resistance and a competing claim, they typically become more aggressive in their arguments. Resistance and competing perspectives, they think, signal that they might lose the debate, so they push on with a louder voice, a stronger argument, a more polished pitch. But this version of debate or deliberation becomes less inclusive, not more. Neither does this dig-in-your-heels approach lead to cognitive flexibility—the "ability to flexibly shift between multiple seemingly incompatible perspectives or descriptions of an object or event" (Farrant, Fletcher, & Maybery, 2014, p. 1)—an important ability for complex problem-solving and for developing the capacity to seriously consider explanations and rationales that might inform a person's own perspectives and behaviors as well as others' (Farrant, Fletcher, & Maybery, 2014, p. 2). Nor does a binary approach lend itself to navigating through complexity, to discovering new understandings, or to fostering the invention of alternative options.

Considering the perspectives of multiple stakeholders is one step toward exploding the notion that there are only one or two ways of seeing an issue, one or two ways of framing a point of stasis, one or two ways of addressing a shared concern—predominant myths that circulate in practices of teaching argument even if language about teaching argument nods at more expansive concepts (Bay, 2002; Knoblauch, 2011; Welch, 2010). Importantly, developing cognitive flexibility is also integral to developing more just relations with the self and others because considering multiple seemingly incompatible perspectives and being able to conceptualize a range of possible values, beliefs, experiences, and rationales that might inform those perspectives is also necessary for casting the self and others in more complex terms than a simple right or wrong.

However, this kind of deliberation is seldom fostered in the ways argument is taught in English Language Arts or First-Year Composition classrooms nor in the ways many of us experience argument with others. It was certainly missing from the Day of Remembrance scene. Students simply saw purple shirts and assumed they knew the central concern—the point of stasis or impasse—that was being raised. Even those who wore purple shirts were not necessarily all expressing concern about the same shared issue. Youth experience and "read" these conflicts in real time, without any way to hit the pause button, so to speak, and freeze-frame the conflicted situations in order to slow down and put competing perspectives up for dialogue, we and the youth we teach often continue to read experiences—our own or others—for the ways they map onto our already existing pet theories. And yet, if we and the youth we teach do not have forums where concerns can be raised and related issues named, the concerns youth express may never get addressed in ways that take their experiences seriously, let alone in ways that bring about change.

Argument and Public Life

In classrooms and in public life, there is little agreement on what the term *argument* might mean, or how critical inquiry and processes of argumentation might be productively supported. An "argument" can be something a person *does* (a process), or something one *makes* (a product); these tend to be the two most common ways of thinking and talking about argument. Argument as a product is often measured by its logic, its ability to hold up to critical scrutiny or probative reasoning; argument as a process is often measured by its persuasive appeals and ability to sway. However, these models often conceptualize and instantiate argument as claim-driven, monologic, and adversarial. Thinking about argument in this way and teaching or operationalizing argument in this way is often not productive for doing the kind of complex problem-solving and deliberation people most often need to do in public life. In an era where disagreement perhaps characterizes public life, simply advancing one's own positions only works to further solidify enclaves where people already agree (Roberts-Miller, 2004) and to fragment and further distance those who disagree.

A priori claims are often insufficient to understand, let alone address, the complexities of shared concerns. In their day-to-day lives, "young people are faced with questions that transcend their own local experiences and are permeated by global forces and factors" (Appadurai, 2006, p. 175), making it difficult for people with strictly local knowledge to improve their circumstances. Like the young people we teach, many of us experience what Moisés Naím, editor of *Foreign Policy*, describes as

> a general anxiety about globalization because there is a sense that there are changes going on that are touching all of us, and we don't know how, at the end of the day, our families, ourselves, our companies, our communities are going to end up being hit or not hit.
>
> *(Barfield, Glassman, & Naím, 2008, n.p.)*

In an era of mass immigration, globalizing technologies, and globalized markets, young people need to be able to make sense of the many systems they find themselves connected to and impacted by, perhaps unknowingly.

To make sense of a complex, rapidly changing world and to ensure the systems they find themselves part of work equitably for them and others, young people also need to be able to enact public life with others in ways that extend beyond circulating ready-made ideas, voting, "like-ing" and sharing something online, and even beyond well-intentioned claim-driven advocacy. Instead, youth need to be able to call on strangers near and far to be in solidarity; to pool their divergent experiences, perspectives, and expertise for collaborative inquiry and problem-solving; and to co-construct equitable ways forward with others, always revisable in the face of new data, changed conditions, or alternative experiences.

While scholars (Foss & Griffin, 1995; Hillocks, 2011; Newell, Bloome, & Hirvela, 2015; Smagorinsky et al., 2011) have noted the insufficiencies of claim-driven argument, something I'll take up more in Chapter 2, as Abby Knoblauch (2011) and Nancy Welch (2010) point out, in practice, even alternative models are often re-tooled as another version of traditional adversarial argument—a version idealized in metaphors of chess matches or fencing bouts and whose end goal is to vanquish opponents. This version is particularly troubling for public life, as adversarial argument, the dominant model taught in ELA and FYC classrooms does not typically value difference. And yet inclusive public life, by definition, includes and values—rather than vanquishes—difference.

People with quite different histories, cultures, backgrounds, and perspectives need public resources like schools, roads, infrastructure for water and sanitation, open spaces and parks, equitable laws, and so on to work for them. Making these work or changing them when they don't work are not things an individual can do on his or her own. Neither, however, are these merely concerns of government; they are, instead, primarily the concerns of everyday people whose lives depend on such systems working for them. In relation to these systems and the human needs these systems support, the lives of strangers are, thus, interdependently intertwined. People tend to become more aware of this interdependence, when systems don't work or when new needs or conditions emerge, and they need to be able to call on strangers to collaboratively work together across difference to create more effective and equitable options going forward.

These tensions between the demands of public life and the aims of traditional models of argument present quite a conundrum if we consider that a broad goal of education is to prepare young people for full participation in economic and public life. Strengthening *a priori* claims and vanquishing opponents are, at best, simply ineffective in a complex and rapidly changing world and, at worst, unjust in a pluralistic society.

The pragmatic bent of public life presents another area of tension with traditional argument. People often have to act under constraints of time and space, with limited knowledge, uncertain of how others will respond, how their choices will impact others, or whether they've chosen the best course of action. Sometimes their decisions impact them and others in ways they didn't anticipate, in ways that are harmful, regrettable. Sometimes they must act in the face of equally painful options and with others who reasonably disagree. And yet in the face of uncertainty, conflict, and difference, people are often faced with needs and urgencies that demand action. Adversarial models of argument, however, often focus on generalizable issues and pretend to more certainty than is helpful or wise in light of the perspectival or pragmatic nature of public life. In fact, scholars have documented that one major reason that megaprojects, like bridges or tunnels, get off budget and off schedule so quickly and reliably is that contractors must pretend to a certainty in their bids that they cannot guarantee; thus, their bids are at best, guesses and at worst, lies (Flyvbjerg, 2005).

Finally, traditional models of argument do little to account for relations of power and the ways those play out not only in everyday life but also in conceptual and practical models of argument. Indeed, adversarial models of argument often enact dominance as a primary and desirable aim of argument without interrogating the ways relations of power inform and produce versions of rationality and reasonability—cuing what aims are worthwhile and possible (or not) and which ideas and people are reasonable (or not).

These conundrums are at the heart of this book. I write in response to my own "felt difficulties" (Dewey, 1998, p. 107) at this intersection of argument and public life. In particular, I take the limitations of current ways of thinking about and teaching argument in English Language Arts and First-Year Composition classrooms as a starting point for conceptualizing argument-in-practice as collaborative and inventive social practices capable of meeting the demands of contemporary public life.

Thus, this book considers *what it might mean to re-think and re-tool argument as dialogue across difference* in classrooms, "where cultures meet, clash and grapple with each other, often in contexts of highly asymmetrical relations of power" (Pratt, 1991, p. 444). Precisely, I ask: What might be entailed in re-thinking and re-tooling argument as dialogue across difference *for public life*, where any of us need to be able to leverage multi-literacies to construct just relationships and practices, to share and distribute common resources, and to interrogate and re-write policies and ways of being together with others who may reasonably disagree?

Limitations as Sites of Knowledge Building

In this next section, I'll describe the ways Nate attempted to construct a discussion about the Day of Remembrance in his classroom. Surely, facilitating productive dialogue across difference is not easy whether it's done in response to something that arises unexpectedly or whether it's part of planned instruction. Our attempts are always in progress and tentative, even at their best and most well-tooled. You'll notice some of Nate's difficulties in what Nate recounts and where he expresses his own frustration. The students in the class, even those he disagrees with, would likely note still other limitations and other frustrations. You may notice still others. You'll also see the ways adversarial argument rears its head even in Nate's well-intentioned work as he initially describes students in oversimplified and stereotypical ways and later casts the discussion in terms of "sides" and winning or losing. Especially in light of the ways Nate and his students brushed up against the limitations of adversarial argument, Nate's attempts to scaffold dialogue across difference raise important questions regarding argument and public life—questions that frame the work of the remaining chapters.

Setting aside his planned instruction on the Day of Remembrance, Nate showed a short YouTube video of a city councilman from Texas who was using the television time of the city council meeting to speak about the 15 suicides. He began with one that occurred near Fort Worth. The councilman was sympathizing with youth who had experienced years of bullying and with their families because their children had taken their own lives in response. As Nate explained it, the city councilman told his own story of "how he had come out and how he had overcome bullying." The city councilman alluded to his own suicide attempt as well. Nate recalled that the video is "powerful, very, very powerful. . . . [The councilman's] kind of just addressing the message that it gets better, it gets better."

Nate recognized this as a timely and relevant issue because of the ways he saw his students relating:

> And you know the dynamic in the classroom, in all of my classrooms, is actually—well, you've got the popular kids and then the slackers, and you've got these kids who are quiet and sit off to the side and don't really fit into any other group. . . . I see that some of these students are in the same class

as the people that bully them. You know, they get bullied and their bullies are a couple of rows down. I know they're bullied because one student complained because I moved the seating chart around a couple of weeks ago and he came to me and said, "I can't sit next to these guys. You have to move me. Please." So I did that. That was in one of the senior classes.

On the Day of Remembrance, students watched the video, wrote reflections, read them out loud and discussed their reflections in class. In the discussion, students framed the issue in different ways, sometimes shifting what someone else had named as a point of stasis—the question the issue turned on. Nate explained:

> There were a couple of outspoken students who, you know . . . were like, "Suicide is dumb. Whoever commits suicide is a coward. They can't face things in their own lives." And as a person—I won't say as an educator—but as a person who has gone through adversity like that, and, you know, having the discussions speak to me so personally, like "Oh, you're just going to address it as cowardice," you know, and say that they're too scared to face their demons or something like that, that's why they committed suicide. How dare these kids—the outspoken ones who are the bullies—say that because they've never experienced that before. They don't know how it feels.

Later in our conversation, Nate described a particularly poignant moment in class that day—one in which students had very different responses to the video they'd just seen, some not even acknowledging bullying as a local issue. Nate recounted:

> There was one student who during the video started crying. She had had a history of being bullied as well. . . . She started crying in class . . . she reacted very powerfully to the video; it was really heartbreaking to see that. So I felt like it was a necessary message and a necessary step to take in the classroom. She [the girl who was crying] was sitting in the corner, the back corner of the classroom.
>
> One of the popular girls on the other side of the room said, "That kind of bullying doesn't happen in this school. This isn't a problem in our community. We are all friends, we all get along at this school."
>
> I asked her, "How can you say that? How can you say that when we've got someone over here crying? This issue clearly touches some people very personally. We've got another person in this classroom crying . . .'"
>
> She said, "Well, my friends and I don't do that."
>
> I said, "But do you do anything about it? Do you do anything when you see it happen? You're not unbiased. If you don't take action, you're passively supporting or submitting to whichever side is winning."

Even as Nate attempts to construct a discussion in which people who ordinarily might not talk with one another will listen and learn from one another, he seems to find it difficult to listen and learn from those students he disagrees with, to construct their differences as sites of mutual inquiry and knowledge building. And it's unlikely that the student who thinks of suicide as cowardice is any more inclined to listen and learn about the experiences of gay youth—especially from gay youth. These instances where we most heatedly disagree often point to concerns that matter a great deal to us or to others and point to concerns where we most need argument to be transformative. But doing argument or teaching argument in ways that don't simply re-instate the status quo or power differentials or staunch positions is no easy task—for Nate or for any of us. And yet, these kinds of instances—where differences are most volatile, where systems bear down unevenly, where people's responses to each other matter, and where some people's experiences indicate that something needs to change—are where our "ways with words" (Heath, 1983) also matter most and where teaching argument in terms of inclusive public life might hold the most promise.

In considering possibilities for transforming practices for doing and teaching argument, think about the ways Nate's efforts, as well as their difficulties and limitations, raise some important questions about argument and public life:

- *How do we co-construct what needs to be deliberated with others?* Some students were disturbed by what they saw as a showing of "gay pride." Others were saddened and angered by the bullying LGBTQ students face on a daily basis across the nation. Others thought the suicides were personal issues that only affected those 15 individuals. Others thought bullying might happen but wasn't something that directly affected them personally. How do they determine what, if anything, needs to be talked about?
- *How do we construct shared concerns? How do we learn to listen for concerns that deserve more public attention?* One student constructed suicide as cowardice and seemed to imply that suicide was a personal, private matter. Another student didn't think talking about suicides or bullying was relevant to her or her friends. And yet 15 youth were dead, a classmate was crying across the room, videos were circulating on YouTube, and students across the country were gathering at flagpoles. What might entice the student talking about suicide or the girl dismissing concerns about bullying to *share* the concerns of the girl crying or the students at the flagpole or of Nate, even if they don't share those concerns in the same way or to the same degree?
- *On what do we base our claims, experiences, conclusions, and lines of reasoning? What do we do with competing claims, experiences, conclusions, and lines of reasoning?* The young woman who insists that bullying doesn't happen at her school based her claim on her own experiences and the experiences of those she knew best. Her insistence and unwillingness to entertain other possibilities, at least on that day, seems to assume that she and her friends know fully what

happens in school and in her town or that she thinks all of her schoolmates' experiences are the same as hers or perhaps even that those who are not her friends don't count. Her qualifying remarks that she and her friends don't bully also suggest some assumptions about who she sees herself responsible for and to and, especially, about the limits of her responsibilities. The claims people say out loud and act on rely on assumptions and values that are often unarticulated and that have to some degree become stabilized for them. The claims people make visible through language, materials, and actions are also often tangled, intertwined with other claims that rest on still other assumptions. These claims and assumptions, however, are not universal but decidedly situated and rhetorical, networked and relational, ideological and agentive. These hidden logics, seldom voiced, are often as much about what we do with people as they are about what we do with data. These assumptions under the surface often become sticking points if they, too, are not discussed, bringing the possibility of productive argument to a screeching halt.

- *How do we make sense of conflicting experiences? What do we do with experiences that don't match ours or that directly contradict our experiences? How do we talk about and with each other—when others' experiences and/or values do not match ours?* The student who calls suicide cowardly marks one familiar way of making sense of others' experiences—framing a person's experiences, and thus, that person, as lacking in character or in morality. The student who says bullying is not a problem at her school marks another way of making sense of conflicting experiences—to distance them in some way. Importantly, these moves shrink public life and dialogue across difference, constructing relationships with strangers around superiority and inferiority or denying a person's alternative experience as worthy of the attention of strangers.

- *How might we imagine the self—our own and others'—in more dialogical ways?* At one point, Nate acknowledges seeing his self as multiple—distinguishing who he is as a human, as an educator, and also as a gay man who has experienced bullying. By marking this distinction, he also acknowledges that his different subjectivities offer him different ways of understanding and responding to the same situation. Though he uses sweeping language, Nate also acknowledges that individual students inhabit multiple subject positions simultaneously, for example, as a popular kid, a bully, and a boy, or as a quiet student, a lesbian, and someone who is bullied. Perhaps the girl crying in the corner is also an ROTC cadet, a cross-country runner, and indigenous. How might her various I-positions (Hermans & Hermans-Konopka, 2010) help inform her and others' thinking? How might she call on different intersectional identities as a self-in-dialogue (Hermans & Hermans-Konopka, 2010)? How might Nate and the other students also engage as dialogical selves transacting with and synthesizing across a whole host of cultural and institutional identities internally and externally? How might they call on their multicultural selves transacting in multicultural contexts to construct more expansive understandings and to offer a more generative range of possibilities for dialoguing internally and externally with the self and with others (Fecho & Clifton, 2017)?

- *How might we re-imagine the work of argument not as a contest or a stand-off of two "sides" but as inquiry and knowledge building?* Nate and the two more vocal students he described all seem to see the discussion they're having as adversarial in some way. Nate seems to be trying to persuade, while the two students try to fend off his claims and launch some of their own. If they and others are going to be in conversation in ways that aren't simply about stand-offs and impasses, they will need to see themselves and others differently in ways that account for the multiplicity and dialogism of stakeholders, histories, and so on, and in ways that re-figure the aims and practices of argument.

These questions, focused on a novice teacher's best efforts at trying to transform grist into a site of knowledge building and dialogue across difference, suggest something about the ways current practices for teaching argument often do not attend to or account for or support the complexities young people encounter when they try to engage in productive argument with others. They also point to the limitations of viewing public life primarily in terms of going public and suggest the possibility of theorizing and *tooling* argument as productive and expansive dialogue across difference in the context of deliberative public life—an intersection that is the focus of this book.

But Why Public Literacies?

Decades' worth of scholarship in literacy studies has shown that a student's ability to remember facts or formulas or forms for a test does not necessarily mean that that student would be able to discern in another situation what to *do* with those facts, or even which facts might be helpful for understanding a phenomenon or for addressing a particular problem in a meaningful way (Barton & Hamilton, 1998; Collins & Blot, 2003; Gee, 1991; Hull, 1993; Scribner & Cole, 1981). To isolate knowing from doing is to limit the ways young people learn to leverage literate practices and, thus, the ways they imagine possibilities for being and becoming.

Literacies are, after all, learned in the doing. None of the subjects we teach in schools or universities are merely a collection of static facts. Each is, instead, its own buzzing ecology of activity systems, or as James Gee (2005) puts it, "a 'game' certain types of people 'play'" (p. 34). Using biology as an example, Gee writes:

> These people engage in characteristic sorts of activities, use characteristic sorts of tools and language, and hold certain values; that is, they play by a certain set of "rules". They *do* biology. Of course, they learn, use, and retain lots and lots of facts—even produce them—but the facts come

from and with the doing. Left out of the context of biology as activity, biological facts are trivia.

(p. 34)

In schools, then, when students are learning biology or art or history, they should be learning to play that "game," to *be* players in that game. The literate practices (Scribner & Cole, 1981) of a biologist are best learned in the context of doing biology, becoming a biologist.

For those of us who teach language and literacies, writing and rhetoric, this raises an important question: What is the "game" of argument? What is argument good for in the world? What role might argument play in our everyday lives, in carving out good work with others, in inviting others to share our concerns, in testing out possible futures? In other words, what might the "game" of argument be in public life?

By framing these questions this way, I aim to focus on and situate argument within a larger need for inclusive and just public life so that the particular work we need to do with strangers informs the ways we think about and do argument—and perhaps especially the ways we re-imagine and re-invent argument and public life. These questions are also deliberately framed in the language of possibility, perhaps the language best suited to public life. The focus, with regard to teaching and learning public literacies, is, thus, not on producing isolated skills or forms, but on how young people become critically and rhetorically savvy in leveraging their literacies-in-practice to do real work they set for themselves. It is the hope of creating possibilities that don't yet exist that coordinates the productive use of argument with others in public life. And this work—of shared hoping and collaborating, of deliberating over the *is* and the *ought to be*—is the project of public literacies. It is this work that creates an impetus for reading, writing, designing, researching, talking, imagining, and acting together in public life.

Situating literate practices in the present need for and hopeful possibility of transformative public life also suggests a need for critical literacy to be embedded within public literacies. As I'll unpack a bit more in Chapter 1, this includes making sense of the rather ordinary ways texts order and reproduce power relations and systems of oppression (Bourdieu, 2000; Dryer, 2008; Hull, 1993) and leveraging literate practices to change relations of power and dominant structures that work for some, but not others (Freire & Macedo, 1987).

If deliberative engagement is to actually do public work, public literacies that coordinate argument as dialogue across difference must support personal and public discovery and change (Young, Becker, & Pike, 1970). Given the predominant models of argument, this must involve not only discovery and change regarding the issue at hand but also about argument itself. Thus, a critical approach to public literacies also looks at the ways discourse *about* argument and public life produces particular versions of argument and public life and orients people as particular kinds of people—opponents, adversaries, winners or losers, collaborators, researchers, etc.—engaged with others in particular kinds of work. These orientations toward public life and toward others also cue people's expectations and demands regarding which concerns "count" as public concerns and which ways of talking, relating, and writing together are "appropriate" or not. As important for sustaining public life under contemporary conditions is the need to attend to the ways systems actively co-opt, usurp, or otherwise re-figure public life as well as the tools and stances—especially the values and reasonabilities—we need to be able to call on with strangers in public life.

Although Enlightenment era models of public life and many pedagogies of traditional argument bracket people's multiple literacies—something I'll unpack a bit more in Chapter 2—public literacies make space for the multiple literacies as well as the situated and value-laden expertise people bring to deliberative publics. Of course, these literacies are not neutral; they are instead ideological, reflecting and enacting social and cultural values, as well as political, differently connected to power relations. Therefore, young people also need to be able to determine which literacies others expect in certain situations, how to enact those literacies wisely and well, what is at stake in enacting those literacies—what stands to be gained or lost and to what degree—and when and how those literacies, including the practices and the relationships they construct, may need to be revised and transformed.

Engaging youth in public literacies transforms and re-contextualizes argument as dialogue across difference in public life, foregrounding rhetorical expertise and its importance in public life rather than isolated text types or cognitive processes. Focusing on rhetorical expertise in public life re-imagines writing instruction and especially argument instruction around the activities of deliberative publics and focuses on real time, iterative judgments and actions (that sometimes involve texts) to construct inclusive public life with others across difference. Rather than valuing the rule-driven model of expertise instantiated in teaching argument as text types or argument as cognitive processes, public literacies recognize:

> True expertise is based on *intimate experience* with thousands of individual cases and on the ability to discriminate *between* situations with all their nuances of difference, without distilling them into formulas or standard cases. Experts do not use rules but operate on the basis of detailed case experience. This is *real* expertise. The rules for expert systems are formulated only because the systems require it; rules are characteristic of expert *systems*, but not of real human *experts*.
>
> *(Flyvbjerg, 2011, p. 312, emphasis added)*

In particular, public literacies frame the expert work of deliberative publics as inquiry and invention—work that, in the context of public life, necessitates dialogue across difference. Rather than stabilize difference or argument or expertise, I invite you to consider with me not only how these do work together in public life but also, and perhaps more importantly, how they *could* work together in public life. In other words, I am inviting you to join me in a space of inquiry and invention about the world as it "ought to be" (Branch, 2007; Horton, 1961)—a quest at the very heart of public life.

Overall, this book offers a framework for public literacies that instantiates five core commitments for young people engaging in public life: (1) accessing and attending to public and yet-to-be-public concerns; (2) fostering inclusive public dialogue across difference; (3) embracing a productive rhetorical pragmatism; (4) becoming agile performers in contemporary public life; and (5) generating conditions, forums, tools, and practices for contemporary public life. The remaining chapters theorize, unpack, illustrate, and tool these commitments, contextualizing argument within the activities of deliberative publics.

What to Expect From This Book

Rather than reading for specific practices—although I think you'll find some useful ones in the coming chapters—I instead invite you to read this book as a heuristic for thinking about what you and the young people you teach most need—and most need to invent—with regard to constructing inclusive and generative practices for argument and public life.

A significant aim of this book is to unpack and bring to the fore important concepts and assumptions that are often tacit in the ways we imagine and operationalize argument and public life. In particular, I attend to those concepts—that is, rationalities, reasonabilities, polity, commons—that have the most significant implications for self–other relations because stranger relationality (Warner, 2005) is both central to public life and often neglected in teaching argument. As media, migration, and the market have at once expanded and shrunk the ways we see and experience the world, so, too, are they impacting the ways we experience uncertainty, conflict, and difference (at the heart of argument) as well as what we share, how, and with whom (at the heart of public life). This book considers what some of these changes might mean for ways we conceptualize argument in public life. Because argument and public life both call on language to address uncertainty, conflict, and difference and to bring about changed minds and changed worlds, *and* as importantly, because our work in ELA and FYC classrooms informs young people's ways with words, I also spend time unpacking some assumptions embedded in common ways of thinking about language, knowing, texts, and social practices.

This book also suggests that there is a significant metacognitive component to argument and public life and the ways they are tangled together; in deliberating publicly about security in schools or student loan debt, for example, we are, in addition to constructing claims about guns or education, also producing public life and operationalizing a theory of how argument does and should work, both of which also always need to be on the table for deliberation. Thus, this book theorizes limitations of argument as sites of knowledge building and aims to support youth in the inventive work of critically re-imagining and rhetorically inventing social practices of argument in public life. That is, I take a means and ends approach to teaching and doing argument as dialogue across difference and to engaging youth in public literacies. When we argue, we argue about *something*. But in public life, the life of the public *is* the thing. The question, then, is, *How do we do argue about a shared concern in a way that fosters healthy publics?* This book offers some possibilities and suggests ways of scaffolding that work with youth.

Chapter 1 focuses on the social aims and social relationships people construct in argument and public life. In addition to teasing out distinctions between rationalities and reasonabilities, I also take up relations of power, especially as they are perpetuated in systematized rationalities and reasonabilities. Marking moments when people experience existing systems as disruptive to their lives, I distinguish the work of "going public" from the work of creating publics that cultivate further argument. As calling a deliberative public into being requires response from strangers who agree, at least temporarily, to share concerns, I theorize some of the difficulties and rhetorical work of constructing polity with others. Finally, this chapter marks a departure from the certainty of claims circulated in traditional adversarial argument and instead prizes contingent knowledge building as the primary work of argument and public life—work that necessitates dialogue across difference.

Chapter 2 turns to predominant models of argument taught in ELA and FYC classrooms, noting the ways even alternative models are often a re-tooling of traditional argument that aim at producing a text type. Expanding Chapter 1's discussion of rationalities and reasonabilities and weaving together contemporary genre theories, Chapter 2 conceptualizes argument beyond text types, emphasizing both the social action and the activity systems of familiar responses to recurring situations. I also note the ways everyday genre ecologies distribute and normalize, cue and produce rationalities and reasonabilities and power relations. With regard to public life, this chapter continues discussion of "life-world disturbances" (Habermas, 1996), which often mark concerns that need more public attention and public dialogue. As mass migration, global markets, and globalizing technologies are impacting and changing the ways people experience life-world disturbances and find themselves interdependently intertwined with others, this chapter also conceptualizes public life—especially polity and the commons—under contemporary conditions.

Chapter 3 considers how an idea becomes a shared, public concern and focuses on public listening as a means of attending to life-world disturbances that may indicate a public or yet-to-be public concern that warrants further dialogue. This chapter considers alternatives to "walking in someone else's shoes" since calling strangers to attend to concerns anticipates response that is not predicated on someone else having the same experiences. In addition to offering three types of critical incidents that might indicate shared concerns, I also introduce possibilities of leveraging inventive, hybridized texts to construct and invite alternative social practices of argument, including dramatizing and freeze-framing incidents in order to cultivate argument and scaffold deliberation that attends to what is situated and systematized, values multiple perspectives, and recognizes and negotiates multiple points of stasis. Ultimately, this chapter suggests and invites practices for critically re-imagining and rhetorically inventing more just and generative options for argument and public life, leveraging tools-in-use to construct and coordinate social activities of public life.

Chapter 4 theorizes the centrality of experience to public literacies—especially the experience of making live, uncertain choices and learning their consequences. In contrast to the certainty and self–other relations often invoked or implied by traditional argument, this chapter demonstrates the limitations of traditional argument in relation to the uncertainties of life-world disturbances youth name and experience. Circling back to provisional knowing and the need for argument discussed in Chapter 1, Chapter 4 distinguishes generalizable or propositional knowledge as insufficient for knowing what to do in the face of the uncertainty of felt difficulties and of public life. The chapter commends experience as the means by which youth gain rhetorical expertise and practical wisdom to re-cast argument as dialogue across difference in contemporary public life.

Finally, throughout the book, you'll find interludes that offer strategies, tools, and case studies as a way of making visible, as well as do-able and teach-able, some possibilities for engaging youth in public literacies. The number of interludes per chapter increases as the book goes along, with Chapters 1 and 2 focusing on creating shared and sustained inquiry that cultivates sensibilities and performative practices for attending to public and yet-to-be public concerns and for making sense of people-in-systems and situations-in-systems. The interludes in Chapters 3 and 4 move toward supporting and showcasing youth conceptualizing and doing argument as dialogue across difference as they call deliberative publics into being around a shared concern and co-construct alternative self–other relations, power dynamics, and social practices of argument with others.

Note

1. Names have been changed throughout unless otherwise requested.

References

Appadurai, A. (2006). The right to research. *Globalisation, Society, and Education*, 4(2), 167–177.

Barfield, C., Glassman, J., & Naím, M. (2008). A Conversation about globalization. Available online at http://iipdigital.usembassy.gov/st/english/publication/2008/08/200808 21172457xjyrrep0.1554376.html

Barton, D. & Hamilton, M. (1998). *Local literacies: Reading and writing in one community*. London: Routledge.

Bay, J. L. (2002). The limits of argument: A response to Sean Williams. *Journal of Advanced Composition*, 22, 684–697.

Bourdieu, P. (2000). *Pascalian meditations*. Trans. Richard Nice. Stanford, CA: Stanford University Press.

Branch, K. (2007). *Eyes on the ought to be: What we teach when we teach about literacy*. Cresskill: Hampton Press.

Collins, J. & Blot, R. K. (2003). *Literacy and literacies: Texts, power, and identity* (No. 22). Cambridge, UK: Cambridge University Press.

Dewey, J. (1998). *Experience and education*. New York: Free Press.

Dryer, D. (2008). Taking up space: On genre systems as geographies of the possible. *Journal of Advanced Composition*, 28(3), 503–534.

Farrant, B., Fletcher, J., & Maybery, M. T. (2014). Cognitive flexibility, theory of mind, and hyperactivity/inattention. *Child Development Research*, 1–10, Article ID 741543, doi:10.1155/2014/741543.

Fecho, B. & Clifton, J. (2017). *Dialoguing across cultures, identities, and learning: Crosscurrents and complexities in literacy classrooms*. New York, NY: Routledge.

Flyvbjerg, B. (2005). Policy and planning for large infrastructure projects: Problems, causes, cures. World Bank Policy Research Working Paper 3781. Available online at http://econ.worldbank.org

Flyvbjerg, B. (2011). Making social science matter. In Georgiaos Papanagnou (Ed.), *Social science and policy challenges: Democracy, values, and capacities* (pp. 25–56). Research and Policy Series. Paris, France: UNESCO Publishing.

Foss, S. K. & Griffin, C. L. (1995). Beyond persuasion: A proposal for an invitational rhetoric. *Communications Monographs*, 62(1), 2–18.

Foster, H. (2005). Kairos and stasis revisited: Heuristics for the critically informed composition classroom. *Composition Forum*, 14(2). Available online at http://compositionforum.com/issue/14.2/foster-kairos-stasis.php

Fraser, N. (1989). *Unruly practices: Power, discourse, and gender in contemporary social theory*. Minneapolis: University of Minnesota Press.

Freire, P. & Macedo, D. (1987). *Literacy: Reading the word and the world*. Westport, CT: Bergin & Garvey.

Gee, J. P. (1991). *Social linguistics and literacies: Ideology in discourses, critical perspectives on literacy and education*. New York: Routledge.

Gee, J. P. (2005). Good video games and good learning. *Phi Kappa Phi Forum*, 85(2), 33–37.

Habermas, J. (1996). *Between facts and norms*. Trans. W. Rehg. Cambridge, UK: Polity Press.

Heath, S. (1983). *Ways with words: Language, life, and work in communities and classrooms*. Cambridge, UK: Cambridge University Press.

Hermans, H. & Hermans-Konopka, A. (2010). *Dialogical self theory: Positioning and counter-positioning in a globalizing society*. Cambridge, UK: Cambridge University Press.

Hillocks, G. (2011). *The teaching of argument writing, grades 6–12: Supporting claims with relevant evidence and clear reasoning*. Portsmouth, NH: Heinemann.

Horton, M. (1961). Myles Horton's talk at experimental citizenship school workshop, February 19–21. Highlander Archives, Box 40, folder 4, n.p. Monteagle, TN: Highlander Folk School.

Hull, G. (1993). Critical literacy and beyond: Lessons learned from students and workers in a vocational program and on the job. *Anthropology and Education Quarterly*, 24(4), 308–317.

Knoblauch, A. A. (2011). A textbook argument: Definitions of argument in leading composition textbooks. *College Composition and Communication*, 63(2), 244–268.

Newell, G. E., Bloome, D., & Hirvela, A. (2015). *Teaching and learning argumentative writing in high school English language arts classrooms*. New York: Routledge.

Pratt, M. L. (1991). Arts of the contact zone. *Profession*, 33–40.

Roberts-Miller, P. (2004). *Deliberate conflict: Argument, political theory, and composition classes*. Carbondale, IL: Southern Illinois University Press.

Scribner, S. & Cole, M. (1981). *The psychology of literacy*. Cambridge, MA: Harvard University Press.

Smagorinsky, P., Joannessen, E., Kahn, T., & McCann, M. (2011). *Teaching students to write: Argument*. Portsmouth, NH: Heinemann.

Warner, M. (2005). *Publics and counterpublics*. New York, NY: Zone Books.

Welch, K. E. (2010). Ideology and freshman textbook production: The place of theory in writing pedagogy. *College Composition and Communication*, 38(3) (1987), 269–282.

Young, R., Becker, A., & Pike, K. (1970). *Rhetoric: Discovery and change*. San Diego, CA: Harcourt College Publishing.

1

PROVISIONAL KNOWING AND THE NEED FOR ARGUMENT

In debates and in argument essays, claims are often presented as "truth-statements" of what is already known; argument as a product or process declares what others should know, what they should see as obvious and true or right. But consider this: We only need to be able to reason together if there are things we cannot know. If all people acted on premises that all others knew for sure to be right and good and certain, there would be no reason for reasoning together. We would all understand and value the same things. Or else those who didn't would simply be inferior in some way (Scott, 1967)—either knowing less or holding less good values. In that case, reasoning together would only involve superiors and inferiors; among equals, argument would be superfluous and irrelevant. Argument, in this case, would simply make what we all know, or should know, to be true, apparent, rendering discourse "a neutral presenting of data among equals and a persuasive leading of inferiors by the capable" (Scott, 1967, p. 10).

Rationalities, Reasonabilities, and Power

These pervasive, if often unarticulated, assumptions about language and argument are not lost on students. In a class focused on argument, a student described argument

> like playing chess where the goal is to put your own pieces (which you could say represent the facts, evidence, and witness testimony) into a position where the opposing player has no more moves to make (which could be seen as their acceptance of your argument or their inability to refute superior logic). . . . [We] fortify our own position while simultaneously dismantling the opposition's argument.

By writing that his pieces "represent the facts, evidence, and witness testimony," he seems to imply that there is really only one sure, best, apparent conclusion to be drawn from those pieces. His goal is that he and others see the certainty and superiority of that conclusion, *his* conclusion. Argument, for this student, is only for superiors and inferiors; it is about dominance of the intellect.

However, when obvious conclusions aren't evident—or when they are obvious to some and questionable, perhaps even unthinkable, to others—there is a deep need to reason together *if* relationships, institutions, and especially public life are going to do more than perpetuate existing power dynamics. In this student's conception of argument and in much of the Enlightenment tradition, rationality is well-defined and context-independent. There is one right, best conclusion that should be obvious to everyone, everywhere. What is rational is somehow singular, clear, known by everyone, constant over time and place. The student who compared argument to a chess match sees part of the work of argument as demonstrating the ways other rationalities are somehow less rational (or not rational at all) and less reasonable (or not reasonable at all). And yet rationalities and reasonabilities—both plural—are deeply tied to ends-in-mind, to potential gains and losses, and to individual and shared values.

After being pinned under a boulder for five days and seven hours in an isolated Utah canyon, exhausting other possibilities for escape, and running out of food and water on the fifth day, rock climber Aron Ralston made a rational decision to cut off his pinned arm with a dull knife. Under other conditions, this choice might not be rational; however, its alignment with his *goal* of survival and with his lack of other *means* to ensure his likely survival and with his *will* to endure the likely as well as the unpredictable potential costs of this choice, makes the logic of the choice, logical, rational. While Aron did live, his decision didn't need to work out the way he hoped in order for his decision to be rational; rather, his decision was rational, regardless of outcomes, in large part, because it was well-informed, well-aligned with his aims, and willfully chosen. While you might not have made the same choice Aron made, you might say his decision is rational: you can follow the logic, and you understand his reasons for cutting off his arm. In this case, where others are not immediately affected by his choice and where the question under consideration is not necessarily a moral question, *rational* and *reasonable* generally mean the same thing.

However, where moral judgments are in play, it can be helpful to distinguish rationality from reasonability, which is more connected to the construction of values with others (Sibley, 1953). For a decision to be reasonable in a way that is distinct from being rational, it must be informed about and *morally attuned* to the ways a decision might possibly impact other people in some way. A reasonable judgment is one that does more than simply "sees" others' perspectives and the ways each person might be affected by possible alternatives; someone making a decision might do this and be a prudent egotist but not necessarily reasonable (Sibley, 1953, p. 557). If a person chooses a course of action that points to some good for herself, she must also be prepared to allow that it results in what another deems harm to himself. If you make a decision that somehow furthers your career at the expense of young people, it is unlikely that the youth or their parents will think you are reasonable even if they understand your rationale for making the choice you did.

To be reasonable, a person must be prepared to be *influenced*, in reaching a decision, by the estimate of the possible ways his decision might affect others (Sibley, 1953). That is, a reasonable person will allow data about the consequences of his proposed decisions upon the welfare of others—what others want and need as well as if and how they might be harmed—recognizing impacts on others as relevant to his judgments. The basis of reasonability is in others' ability to appeal to some moral principle(s) that informed—or should have informed—a person's decision; it is the construction of "some principle[s] from which we can reason in common" (Sibley, 1953, p. 557). To be reasonable in determining what to do in a complex situation, you must weigh your options in terms of the possible impacts on all those involved, and some moral principle(s)—of kindness, of wisdom, of personal responsibility, of justice, of candor, or some such—must govern your estimation. Reasonability, thus, assumes, requires, and structures a stranger relationality (Warner, 2005); it necessitates and creates some moral basis that frames how you will relate with others and how they will relate with you. Reasonability calls on people to construct some version of equity together. But this call is not tied to rationality; it is derived instead from desire. A person will only act reasonably if he has a *desire* to be reasonable, a *desire* to act morally, a *desire* to be in some way connected to and bound by a certain kind of relationship with others (Sibley, 1953, p. 558).

Even so, being rational does not necessarily guarantee a good result. Aron Ralston lost his arm; he could just as easily have lost his life. Neither does being reasonable necessarily secure a happy end. Sometimes there are no good options, none we would actively want to choose anyway. Sometimes it seems clear that helping one person means that someone else's needs will not be met. Worse, sometimes the only options available are harmful. This is often the terrain of medical decisions or military decisions. In these situations, a person may be quite rational, quite reasonable, and left with only horrible, heartbreaking options, and varying degrees of uncertainty (cf. Clifton, 2013). Argument is, thus, not about knowing with any certainty what the best course of action is or how things will pan out. It is, instead, about deliberation—being deliberate in considering "what could be," weighing values, contingencies, and possible futures with others.

While reasonability recognizes a need to listen and learn from others a person might not have otherwise been inclined to attend to, "power unavoidably spoils the free use of reason"; further, "more power spoils reason even more" (Flyvbjerg, 1998, p. 5). Power—dense and dynamic nets of omnipresent relations embodied and enacted through strategies and tactics (Foucault, 1990, pp. 95–96)—often avoids the demands of reasonability and rationality by blurring the dividing line between rationality and rationalization. Rather than allowing for reasoning or recognizing the need to re-open or continue reasoning together as goals or constraints change or as data is presented about a decision's impact on others, reasoning together is set aside or feigned. Rationalizing a past decision—one not up for dialogue or revision in the here and now—takes the place of reasoning together, and persuasive strategies and "woolen language" (Welch, 2011) take the place of dialogue.

Indeed, "rationalization is shown to be a principal strategy in the exercise of power" (Flyvbjerg, 1998, p. 228). If you've ever been asked for your input about a decision and, after offering your thoughts, realized that a supervisor or someone else had already made a decision, then you've experienced this kind of rationalization at work. Those leveraging or caught up in strategies and tactics of power often operate *as if* reasonability were valued, but often without any interest in allowing others' perspectives to influence the decision-making or outcomes in any significant way (Flyvbjerg, 1998). Further, as strategies and tactics of power become normalized in processes and systems, they come to seem monolithic, as universals. However, according to Foucault, "universals do not exist. . . . Where universals are said to exist, or where people tacitly assume they exist, universals must be questioned" (as qtd. in Flyvbjerg, 2001, p. 100). With regard to power and argument and public life, the important question, then, is not only "Who governs?" but "How is power exercised? What 'governmental rationalities' are at work when those who govern govern?" (Flyvbjerg, 1998, p. 273).

The "strategies-and-tactics" (Flyvbjerg, 1998; Foucault, 1990) of power relations often work by avoiding reasoning with others since the nature of relations of power is to perpetuate existing power relations rather than to be bound by the moral reasonability others might insist on. Rationalizations operationalize power relations, diffusing and obscuring arguments as they are distributed across and through interconnected technologies, materials, texts, practices, and relations. Think about a school's student dress code, the ways teachers and principals monitor and enforce that dress code, the ways Student Resource Officers might talk about the dress code, and the ways parents buy clothes that fit the dress code. Rationalities and reasonabilities are distributed across the entire ecology of practices related to the dress code—and yet the code and its surrounding practices are rarely a site of the shared use of reasoning about the goals of the dress code, about the impacts of the code or related practices on different people (Ewing, 2014; Pinnow, 2013), or about the moral principles that guide the kind of relationships constructed through the practices surrounding the dress code (Fecho & Clifton, 2017). Instead, rationalities and reasonabilities are distributed and normalized through recurring social situations, diffused across time and space, texts and technologies (cf. Brandt & Clinton, 2002).

These recurring social situations—something I'll return to in the next chapter about conceptualizing argument and genres beyond text types—and people's responses become familiar and normalized in their recurrence. In the familiarity of recurring situations, say, in a church or in a classroom or at the dinner table, people come to recognize what others expect and are cued—by people but also by things like signs or lighting, proximity or time of day—to produce certain conventional and routine ways of being in those situations. In a situation that is very familiar, you likely don't give much thought to rationalities or reasonabilities—to what it makes sense to do or to how others are affected or how you expect to relate together; you simply know. You've been at the dinner table with the same family members every day for years; if your family engages in some ritual before you eat together, you might find yourself at times bowing your head or putting your napkin in your lap or telling about your day without even realizing what you're doing unless something, like a doorbell or a son taking too long in his room, interrupts the routine. That familiar situation cues what genre theorists call "uptake": you are "caught up" in the recognition of a situation and take up acquired dispositions, behaviors, relations, and so on (Dryer, 2008). You've stepped into and produced distributed arguments—rationalities and reasonabilities distributed across people, institutions, technologies, materials, and texts, cuing and producing as well as surveilling and disciplining what should be, how it should be, for whom, and by whom.

Over time distributed arguments come to shape what seems—and is—normal and right; they define and produce what counts as rational, what counts as reasonable within and across social ecologies. The power of these distributed arguments is in their capacity to create realities as something stable and enduring rather than something tentative and contingent. Together, the diffusion of arguments and rationalization presented as rationality make this possible; what "should be" is rendered procedural, a matter of course, a matter of fact—the way things are (Grabill & Simmons, 1998). Of course, we often need the stability of distributed arguments for efficiency, for collective memory so we don't have to "re-invent the wheel" each day, and for navigating uncertainty. Indeed, distributed arguments, at their best, carry and produce value-oriented wisdom, charted over time and across familiar and changing circumstances, people, resources, and exigencies. They scaffold and coordinate how we manage "the circumstances which [we] encounter day by day" (Isocrates, *Panathenaicus,* 1929/1980, 12.30).

However, some of the most significant work of distributed arguments is in their regulation of power relations. In a world of limited resources, foibled people, global demographic shifts, and rapidly changing technologies, distributed arguments create truces in which people put aside uncertainty, conflict, and differences with colleagues, bosses, neighbors, and students to get things done. Recognizable features of recurring social situations help cue and produce rationalities and reasonabilities that create a rough kind of equilibrium that maintains and reproduces existing power relations.

Cultivating Argument

However, *stable* realities and power relations are not necessarily *equally distributed* or balanced power relations; stability does not imply justice (Flyvbjerg, 1998). Nor does stability imply that power relations are fixed and unmoving. They are continually being cultivated, maintained, produced, resisted, and re-written. Further, since power often relies on rationalization and defies reasonability, people have very different experiences of those power relations and of the realities distributed arguments put in place. In fact, a danger of distributed arguments is that they wear down differences—making the range of people's aspirations and experiences less vivid and distinctive, folding differences into what has been uniform by re-directing them back to the routine. However, sometimes different experiences of distributed arguments are different enough to destabilize and call into question current realities—to create what Bob Fecho (2011) calls "wobble," a liminal experience of confusion, doubt, conflict, disturbance, or dissonance of some sort so jarring that it demands attention and re-calibration.

When people object to something about distributed arguments, often what they're objecting to are not only pragmatics—the policies and practices for accomplishing tasks—but also, and primarily, particular reasonabilities: the self–other relations, the *morality* that distributed arguments render normal. First experienced as pressing problems (Habermas, 1996), the effects of violated interests and threatened identities point toward rationalities and reasonabilities that are askew. When these "felt difficulties" (Dewey, 1998) or "life–world disturbances" (Habermas, 1996) are experienced as urgent and significant, when they violate a reasonability that people think they should be able to rely on, and when they are well beyond an individual's capacity to fully understand or remedy, people go public in an effort to garner more public attention and to construct new reasonabilities and rationalities.

Consider a mother's indictment of a school's policies for dealing with bullying. Just as a new school year was underway and teachers and students settled into familiar routines, a high school senior committed suicide, already overwhelmed—in September—by bullies at his school. His best friend's mother grieved with the family privately but also spoke out to the local newspaper: "Children are bullied, and then when they retaliate after talking with teachers and principals . . . they fight back, and then they are suspended—there is something severely wrong with that" (Alcedo, 2013).

In what otherwise might have been an intensely private time of grieving, a mother speaks out to raise this young man's suicide and the circumstances surrounding his death as a concern that she thinks others should—and hopes others will—share. She *goes public* to call others—strangers—to attend to a concern that she hopes will change, a concern she does not have the capacity to change on her own. Her grievance is certainly about how ineffectual the school's policies are, but her greater concern is about the ways youth relate to each other, the ways teachers and principals address youth in these situations, the ways a public institution entrusted with the care of sons and daughters somehow fails.

She is *making* an argument (as a product)—"something is severely wrong"; in going public, she is also *cultivating* argument by marking this practical and moral conflict as a distinctly *public* problem. And yet for this concern to become a distinctly public problem (Habermas, 1996), for it to enter what Habermas (1991) called the *public sphere* requires both call *and* response (Warner, 2005). Publics are not found but called into being by discourse. Michael Warner (2005) notes, "Public discourse says not only, 'Let a public exist,' but 'Let it have this character, speak this way, see the world this way. . . . Run it up the flagpole and see who salutes. Put on a show and see who shows up" (p. 14). *Going public* is simply not enough. Circulation is not enough. Response is required.

To pursue changes in practices, policies, and ways of relating requires more focused and sustained engagement with others—youth, parents, teachers, principals, school counselors, youth mentors, student resource officers, and others—who may reasonably disagree. She must *call into existence* a conflict where people had not previously seen or experienced conflict. Others must recognize this as a concern they share and a conflict they're willing to engage. And she must *cultivate* further *argument* among people, likely strangers, who experience existing distributed arguments very differently in order to create a *deliberative* local public (Long, 2008; Flower, 2008) where one had not existed before. And yet calling together this range of people is no easy feat despite the fact that they may sometimes find themselves in the same building. Neither is it easy to get them to share a concern—for each of them, somehow grave enough and shared enough—that they would be willing to problem-solve with—to listen to and learn from—people they don't know and otherwise might not have anything in common with. And yet nothing changes if they don't, if they won't.

Deliberative Publics and Argument as Dialogue Across Difference

For quite some time, English Language Arts and First-Year Composition teachers have recognized something valuable about "going public"; the "letter to the editor" or government official or literary author and the more recent use of social media like Twitter, Facebook, Buzzfeed, blogs, and YouTube are possibly evidence of this. For some, the value of going public, and perhaps especially with contemporary technological tools, is primarily about keeping students' interest; for others, going public, even among classmates in a writing workshop, has the capacity to construct more tangible audiences and thus, maybe, more tangible and worthwhile purposes for writing than those of a mere assignment and grade. For still others, going public is related to a kind of civic engagement or 21st century global citizenship that asks young people to attend to and attempt to change the world around them. These instructional purposes and methods for "going public" often frame the work of argument as expression or persuasion, but not as inquiry or collaborative knowledge-building.

When instruction connected to public life centers only, or primarily, on going public, the work of public life is primarily cast in terms of circulating ready-made claims by sharing texts, voting on an issue, mobilizing people, or performing acts of service for a predetermined cause. While going public is often an important and necessary part of the social practices of argument in public life, circulation alone is often insufficient to construct new ways of knowing, to change minds, to transform relationships, to bring about new possibilities.

This paradox is one that has puzzled scholars for a while now. As Eli Goldblatt (2007) explained about his work at the New City Press at Temple University:

> We immediately recognized that printing new authors wasn't enough. The problem of distribution hit us full in the face: we still have hundreds of copies [of our initial anthology] sitting in storage, with no way to get them into the hands of new readers.
>
> *(p. 200)*

John Trimbur (2000) notes that the challenge of going public is motivated by "the democratic aspiration to devise delivery systems that circulate ideas, information, opinions, and knowledge and thereby expand public forums in which people can deliberate on the issues of the day" (p. 190). However, mere circulation does not necessarily call a public into being. Consider the circulation you encounter on your Facebook or Twitter feed. You read some of what's circulated, likely ignore much more of what makes its way to your screen, occasionally "like" or re-circulate something. You are involved in the work of circulation, but not necessarily the work of a public, let alone a deliberative public. Swirling discourses do not a public make. This marks an important, if somewhat counter-intuitive distinction about *publics* as well as an important aim of this book.

Rather than defining publics in terms of a ready-made list of people or a nebulous audience out there somewhere, the best way to define a public is by how it functions—by its rhetorical work (Asen, 2000; Flower, 2008; Hauser, 1999). In some cases, a public can be said to exist if people are merely paying attention to a circulating discourse (Warner, 2005). This version of public is most often invoked in the work of "going public" and, in classrooms, often reifies an adversarial, text-type model of argument. Other publics, like a city council or school board, function as decision-makers (Flyvbjerg, 2011; Tracy, 2010). These publics often come to a "majority rules" vote or to consensus, fronting deliberation even as decisions are made elsewhere and before a vote.

In contrast, I contextualize the teaching of argument in terms of *deliberative publics*—rhetorically constructed, poetically sustained hybrid domains that do the hard and necessary work of argument as dialogue across difference in the face of shared exigencies *"within concrete contexts of struggle"* (West, 1993, p. 108, emphasis in the original). Rather than demanding consensus, *deliberative publics* construct, to some degree, shared understandings, actively value individual differences, and work toward shaping participants' choices in their different, distinctive spheres of their personal and professional lives (Higgins, Long, & Flower, 2006).[1]

Deliberative publics are connected to Iris Marion Young's (1997) notion of the polity, of "people who live together, who are stuck with one another" through proximity and/or economic and political interdependence (p. 126). When Bob Fecho and I dialogued about this concept in a sidebar of our book about dialogical selves, Bob noted (Fecho & Clifton, 2017), "the *stuck* part can be troubling." He expounds:

> The concept of being stuck together conjure[s] up images for me of someone saying to someone else in a resigned way, "Oh well, I guess we're just stuck together," the implied meaning being that they wish it weren't so, but here we are nevertheless. To me, being *stuck together* [feels] just a tad better than being *stuck with*, but neither term [makes] me sense a welcoming relationship. . . . There's nothing voluntary about it, nor does it suggest movement of any kind. Instead I see tires stuck in the mud, cars stuck in snow, gum stuck in a toddler's hair, keys stuck in a lock, windows stuck in the frame, fingers stuck in my face. The idea of *stuck together* remind[s] me of why I and so many educators have issues with the idea of teaching tolerance of other cultures. Teaching tolerance is such a low bar to set. If I tolerate something or someone, I'm barely disguising my dislike for it and merely putting up with it. True, tolerance is better than aggression, but far below acceptance, understanding, and love. I just [feel] that when people engage across cultures in daily transactions that they should aspire to more than feeling stuck together.
>
> *(Sidebar 2.1)*

What is perhaps most lovely and troubling about Bob's reflection is that he has precisely grasped a central conundrum of deliberative publics: what will we do with the volatile presence of difference? To be sure, people do not always want to be *stuck* with the people they're stuck with. I've certainly felt this way at times about others; I'm sure others have felt this way about me, too. As Bob recognizes, being stuck with others is not always a pleasant affair, and often not of our choosing.

And yet, if a policy informing, say, quality control of water in Flint, Michigan, is not working for some people, those folks need to be able to get others in Flint or beyond Flint to share that concern if anything is going to change. This is also true in relation to some of our most private experiences, like domestic abuse or child abuse or which bodies can use which bathrooms at school or at McDonald's. The likely fact is that others around us—in our towns, in our schools, in our churches and mosques and synagogues, in our economies, in our mayor's office—do not share our experiences or our perspectives, and perhaps don't agree with us or necessarily think they have any reason on their own to pay attention to someone like us. They haven't necessarily *chosen* us; we are strangers—strange and unknown to each other. But clean water, safe buses, school funding, and more all depend on us being able to construct what Warner (2005) calls *stranger relationality*—ways of relating with strangers—that relies on far more than mere tolerance.

With regard to being stuck together, this also means we must construct some reason to share each other's concerns, especially concerns that might not directly impact our own practical goals but that have a profound impact on the people we are, in one way or another, stuck with. As Callie, an eighth grader, put it in a classroom conversation her teacher and I were fostering about what every community needs: "People need a reason to come together. If you're my neighbor, whoop-ti-do! I'm not going to talk to you. And if we don't have a reason to talk together we're not a community; we're just a bunch of people living side by side." Despite using the more familiar language of "community" rather than public,[2] Callie recognizes that this interdependence, this stuckness is not simple empirical fact; it is rather a discursive construction of the intersection of rationality and reasonability, sometimes weighted more toward goal-driven rationalities and sometimes more toward moralities guiding how people will relate with one another.

However, any teacher at a faculty meeting, any parent at a parent-teacher conference, any young person in a principal's office can tell you that it is also not enough to simply get concerned people in the room, even if they all have a compelling reason to be there together. Put a grief-stricken, angry mother in the room with the kids who bullied her son, her son's best friend, a principal, and teachers who may have done all they knew to do but whom she sees as responsible for the danger and hopelessness that led to her son's death, and it's not hard to imagine that that conversation could degenerate in a hurry into a blame game or heated arguments that others won't take to heart or an impasse in which they "agree to disagree" and walk away with no better options on the table and no better ways of relating. In fact, in the face of heated disagreement—over bullying, police shootings, dress codes, standardized testing, marriage rights, genderless bathrooms, water rights, or suspension policies—and when any of us most need argument to be productive, these are the outcomes many people have come to expect (Bay, 2002; cf. 694).

And yet, like the mother who voiced her complaint to the newspaper, or Black youth and their families calling for changes in police training or suspension policies, or teachers and parents resisting a culture of testing, or graduate students insisting on a fair wage, or a battered wife in need of protection from an abusive spouse, we all sometimes need to be able to:

- call strangers to share our concerns;
- make sense of situations characterized by uncertainty, conflict, and difference;
- pool resources beyond what we alone can bring to bear;
- problem-solve among people who may disagree;
- invent alternative ways forward; and
- put our best options in place, always attentive to ways they may need to be responsive to new data.

1.1 Creating Contexts for Individual and Shared Inquiry

These interludes focus on instructional possibilities of engaging youth in public literacies. Importantly, the pedagogy I hope to commend is grounded in *praxis,* or well-informed and morally committed action in public life, and *phronesis,* or practical wisdom—two concepts I unpack more fully in Chapter 4. The gist of this is that a pedagogy of public literacies aims to engage youth from the get-go in *doing* the work of public life, thus creating a rhetorical context in which to put public literacies to use. *Praxis* engages youth in deliberative publics now; *phronesis* invites them to be better at it next time.

Likewise, constructing a pedagogy of public literacies is an act of *phronesis*; it *follows praxis*, it is something we pursue (Kemmis, 2012; Lynch, 2013, p. xviii). And yet, at least some of what I may be commending may be unfamiliar to you and your students; that is, for you, some of what you read may come before *praxis*. So where does that leave us? Dewey would say that leaves us with *experience.* And so I offer some approaches and strategies for engaging youth in public life not so that they *gain* experience but so that they *become* experienced by learning from—reflecting on, tooling and re-tooling, artfully inventing and re-inventing—experiences of argument and public life. As Paul Lynch (2013) notes, "Everyday living becomes method when we examine the world around us, when we make guesses as to the consequences our various choices might produce, and when we make choices and see whether they work" (p. 80). With regard to public life and argument as dialogue across difference, these are the methods and experiences I most hope to commend to you and the youth you teach.

Framing a rich problem space for shared and sustained dialogue

To create a shared dialogue is to create a compelling reason for young people to read and write, listen and learn, design and deliberate together. Creating a sustained dialogue means that shared meaning making is extended over time and across texts, increases in complexity over time, and is responsive to the connections and questions that emerge along the way.

Inquiry and public life begin in the experience of doubt—what Fecho (2011) calls "wobble." Wobble marks a site of change, of transition, and often, of discomfort. With regard to creating an atmosphere in which wobble occurs, the idea is not to bring someone's world crashing down, but to get previously firmly held beliefs "to sway enough that the wobble grabs the person's attention and compels some level of reflection on the contexts that created that belief system" (Fecho, 2011, p. 54).

And yet not all experiences of wobble may merit more *public* attention and *public* dialogue. Wobble experiences that mark public concerns or yet-to-be-public concerns often occur when interactions go awry with strangers or with systems; wobble experiences often merit public attention when they are not one-off experiences but patterned or when they are so harmful that the harm creates a felt sense of urgency, *and* when the difficulty is not something that an individual person can resolve on his own.

In your class, having youth read about and document these kinds of *critical incidents*—specific dramatic moments when these felt difficulties play out—invites students to pay attention to wobble experiences they and others have. Interactions with strangers or systems (and their people, policies, and practices) in which young people have found themselves asking, "What the heck just happened there?" or saying, "That's not right!" or "I can't believe that just happened [to me or to someone else]!" or "That doesn't really make any sense. Why do we do it that way?" often indicate wobble experiences that might also point to concerns others share, or should share. You'll know you're on to a rich problem space when students share concerns—or urgently need others to share their concerns—and ask: *So, what do we do?!*

Consider some of the concerns of the other eighth graders in Callie's class and the limitations of a chess match model of argument for addressing their concerns. Around the room, tables and chairs were clustered to foster small group discussions; on each table was one of the following questions.

- *What does every community need?*
- *What are your community's or schools' strengths (and how do you know)?*
- *What are your community's or school's values (and how do you know)?*
- *How do you see your role in your community or school? How do you think others (principals, teachers, peers, parents, etc.,) see your role?*
- *What concerns do you have about your community or school (and can you describe "a time when" this concern seemed especially important)?*

Students talked for several minutes together about the question at their table and then rotated to the next set of tables and chairs with the next set of questions, jotting down notes to record their groups' responses:

- An African American girl was concerned that her use of African American Vernacular English (AAVE) was policed in the hallways. A principal heard her talking in the hall, called her over, and wouldn't let her leave until she abandoned the grammar and dialect of AAVE and spoke in Dominant American English.
- Another group of students were concerned about their neighborhood. They noticed that the houses and yards were well-cared for until they reached a particular section of the neighborhood, where the houses' paint was peeling, yards were un-mowed, shutters were missing or dangling, sidewalks were broken or nonexistent, and roof shingles were loose or gone. Their

parents told them to be careful walking along the streets in that part of their neighborhood.

- A White boy was concerned about the future of his town and if there would be a place for him there later. He noticed that when people graduated from high school, they seldom returned.
- A group of African American boys talked about a White police officer stopping them as they walked home from the local mall. They described the experience as one that made them nervous and angry since they said there wasn't any reason for the police officer to stop them.
- A group of Latina and African American girls worried about their mothers being sexually harassed. They also worried about their own safety as men began to notice their bodies differently.
- Another group of students, scattered across several small groups, was frustrated that the Student Council wasn't actually allowed to make decisions about anything going on in the school; they said they were simply being used to raise money for things the adults in the school wanted to fund.
- Another girl was bothered that stores selling clothes for young adults posted signs saying they didn't allow youth under 18 in the store without an adult. She and her friends wondered why they were viewed suspiciously, as troublemakers. The girl who'd been turned away from a store explained, "[Adults] immediately stereotype you, think you're up to something, in trouble." A friend of hers at the table added, "On the news, youth are usually shown doing something bad." A third girl chimed in, "But I see them as good, but [shifting her tone to indicate she's talking to adults], don't just assume." The girl who started the conversation concluded, "They don't listen to us because we're 'kids' [she makes air quotes with her fingers]. But our voice and opinion matters even if we are 'kids.'"

In these situations, there is no universal reasoning that will or should prevail. The chess match version of argument is simply not helpful. Who should be painted into a corner? What one idea should they all clearly recognize as the right one?

In deliberative publics, the chess match version of argument is most closely linked to Jürgen Habermas's (1996) deliberative ideal. Many of the norms shaping how we teach humanities and argument writing are derived from Habermas's (1991) image of the bourgeois public sphere in the form of discussions in 18th century coffeehouses, salons, and newspapers (Atwill, 2010; Jarratt, 1991). In this ideal of public discussion, valid arguments are based not on local particular experience or opinion but on universal premises to which all men would agree (Flower, 2008). This "traditional-universalist" model (Roberts-Miller, 2004) insists on general principles that are self-evident—as in Jefferson's "We hold these truths to be self-evident: That all men are created equal"—and tied to a focus on public topics that deal with general interest or affect the common good.

However, the *common good*—something I'll return to Chapter 2's discussion of the commons—was defined narrowly as the rights and interests of the White middle-class male business world, shutting out the interests of people marginalized by age, gender, race, sexuality, class, religion, or status. Further, universalist principles or "common sense" approaches to public argument, which rely on one best proposition to vanquish all others, tend to reflect the assumptions and traditions of the majority, not the marginalized (Roberts-Miller, 2004, p. 43). This narrow intersection of public life and argument has excluded issues of marginalized people; discounted the logics or means of discourse of those who are marginalized; and invoked a cool, uninterested rationality that supposes that the superior claim will rise to the surface regardless of who makes the claim (Fraser, 1989).

In practice, this "traditional-universalist" model has proved to be both insufficient and harmful. The Habermasian salon separated the deliberations of public life from the workings of the family, the economic market, and the state. This public/private split closed off discussions of "private" matters, like domestic abuse, child labor, or workplace safety; instead, these were matters for families and employers to discuss and resolve (Fraser, 1990). More recently, this conceptual public/private split has framed the destructive effects of globalization (Dingo & Scott, 2012; Payne, 2012)—like the privatization of water in Bolivia that made water unaffordable to its citizens; slave labor conditions in the *maquiladoras* in Juarez, Mexico; the destruction of local traditions (Kellner, 1998); harmful agricultural methods and the bankrupting of small farmers (Schell, 2012a, 2012b)—and the effects of austerity (Scott & Welch, 2016)—the systematic de-funding and privatization of social services and public enterprises like schools, prisons, water, pensions, foster care, and so on—as purely economic concerns to be resolved by workplace managers.

These public/personal splits are deeply connected to reasonability—the moralities underlying our relationships with one another. In the eighth grade classroom described earlier, as students named some of their concerns, their classroom teacher asked them to focus on one concern they wanted to spend some more time thinking about. The concern could be something that affected them personally, like some of the concerns I narrated earlier, or it could be something that most directly impacted someone else. Regardless, it had to be a concern others of us should care about, too, and a concern they would like to think and talk about with others in order to make better sense of what's going on and to consider ways of addressing this concern.

We asked them to think about "a time when" they experienced the difficulties—the tensions, conflicts, and confusions—of the concern they had in mind. Then they worked on dramatizing those *critical incidents*—something I'll return to in more detail in Chapter 3—in order to *freeze-frame* a typical moment and re-visit some of the decisions that different stakeholders were making in real time. Some students began to work on drafts right away; others spent more time conferencing about their ideas.

Then something surprising happened. A few parents, primarily White and middle class, came by after school, worried that their children were having difficulty naming and writing about experiences they might want others to attend to, experiences where systems or relationships might not quite be working for them or for others. Their child's teacher explained the work students were doing and how it related to the Common Core State Standards. He also explained that we were asking students to pay attention to their own lives and the lives of others, that we were asking them to dramatize moments of uncertainty, conflict, and difference that merited more public attention and dialogue. He also gave examples of some of the things students were writing about. Invariably, these few parents all said something along these lines: "My son/daughter is a good kid; he/she hasn't encountered these types of things [relating to uncertainty, conflict, and difference] in his/her life." This is significant because it illustrates the deficiencies of a universalist model of public life and argument. The logic goes something like this: *My son/daughter is a good kid. He/she hasn't experienced uncertainty, conflict, or difference. People who do experience uncertainty, conflict, and difference are not good kids. They either are in trouble or they should be.*

The implications are that the concerns of youth who experience uncertainty, conflict, and difference should not be shared by those who do not have similar experiences; that it is unreasonable to share those concerns because they are the concerns of bad people; if those bad people would be more like me, they would not have those concerns either; therefore, these are not *public* concerns—except perhaps as concerns related to surveillance, enforcement, and personal responsibility of the bad youth—but *personal* concerns. Effectively, this logic pushes people who are different—and their concerns—out of public life. These parents (and their children) who say they do not experience uncertainty, conflict, and difference cannot imagine a reason to attend to, let alone share the concerns of youth who do. A "traditional-universalist" model of public life and of argument prepares people, especially those of the dominant culture, to dismiss any experiences, rationalities, or reasonabilities that do not fit their own, often on grounds that cast those who disagree as deeply flawed in character—unpatriotic, ungodly, lazy, irresponsible, or criminal—framing the superiority of the chess match version of argument in terms of a moral high ground.

Argument and Contingent Knowledge-Building

However, if a singular superior argument always emerges as clearly right and best, then questions and difficulties don't need to be considered and worked through or necessarily even talked about. Only inferior intellects or inferior characters would have questions and difficulties. There would be no need for argument. Superior intellects or superior characters would simply be involved in the boring drudgery of explaining what should be clear to people who don't understand, or if a more smug, or well-schooled, attitude were taken, of dismantling others' ideas and trapping them in a corner until they have nowhere else to go and they finally succumb to the obvious superiority of their better.

Further, anyone who was utterly convinced of his own preconceived position as a "truth"—as certain, as apparent, as unassailable—would not genuinely enter into critical inquiry with others. There would be no need. There would also be no good reason for disagreement; deviations from what is certain might, in fact, even be ethically questionable (Scott, 1967). This appraisal is implied in the parents' concern. But what a person knows is not immutable, completely and utterly unassailable, and superior but rather contingent, mediated, and dependent on time and place and experience. Our primary tools of thought—languages and texts—are themselves socially constituted, what Bakhtin would call *dialogic*: words are given to us and carry with them the traces of their prior meanings, their prior contexts, their prior applications.

Ask any five students to tell about a fight they saw in the cafeteria at lunch; even those who describe the same scene, the same events, and the same people will describe them differently. They will contextualize and interpret and name what they saw and heard differently. They *know* what happened differently. Faced with those different takes, how will you know what happened? Based on what they say and perhaps other information or accounts, you will construct a *likely* scenario. Depending on how you weigh what the students have said in relation to other things you know, or think you know, you may feel quite certain of what happened. And yet the moment, now passed, is a construct, told and re-told, symbolized and re-symbolized through words and gestures. How will you know what to do next—who to comfort, who to counsel, who to reprimand? Or what version or combination of comforting, counseling, or reprimanding to enact? Or how that will play out or what consequences might unfold for you and others? These multiple, overlapping, competing symbols are all you have to make sense of the past, to weigh possibilities, to create a future; they are what you act on.

This is the nature of argument; it arises in response to open questions marked by uncertainty, conflict, and difference in the face of issues that demand deliberation because of their urgency and importance for personal and shared well-being and because there are no certain, ready-made answers to be found. We are motivated to inquiry—and argument—when current solutions don't work, when we are willing or forced to stand a while in the vulnerability of deliberate uncertainty. Rather than seeing questions and conflicts as closed or having definitive answers or solutions, which is something that argument as product and process often condition, this version of argument motivates a decision to see questions and conflicts as open and in need of dialogue across difference precisely because there are no easy answers to be found.

Argument as dialogue across difference is, then, not a merely persuasive contest but rather a constellation of collaborative practices that create meaning out of conflict and confusion. These practices go beyond sussing out available means to support a person's initial position; instead, stakeholders raise differences to the surface, pose problems and questions, consider and weigh strong rivals to their pet theories and personal experiences (Flower, Long, & Higgins, 2000), and seek the available means of persuading themselves and others (Miller, 2000). Argument as dialogue across difference is, thus, about constructing meaning in a contingent world.

In determining what to do in the aftermath of the fight I mentioned earlier, you might be engaged in this kind of argument. To decide what to do, you might talk with your principal or ask your fellow teachers about how they've handled something like this in the past. You might question the later impacts of their choices or wonder about the goals they had in mind. You might realize some of those options are not really available to you as a new teacher at the school. You might consult the student handbook, or think about your previous experiences with the principal or parents when you've written up a student. Perhaps, you know these students' parents and anticipate how your relationship with some of them might change. Maybe you consider your history with these students and how your handling of this situation might affect the classroom environment.

As you weigh possible options and outcomes, you might also feel divided about what to do. Perhaps part of you thinks that it might be best to send one of the students to detention or even to the principal for In-School Suspension (ISS), but another part of you wonders if he might be better served with a warning. Maybe, as a friend of his parents, you worry that ISS would damage your friendship. As a new teacher, you might wonder how the principal and your colleagues will view you, depending on what you choose. As a person of color, maybe you worry about disciplining a White student in a small rural town. Perhaps, as a coach of one of the students, you think it might be better to handle any counseling or discipline in practice. You are engaged in a kind of dialogue across difference with yourself, with others, with the broader community, with the district policies, and perhaps with broader dialogues about the school-to-prison-pipeline (Alexander, 2010) or suspension policies (Flower, 2008) or the ways African American students and Native American students are silenced and re-purpose silence in schools (Kirkland, 2013; San Pedro, 2015).

As you talk with others, consult policies, and recognize school and community pressures, you are engaging in the *work of reasoning*—with yourself, with others, with institutions—and you are likely trying to determine a *rational* as well as a *reasonable* course of action. And yet the ways you go about this are likely different on this occasion than the ways you engage in argument in other situations and networks where you must make judgments and determinations. Who you consult and how, what you value and why, how you recognize what others value, what you write down (or don't), what documents you access, what you circulate broadly or keep private, how you think through the web of conflicting testimony as well as potential immediate and systemic consequences are all part of the literate practices (Scribner & Cole, 1981) of argument in this situation. So, too, are the histories, relationships, unspoken policies, statewide pressures, and national outrage that might condition, color, and limit the conclusions you might draw.

If everything could be known with certainty, there would be no need to *determine* what to do about the fight; things would simply unfold as they should and be apparent and apparently good to everyone. But even what may appear to be universal must be acted on in a world we cannot fully know or predict. You—all of us—must step into the "yet-to-be-created" as something unknown, something yet to unfold. When our actions involve the beliefs and actions of others, as they do in the situation I've just described, what we can know is constrained even further. Even so, despite uncertainties, much of the time, we must find some way to navigate these complexities and act in the face of conflicts. There is no guarantee of finding or constructing a clear way through, and yet, we must act. The complexities we face and the uncertain and contingent nature of knowing are what render argument as dialogue across difference necessary and important.

Note

1. For readers interested in social practices and rhetorical work of different kinds of local publics, see Linda Flower's (2008) Community Literacy and the Rhetoric of Public Engagement and Elenore Long's (2008) Community Literacy and the Rhetoric of Local Publics.
2. See Linda Flower's *Community Literacy and the Rhetoric of Public Engagement* (pp. 21–29) for available versions of "community" and distinctions between "communities" and "publics." While I used the familiar language of community here with eighth graders, conceptually I am employing community here as the polity of deliberative publics.

References

Alcedo, M. (2013, September 24). Parents voice bullying concerns at Ashland school board meeting. *Missourian.* Available online at http://www.columbiamissourian.com/news/parents-voice-bullying-concerns-at-ashland-school-board-meeting/article_ef1c4f3f-1c1d-59e7-8869-b2764a6c606c.html

Alexander, M. (2010). *The new Jim Crow.* New York: The New Press.

Asen, R. (2000). Seeking the "counter" in counterpublics. *Communication Theory*, 10(4), 424–446.

Atwill, J. M. (2010). *Rhetoric reclaimed: Aristotle and the liberal arts tradition.* Ithaca, NY: Cornell University Press.

Bay, J. L. (2002). The limits of argument: A response to Sean Williams. *Journal of Advanced Composition*, 22, 684–697.

Brandt, D. & Clinton, K. (2002). Limits of the local: Expanding perspectives on literacy as a social practice. *Journal of Literacy Research*, 34(3), 337–356.

Clifton, J. (2013). Mastery, failure and community outreach as a stochastic art: Lessons learned with the Sudanese diaspora in Phoenix. In J. Restaino & L. Cella (Eds.), *Unsustainable: Re-imagining community literacy, public writing, service-learning, and the university* (pp. 227–252). Lexington, MA: Lexington Press.

Dewey, J. (1998). *Experience and education.* New York: Free Press.

Dingo, R. & Scott, B. (2012). *Megarhetorics of global development.* Pittsburgh, PA: University of Pittsburgh Press.

Dryer, D. (2008). Taking up space: On genre systems as geographies of the possible. *Journal of Advanced Composition*, 28(3), 503–534.

Ewing, L. (2014). (De)Constructing the student body: A post-structural analysis of dress codes in secondary schools. Master's thesis. Available online at https://libres.uncg.edu/ir/uncg/f/DrewiczEwing_uncg_0154M_11507.pdf

Fecho, B. (2011). *Teaching for the students: Habits of heart, mind, and practice in the engaged classroom.* New York: Teachers College Press.

Fecho, B. & Clifton, J. (2017). *Dialoguing across cultures, identities, and learning: Crosscurrents and complexities in literacy classrooms.* New York: Routledge.

Flower, L. (2008). *Community literacy and the rhetoric of public engagement.* Carbondale, IL: Southern Illinois University Press.

Flower, L., Long, E., & Higgins, L. (2000). *Learning to rival: A literate practice for intercultural inquiry.* New York: Routledge.

Flyvbjerg, B. (1998). *Rationality and power: Democracy in practice.* Chicago: University of Chicago Press.

Flyvbjerg, B. (2001). *Making social science matter: Why social inquiry fails and how it can succeed again.* Cambridge, UK: Cambridge University Press.

Flyvbjerg, B. (2011). Making social science matter. In Georgiaos Papanagnou (Ed.), *Social science and policy challenges: Democracy, values, and capacities* (pp. 25–56). Research and Policy Series. Paris, France: UNESCO Publishing.

Foucault, M. (1990). *The history of sexuality: An introduction.* Trans. Robert Hurley, 1978. London: Penguin Books.

Fraser, N. (1989). *Unruly practices: Power, discourse, and gender in contemporary social theory.* Minneapolis: University of Minnesota Press.

Fraser, N. (1990). Rethinking the public sphere: A contribution to the critique of actually existing democracy. *Social Text,* 25/26, 56–80.

Goldblatt, E. (2007). *Because we live here: Sponsoring literacy beyond the college curriculum.* New York: Hampton Press.

Grabill, J. T. & Simmons, W. M. (1998). Toward a critical rhetoric of risk communication: Producing citizens and the role of technical communicators. *Technical Communication Quarterly,* 7(4), 415–441.

Habermas, J. (1991). *The structural transformation of the public sphere: An inquiry into a category of bourgeois society.* Trans. T. Burger. Cambridge, MA: MIT Press.

Habermas, J. (1996). *Between facts and norms.* Trans. W. Rehg. Cambridge, UK: Polity Press.

Hauser, G. (1999). *Vernacular voices: The rhetoric of publics and public spheres.* Columbia, SC: University of South Carolina Press.

Hermans, H. & Hermans-Konopka, A. (2010). *Dialogical self theory: Positioning and counter-positioning in a globalizing society.* Cambridge, UK: Cambridge University Press.

Higgins, L., Long, E., & Flower, L. (2006). Community literacy: A rhetorical model for personal and public inquiry. *Community Literacy Journal,* 1(1), 9–43.

Jarratt, S. C. (1991). *Rereading the sophists: Classical rhetoric refigured.* Carbondale, IL: Southern Illinois University Press.

Kellner, D. (1998). Globalization and the postmodern turn. In R. Axtmann (Ed.), *Globalization and Europe* (pp. 23–42). London: Cassells.

Kemmis, S. (2012). Phronesis, experience, and the primacy of praxis. In E. A. Kinsella & A. Pitman (Eds.), *Phronesis as professional knowledge: Practical wisdom in the professions* (pp. 147–162). Rotterdam, Netherlands: Sense Publishers.

Kirkland, D. (2013). *A search past silence: The literacy of young black men.* New York: Teachers College Press.

Long, E. (2008). *Community literacy and the rhetoric of local publics.* West Lafayette, IN: Parlor Press.

Lynch, P. (2013). *After pedagogy: The experience of teaching*. Urbana, IL: Conference on College Composition and Communication/National Council of Teachers of English.

Miller, C. (2000). The Aristotelian *topos*: Hunting for novelty. In A. Gross & W. Walzer (Eds.), *Rereading Aristotle's rhetoric* (pp. 130–146). Carbondale, IL: Southern Illinois University Press.

Payne, D. (2012). Pedagogy of the globalized: Education as a practice of intervention. In D. Payne & D. Desser (Eds.), *Teaching writing in globalization: Remapping disciplinary work* (pp. 1–16). Lanham, MD: Lexington Books.

Pinnow, R. (2013). An ecology of fear: Examining the contradictory surveillance terrain navigated by Mexican youth in a U.S. middle school. *Anthropology and Education Quarterly*, 44(3), 253–258.

Roberts-Miller, P. (2004). *Deliberate conflict: Argument, political theory, and composition classes*. Carbondale, IL: Southern Illinois University Press.

San Pedro, T. (2015). Silence as shields: Agency and resistances among Native Americans in the urban Southwest. *Research in the Teaching of English*, 50(2), 132–153.

Schell, E. (2012a). Framing the megarhetorics of agricultural development: Industrialized agriculture and sustainable agriculture. In R. Dingo & B. Scott (Eds.), *Megarhetorics of global development* (pp. 174–198). Pittsburgh, PA: University of Pittsburgh Press.

Schell, E. (2012b). Think global, eat local: Teaching alternative agrarian literacy in a globalized age. In D. Payne & D. Desser (Eds.), *Teaching writing in globalization: Remapping disciplinary work* (pp. 39–56). Lanham, MD: Lexington Books.

Scott, R. (1967). On viewing rhetoric as epistemic. *Central States Speech Journal*, 18(1), 9–17.

Scott, T. & Welch, N. (2016). *Composition in the age of austerity*. Boulder, CO: Utah State University Press.

Scribner, S. & Cole, M. (1981). *The psychology of literacy*. Cambridge, MA: Harvard University Press.

Sibley, W. M. (1953). The rational versus the reasonable. *The Philosophical Review*, 62(4), 554–560.

Tracy, K. (2010). *Challenges of ordinary democracy: A case study in deliberation and dissent*. University Park, PA: The Pennsylvania State University Press.

Trimbur, J. (2000). Composition and the circulation of writing. *College Composition and Communication*, 52(2), 188–219.

Warner, M. (2005). *Publics and counterpublics*. New York, NY: Zone Books.

Welch, N. (2011). La langue de coton: How neoliberal language pulls the wool over faculty governance. *Pedagogy*, 11(3), 545–553.

West, C. (1993). *Prophetic fragments: Illuminations of the crisis in American religion & culture*. Grand Rapids, MI: Wm. B. Eerdmans Publishing.

Young, I. M. (1997). *Intersecting voices*. Princeton, NJ: Princeton University Press.

2

DYNAMIC AND DISTRIBUTED ARGUMENT

Youth and Contemporary Public Life

That impasses and stand-offs characterize the ways many people think about navigating disagreement indicates that we are facing a deep crisis of imagination in the ways we think about argument and public life. Our (in)ability to imagine, to take seriously, and to some degree share and navigate the interests and experiences of others across deep differences limits not only how we understand domestic and global citizenship, but also how we enact that citizenship with others. In talk and in practice, the inability to take seriously the interests and experiences of others leads Americans—in English Language Arts classrooms and in public life—to cast those who disagree as deeply flawed in character. As we've seen on the Senate floor or in presidential campaigns, casting disagreement as morally wrong brings democratic deliberation to a screeching halt. More disturbing, the suicides of gay youth across the nation (Erdely, 2012), the criminalization of Black bodies (Alexander, 2010), and the proposed expulsion of immigrants (Leopold, 2015) remind us that casting disagreement as immoral is a kind of annihilation that makes difference—and anyone who embodies difference—an enemy to be squashed. This chapter takes up these concerns in three sections: Part I focuses on limitations of current models of argument instruction, including more expansive models; Part II theorizes how contemporary theories of genres as ecologies of recurring social action offer ways of thinking about argument and power relations as distributed; and Part III looks at distributed arguments affecting youth and threatening and re-writing contemporary public life.

Part I: Current Models of Argument Instruction

Many of the logics underlying an adversarial model of public life are perpetuated—among other places—in our writing pedagogy and *praxis*. These ways of handling differences are perhaps especially prevalent in the ways argument writing is often taught in ELA and FYC classrooms. Consider the classic issue debate, an instructional mainstay in the English classroom. While a debate has *potential* to generate dialogue across difference and aid participants in arriving at new understandings, it typically serves to further isolate participants from those taking an alternative stance. Literacy scholar Bob Fecho (2011) reminds us:

> [A] debate is mostly about destruction. Debaters listen to the other team, not necessarily to learn from them, but, instead, to dispute, refute, and ultimately defeat their argument. Instead of ideas comingling and trans-acting, a debate proclaims a winner and a loser. But, as Bakhtin suggests, vanquishing the opponent also vanquishes the dialogue.
>
> *(p. 17)*

The issue debate is often part of a larger unit related to teaching argumentative writing. The underlying goal of the unit is for students to learn to create an airtight argument—a text type—that is impervious to the ideas of others. This view of "traditional argument" so prevalent in classrooms also "predominates in American culture, and it is what you are used to when you listen to people argue on television or when you read arguments in current periodicals or books" (Wood, 2006, p. 315). Traditional argument, according to Nancy Wood, author of a number of textbooks on argument, is the type in which

> the object is to convince an audience that the claim is valid and that the arguer is right. In this traditional model, the arguer uses the rebuttal to demonstrate how the opposition is wrong and to state why the audience should reject that position. Thus the emphasis is on winning the argument.
>
> *(p. 315)*

This emphasis on convincing, rebutting, and winning marks much of tradi-tional argument and is closely connected to teaching argumentative writing as the production of a particular structure and set of components, conceptualizing and operationalizing argument as a kind of tidy mathematical equation. Regardless of whether this shows up in the form of the traditional five-paragraph essay or some-thing more elaborate, instruction focuses on the pieces and how they fit together (Newell, Bloome, & Hirvela, 2015).

Consider, for example, the ways research is often integrated into the teaching of argument. Students are asked to produce a thesis, articulate some supporting reasons, collect and explain data that supports those reasons—in this order. This approach, prevalent in many ELA and composition classrooms, is problematic for a couple of reasons. One concern, as George Hillocks (2011) has explained, is that much of teaching argumentative writing is claim-driven rather than inquiry-driven. Hillocks (2011) wrote in his book, *The Teaching of Argument Writing*:

> Although many teachers begin to teach some version of argument with the writing of a thesis statement (a claim), in reality, good argument begins

with looking at the *data* that is likely to become the *evidence* in an argument and which gives rise to a thesis statement or major claim. That is, the thesis statement arises from a question, which in turn rises from the examination of information or data of some sort.

(p. xxi)

While Hillocks' point is important, his explanation is perhaps a bit too tidy. With regard to public life, inquiry and argument start with cognitive dissonance about the data of our lives, with "felt difficulties" (Dewey, 1998) or "life-world disturbances" (Habermas, 1996) that are often difficult to name and even more difficult to get others to recognize and value (Fraser, 1989; Higgins & Brush, 2006). Rather than embracing the uncertainty inherent in dissonance to propel deep inquiry and dialogue, instructional models more often invoke conquest or avoidance and separate inquiry and dialogue from argument.

When students stake out a claim without engaging in deep inquiry and dialogue first, their claims are "likely to be no more than a preconception or assumption or clichéd popular belief that is unwarranted and, at worst, totally indefensible" (Hillocks, 2011, p. xxi). These initial pet theories, when touted and clung to, often have the effect of shutting down inquiry and shutting down internal and external dialogue, especially dialogue across difference where new meanings and understandings can be constructed. It is only when those initial claims—and the people who make them—are open to new data and new interpretations that dialogue begins and that discovery and change are possible. That is, for argument to be dialogic, the people involved must be willing to consider data and different ways of understanding and interpreting data *and* must be willing to listen to and be affected by the arguments of others.

A claim-driven rather than inquiry-based and data-driven approach to argument is not very different from the classic debate. Both have in mind to advance already engrained thinking and to vanquish an opponent, and thus, real dialogue, discovery, and meaning making. Adults recognize this kind of phenomenon when they say that those who organize "town hall meetings" and "planning discussions" aren't really going to do anything differently anyway. In those cases, argument starts with the claim, not with data and certainly not with inquiry and dialogue, which raises another critical point. Claim-driven argument is often more about those in power rationalizing their foregone conclusions and about maintaining relations of power than about applying rationality in ways that are responsive and accountable to new information and experiences and perspectives. For argument to be dialogic, it must also attend to and interrogate ways of reasoning together, and ways of reasoning together must also be on the table for deliberation.

As Hillocks (2011) points out, argument begins with inquiry; it begins with the data of people's lived lives, often first experienced as felt difficulties (Dewey, 1998; cf Habermas, 1996). As Fecho (2011) notes in his discussion of the classic debate, argument is also about what people do with each other. And as experiences with institutions have likely reminded many of us, argument is also about power. And yet, textbooks and classroom practices rarely address attending to the data of people's lives and the felt difficulties people encounter in ways that lead to inquiry with others, leveraging and developing well-tooled possibilities for making sense of data, unpacking and co-constructing ways of reasoning with and relating with others, or interrogating, navigating and re-writing power relations. More often, definitions and practices of argument limit the goals of argument to an intent to persuade and the shape of argument to a preset form, often a fixed text type that relays a preconceived claim.

While a form-driven approach to argument may offer useful concepts and language for understanding arguments and argumentative writing, conceptualizing and teaching argument solely in terms of a particular form—or even multiple forms—often oversimplifies the complexity and uncertainty of argument, renders relationships with those who disagree as zero-sum games in which someone must always lose, makes reasonability about a pre-set form and dominant versions of "common sense," and disconnects argument from inquiry and knowledge-building.

Likewise, a cognitive approach that focuses primarily on cognitive processes—like developing "argument schemas" (Reznitskaya & Anderson, 2002); analyzing "facts and abstractions" (Fleming, 2010); and identifying enthymemes, syllogisms, deductive reasoning, and logical fallacies (Gage, 1983)—offers language and schemas that are potentially useful but neglects the situated, networked, and relational aspects of argument as well as the cultural, historical, and political complexities that inform and shape what any of us experience as conflict and difference. Further, a cognitive approach, which often leads to producing a pre-set text type, often renders argument as a mere exercise to be done neatly in a classroom under laboratory-like conditions, which may help young people become skilled at reproducing those practices and texts under similarly contained conditions, but may not do much good elsewhere in the charged and uncertain situations in which young people most need to be able to reason together with others. Further, in practice, a focus on cognitive processes often invokes a fencing metaphor (see the cover of Hillocks (2011) book *Teaching Argument Writing*) or a chess match and continues to focus on intellectual moves that are still ultimately about winning.

Socio-cognitive models and feminist models of argument—alternatives that focus on problem-solving, negotiation and understanding and that highlight social relationships as well as knowledge building—"point toward a more expansive definition of argument, one that challenges the primacy of persuasion or pro-con debates" or traditional forms of argument "in which a rhetor attempts to convince or convert an opponent" (Knoblauch, 2011, p. 245). Consider some of the alternative definitions circulating in popular textbooks focused on argument:

- *Invitational rhetoric*—a process in which one seeks understanding rather than persuasion (Foss & Griffin, 1995)
- *Mature reasoning*—working toward a position rather than starting with a position to defend (Crusius & Channell, 2009)

- *Civil conversation*—treating an issue as open instead of settled; arguing rather than quarrelling (Charney et al., 2006)
- *Middle ground*—seeking middle perspectives not oversimplified by widely divergent views (Palmer, 2009)
- *Weighing perspectives*—carefully considering a full range of perspectives before coming to judgment (Lunsford, Ruszkiewicz, & Walters, 2010)
- *Clear reasoning*—clarifying and supporting reasons to find and promote the best belief and course of action (Ramage, Bean, & Johnson, 2010)

These definitions seem to focus on social practice and social action with others, defining argument in terms that are not solely or primarily about opposition and persuasion but instead in terms of shared inquiry, discovery, and negotiated meaning making without necessarily situating argument in public life.

While this theoretical turn is promising and hopeful, it's operation is less so; even when composition textbooks include "alternatives like Rogerian argument and invitational rhetoric, the processes by which these texts are 'teaching' argument are rarely expansive" (Knoblauch, 2011, p. 245). In a survey of current textbooks popular in high school writing classes, dual enrollment composition courses, and university First-Year Composition courses, Abby Knoblauch (2011) found that "a closer look shows that more expansive definitions [of argument] are often retooled as another form of traditional argument, one that privileges arguments as winning and under-cuts the radical potential of argument as understanding across difference" (p. 245). For example, consider the common re-tooling in which Rogerian argument, sometimes called conciliatory argument, tends to be turned toward persuasive purposes, a trend, Knoblauch (2011) points out, that troubled Car Rogers himself: acknowledging another's perspective becomes a means for disarming an opponent and ultimately winning that person over with a "delayed thesis."

This re-tooling also reveals how pervasive are the models of argument as text type and argument as cognitive processes—models that too often oversimplify and distort:

- the conditions under which arguments are constructed;
- the ways of knowing and ways of relating underneath certain versions of argument;
- the ways arguments circulate and their meanings twist and flip (Dingo, 2012);
- the cultural logics informing different ways of reasoning;
- complex social practices of argumentation;
- the ways models of argument come up short;
- power relations inherent in social relationships;
- the tentative and symbolic nature of language;
- the stochastic nature of argument; and
- the need to invent alternative means of negotiating uncertainty, conflict, and difference with others when current means come up short.

Rather than focusing on argument as a text type or isolated cognitive process, what might it mean to shift the figure-ground and focus on the social practices of argument in public life? While I will continue to unpack some possibilities in the coming chapters, for now, it's instructive to consider this kind of shift more broadly in terms of genres.

Part II: Recurring Social Practices and Distributed Arguments

In ELA and FYC classrooms, talk about genres often gets conflated with talk about text types. This kind of talk, often centering on textual features readers can expect to encounter, can offer some useful touch points, especially for writers and readers approaching previously unfamiliar text types. The difficulty is that talking about genres as text types hides the social systems and coordinated activities—along with their aims, values, and relations of power—that call for and produce a given text with particular conventions. It is often precisely around texts—suspension policies, truancy letters, insurance claims, medical bills—that people most experience systems working or not working for them. Sometimes the difficulty is with the text itself, but more often, the difficulty is with the coordinated activities and networks of relationships of which the text is merely one artifact.

Normalizing the text and fixing our gaze on the text turns our attention away from the activities that are really at issue and, by rendering them invisible, also makes them seem monolithic and unchangeable. In the next section, I draw on the work of contemporary genre theorists to consider what might be gained with regard to argument and public life if we adjusted our focus to instead highlight constellations of social situations. In particular, this shift points to what we stand to learn about how systems work and how people navigate the systems they find themselves part of, sometimes using what we typically think of as texts but often using other symbol systems and tools, and usually in more kinetic and visceral ways than we give them credit for.

Conceptualizing Argument Beyond a Text Type

Consider the following snapshot from a composition classroom that explores the intertextuality of even the most mundane texts (Witte, 1992). In a small computer classroom filled with 24 students, I ask students to create three different pen-and-paper texts: Eight make a grocery list, eight write directions to another building on campus, eight create an invitation to an upcoming event. After three minutes, I ask students to organize themselves in groups of three where each kind of text is represented. Students exchange documents. I ask them to read the document and without talking to anyone else, to take a minute to think about what they're thinking as they approach the piece of paper in front of them. I ask them to jot down on the backside of the paper responses to these questions:

- What are your impressions?
- What do you notice first?
- Are you making any decisions or evaluations?
- What does this paper invite you to do (and how does it do that)?
- Are there things you need that it doesn't offer?

After brief small group discussions, we talk together as a class.

Jen Clifton:	What did you notice? Let's talk about how you found yourself approaching the text in front of you.
Diego:	Well, I had directions. It was to the library, so that was good because I knew where that was. In my head, I was walking the way they told me and thinking, *Is this the way?* And trying to picture landmarks.
Ilsa:	Yeah, I was doing that, too. Taking the steps, thinking if I knew of shortcuts.
Jen Clifton:	Okay, so in your head, it sounds like you were kind of testing out the directions to see if they worked for you, and it sounds like you could know if it worked because of other times you'd been to that building, other times you'd had a similar experience.

Several students nod their heads.

Jen Clifton:	What about those of you with grocery lists? How did you approach those?
Charlie:	I was trying to see if they were healthy or not, or what kind of things they were eating.
Jen Clifton:	Okay, so you're coming at it with a critical eye, trying to judge if your peers are health nuts or not . . .
Chad:	I was trying to see what they were making.
Jen Clifton:	All right, yeah. So Chad wants to know what's for dinner? Should he come over?
Dania:	I was trying to see if I actually would know what to buy—do I know this food? Or is there a certain brand? Would they have this at my store?
Jen Clifton:	What did you decide?
Dania:	I don't know. Some things I think I would know—apples and bananas. But like cereal, I have no idea. I mean, what does this person like? What kind should I get? And there was something on the list— pecorino? I don't even know what that is. Maybe they don't have that at my store, maybe I'd have to go somewhere else, but I don't know.

Jen Clifton:	Okay, so you had some experience you could draw on to figure out what you might do, but for some things you'd need more information. How did you know to go to a store?
Dania:	Well, I mean, that's what you do with a grocery list.
Jen Clifton:	How do you know?
Dania:	That's what it's for. I mean that's what people do.
Jen Clifton:	Okay, so that's what you've done with a grocery list before? Is that what you mean?
Dania:	Yeah—
Charlie:	It helps you remember, and you go to the store because that's where the food is, the stuff you need.
Jen Clifton:	Okay, okay. Anyone else? Other approaches?
Julie:	I was going down the list and making my own list. I kept thinking, mmm, do I need some of that? Am I out of that?
Jen Clifton:	So you've got some purpose of your own you're thinking about and using this list as a jumping off point. What about the invitation? How did some of you approach those?
Adrian:	You know, where's this party? Who's gonna be there? What's happening?
Jen Clifton:	And what are you thinking about when you're getting that information?
Adrian:	Well, I mean, can I go? Will it be fun?
Jen Clifton:	Sure. You're evaluating, thinking about what's fun for you and seeing if what's on this invitation fits in some way. It sounds like you were trying to decide about your schedule, too?
Adrian:	Yeah, do I have time, is it sometime when I'm free?

Genres as Social Action

In this discussion, it's easy to see that there is something about a particular text type that signals certain ways of approaching the text and that limits others. No one who read the grocery list expected to go to a party, although it's possible that the items on the grocery list could have indicated that someone was planning a party. No one who read directions expected to buy food, unless perhaps they were being directed to the cafeteria. The text invited certain kinds of actions and put other kinds of action on the sideline. But the text *alone* didn't do that. On its own, there's no reason that a vertical list of food items would send someone to the store. As Charlie points out, a person makes a list for himself or someone else *to do something*, in this case to remember the items needed and to find those items in a place that sells those items and many more. That is, a particular need in a particular context creates a reason to produce a particular text in a particular way. The text emerges out of a recurring social need and fulfills a social need by scaffolding social action. This is true of mundane texts like grocery lists, invitations, and directions, but it is also true of other texts, including email memos, op-ed pieces, text messages, grade reports, parent-teacher conferences, remixed videos, blog posts, web sites, policy briefs, job interviews, Instagram posts, online comments, billboards, graffiti, radio essays, and others. Genres, then, are not just text types; they are instead "typified rhetorical responses to recurring social situations" (Spinuzzi, 2008, p. 17). Genres are typified social actions involving "tools-in-use" in particular social situations.

It is also easy to see from the classroom exchange that some rhetorical responses and texts become fairly calcified over time. The social action and the tools supporting the social action become somewhat standardized. In the United States at least, when a person creates a grocery list, as Dania explains, that person goes to the store—"that's what people do." A need for food cues a need for a list, which cues a trip to the store for the food. When a person makes a grocery list, he or she likely makes a vertical list so that each item is more easily visible. People may organize their lists differently—according to food groups or the layout of the store perhaps, but nearly anyone who's encountered grocery stores and needed to remember more than three items will recognize the list as a "grocery list" at first glance.

Genre Ecologies as Distributed and Distributing Arguments

If a text—or some other typified response—is used often and is familiar to a person, he or she also comes to have certain expectations about how that genre—the recurring social action and the texts, materials, and relations that support that social action—*should* be performed because of how it *has been* performed. These judgments about how something *should be* are arguments involving rationalities and reasonabilities embedded, produced, taught, and policed or resisted in social practices, texts, materials, and technologies.

These judgments are as much about social practices and relationships as they are about the thing at hand. For example, if you offer to pick up someone's groceries and that person hands you something that looks like this (see Figure 2.1), you may spend longer than ordinary deciphering what that person wants since it is in a less familiar form, and you may also think, perhaps to yourself, that this person has "done it wrong" even if you're able to figure out exactly what that person needs you to buy.

Eggs bread milk pimento cheese flour bacon bits raspberry vinaigrette spinach baby asparagus chocolate chip cookies coffee cream chicken filets butternut squash fettuccine noodles creamer granny smith apples bananas blueberry syrup butter

FIGURE 2.1 Grocery List With Unexpected Conventions

In light of your previous experiences grocery shopping, you likely want to be able to shop quickly, efficiently, crossing off items as you go. Anything about the text—messy handwriting, too little information, horizontal listing, bunched spacing, unfamiliar organization of foods—that inhibits the social action you anticipate is probably a little uncomfortable for you if not downright frustrating. After all, over time, the tools you're used to and the social action you're used to calcify together. The more we grocery shop in a particular way and create grocery lists in a particular way, the more we get into a habit with the text and with the activities the text supports. Over time, we may come to expect others to do things like shop and create with tools-in-use like lists in the same ways (or nearly the same ways) we do. We may, thus, develop a sense of correctness about a given text, even something as seemingly innocuous as a grocery list, and we may come to see certain social actions around that text as normal or similarly, as correct, standard, appropriate, neutral, even necessary.

These recurrent forms condition particular dispositions, particular responses that over time people come to see and value as the only or best or right responses. Charles Bazerman (2002) describes the moment in which we recognize a familiar recurrence:

> In perceiving an utterance as being of a certain kind or genre, we become caught up in a form of life, joining speakers and hearers, writers and readers, in particular relations of a familiar and intelligible sort. . . . It is like going to a dining room or a dance hall, or seminar or church. You know what you are getting into and what range of relations and objects will likely be realized there. You adopt a frame of mind, set your hopes, plan accordingly, and begin acting with that orientation.
>
> *(p. 14)*

Bazerman (2002) contextualizes recurring situations as fields with implications for those who encounter them (Dryer, 2008, p. 504). Put more colloquially, Bazerman (2002) explains: "if you hang around a certain place long enough you will become the kind of person who hangs around that kind of place" (p. 14).

Genres position and order people as they cue and orchestrate activity; they teach and condition and produce the kinds of responses that are possible, or not possible. As Carolyn Miller (1984) writes in her landmark essay "Genre as Social Action":

> What we learn when we learn a genre is not just a pattern of forms or even a method of achieving our own ends. We learn, more importantly, what *ends we may have*: we learn that we may eulogize, apologize, recommend one person to another, instruct customers on behalf of a manufacturer, take on an official role, account for progress in achieving goals. We learn to *understand better the situations in which we find ourselves*.
>
> *(p. 165, emphasis added)*

Miller (1984) saw that genres and the social relations they routinize persist because they frame what they permit as that which is possible. Miller (1984) suggests that "we are constituted by and through the genred sites in which we 'find ourselves' readers and writers of texts whose conventions precede us and whose historical and material origins are usually effaced" (as qtd. in Dryer, 2008, p. 506). In interpreting, producing, and using texts—like a grocery store list, a syllabus, an administrator's checklist—we find ourselves and others to be certain kinds of readers and writers in recurring situations. The familiarity of recognition that happens in recurrence and that cues uptake also "makes different situations *appear* similar" (Dryer, 2008, p. 506). Situated communication, always in some way unfamiliar, then becomes "*capable of reproduction*" (Miller, 1994, p. 71). That is, genres are recurring social situations + familiar responses and tools-in-use. Genres are more than mere situated social tools that we employ; they also produce us. They persistently order social relations in and through routinized practices; they cue, structure, and produce arguments about what is and what should be and what could be. As Dylan Dryer (2008) notes, calling on Bourdieu (2000), genres create "pressure or oppression, continuous and often unnoticed, of the ordinary order of things" (p. 141).

While sometimes not appearing to be arguments, texts and other artifacts that coordinate social relationships and activities produce rationalities and reasonabilities and teach us—let us know—what is for us and what is not for us; they teach us to know our place, or as Bourdieu put it, to develop a practical comprehension—to "know confusedly what depends on me and what does not, what is 'for me' or 'not for me,' or 'not for people like me,' what is 'reasonable' for me to do, to hope for, and to ask for" (p. 130). Consider your own interactions with tax forms, student evaluations, insurance policies, zoning ordinances, ingredient lists on packaged foods, or consumer warning labels. If you cannot put this instrument to use or adapt it in some way to accomplish the particular social activity you have in mind in a particular social sphere, you might feel, rather quickly and frustratingly, as inexpert or excluded, or have a vague sense that this activity and this tool are "not for me." You "*practically* comprehend that this is text with which it is impossible to interact, an unresponsive [tool-in-use] that constitutes without being constituted, a closed system not subject to revision" (Dryer, 2008, p. 517)—at least not by you. Your own frustration *manufactures the evidence* that allows you, indeed in some way tells you, to come to this conclusion. Instrumentally, arguments about your place in the world—about your relationship to textual propositions; about your relationship to the activities and systems that perpetuate and circulate them; and about the consequences of your place in the world—are produced and re-produced every time you experience that frustration and anticipate or experience those consequences (Crick, 2010, p. 150).

Of any writing assessment, Kathleen Yancey (1999) writes that we should ask, "Which self does [this] writing assessment permit . . . which self does [this] assessment construct?" (p. 484). We might ask this not only about writing assessments, but also about all of the situations texts, tools, and activities we encounter and create, circulate and perpetuate. The texts a person reads and writes, the activities a person engages, the recognizable social situations—the genres and genre ecologies—a person finds himself navigating teach a person more than forms, conventions, or methods; they produce arguments about what is possible—what a particular person can do (or not) and what a particular person must do (or not) in particular situations. They argue, then, what kinds of selves, what kinds of relationships, what kinds of systems, what kinds of worlds are possible and necessary, and in so doing, routinize identities and social relations.

Even a text as familiar and universal and seemingly neutral and "common sense" in the U.S. as a grocery list embeds and coordinates arguments, which is to say that it supports activities and social relationships that are full of implicit claims. When a person creates a list with a particular grocery store in mind, that person has made a judgment, a claim, that this store is the "best" place for her to shop for food for her family. Perhaps her choice is based on that store's convenient location around the corner from her house, or on the particular brands that store carries, or on the number of brands available, or on the low prices, or on the store's commitment to carrying locally grown food, or organic foods, or something else. Regardless, based on some accumulated data, the grocery list reflects implicit judgments, implicit claims about the relative value of this store in relation to other possible stores where she could shop, or even in relation to other possible ways of securing food (like, say, urban farming or hunting or going to a local farmer's market or going to a soup kitchen or a going to a food pantry or buying fast food meals or partnering with a regional Community Supported Agriculture cooperative).

These kinds of judgments are, of course, also included in the kinds of foods, the brands named or not named on the list. A particular text crafted for a particular social situation, then, embeds a host of arguments—claims that support and invite some kinds of actions with others and discourage or limit other kinds of action with people who are making their way among complex systems. These arguments are produced through content—in this case, where to shop, what kinds of foods to buy, how much to buy, what brands to select, etc.—through conventions—in this case, a vertical list, perhaps ordered in a particular way—through language choices and choices of medium and, as we'll see later, also through complex social networks that are increasingly as transnational as they are local.

Through recurrence and use, genres weave together networks (Spinuzzi, 2008, p. 17) and "interrelate with each other in intricate, interweaving webs" (Freedman & Smart, 1997, p. 240). They may be connected and used in rather different ways in response to different exigencies, producing what is rational and reasonable, what is possible and good, and for whom. Think about the multiple exigencies and tools-in-use surrounding standardized tests: a state's assessment and accountability program includes

> the production of tests, testing materials, distribution, scoring, dissemination
> of results, school grading, prep materials, and supplementary test materials

to support the retake process, and communication and enforcement of stringent testing protocols.

(Strauss, 2012)

No single tool or text functions on its own, neither do any of the recurring social situations related to producing tests and testing materials, selling and distributing those materials, scoring, etc. Further, a single text/tool, like a test, might be involved in multiple exigencies and might take on an agency of its own to determine "good" or "bad" teachers, determine funding eligibility of schools, measure a student's "success," profit Pearson Education, determine middle school or high school graduation or grade promotion, shape classroom instruction, and so on.

Genres are not simply performed or communicated; they represent the "thinking out" of complex networks of communities and institutions—a "thinking out" that qualitatively shapes the entire set of activities in which people engage (Spinuzzi, 2004, p. 38), "materializ[ing] the situated knowledge work of the past and us[ing] it to organize *and produce* the present and future" (Johnson, 2012, p. 1). These kinds of clusters of interactions, what Clay Spinuzzi (2004) calls *genre ecologies* (Figure 2.2), thus, *encode* the values of the past into what become institutional habits and ready-made practices, mechanisms, and relationships.

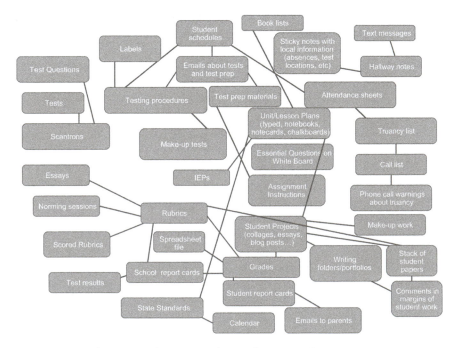

FIGURE 2.2 Tools-in-Use That Cue and Coordinate Social Practices Across a Genre Ecology

They operationalize warrants—logics embedded in processes and social activities that allow, perpetuate, and shape what *is* possible as well as what *seems* possible—without requiring deliberation over the warranted assumptions that supported the move from past exigencies to current possibilities, or impossibilities (Clifton, Loveridge, & Long, 2016). Genres and genre ecologies act just as much as they are acted upon, often in relatively stable ways (Spinuzzi & Zachry, 2000).

When we teach a particular text type, we are not simply teaching students to produce a text in isolation. When we perpetuate recurring social situations—prom, homecoming, pep rallies, homeroom rituals, parent–teacher conferences—we are engaged in genre ecologies, cuing, structuring, and producing distributed arguments, teaching young people to take up and produce particular activities and social relationships that are bound up in implicit goals, values, judgments, and systems. These ordinary texts, tools, materials, and activities cue us about norms as they order, classify, and normalize relationships and activities. These coordinated activities gain efficiency and constrain imagination through repetition and recurrence, which produce what seem to be fixed boundaries, limiting what is possible as well as what is reasonable. The values underlying coordinated activities are held together and operationalized in the most mundane and ordinary ways—through emails, memos, meetings, databases, tallies, lunches, checklists, handwritten notes, and so on.

As responses to familiar situations and activities recur and become routinized, so, too, do particular ways of knowing and being and doing. As we recognize and take on those mindsets and practices, we reproduce the value-laden warrants—the rationalities and reasonabilities—underlying them. Our imaginations are, then, constrained not only by the activities that seem possible but also by the rationalities and reasonabilities informing what activities and possibilities might be desirable. In perceiving and recognizing what we are now part of and in taking up an institution's call for particular kinds of relationships and particular schemas of activities, over time, we see and learn and produce the kind of institution and infrastructure we've come to recognize.

However, when a person is "caught up" in recurring situations, he doesn't find the situation exactly the same each time; indeed, he is not exactly the same each time. Nor does he perform in these familiar situations the same way every time. Instead, the activities and relationships as well as their rationalities and reasonabilities become his own when they are appropriated and adapted for his intentions. And yet the encoded rationalities and reasonabilities he encounters do not simply lay dormant or neutral or impersonal, waiting for him—or any of us—to put them to use. They are, rather, "in other people's mouths, in other people's contexts, serving other people's intentions" (Bakhtin, 1981, pp. 293–294)—"a part of social and political structures" that articulate the nature of the "individual within those structures and the distribution of power" (Berlin, 1987, p. 4). It is from there that a person must both "make it one's own" and simultaneously build a world together with others, a world as it "ought to be" (Branch, 2007; Horton, 1961). These are not, however, merely social endeavors; they are, rather, deeply political, tied to the ways people find and construct their lives as interdependently intertwined with others—in other words, deeply tied to public life and especially to polity and the commons.

Part III: Distributed Arguments and Contemporary Public Life

The following sections conceptualize the construction of public life as well as contemporary threats to public life by weaving together several ideas: (1) "life-world disturbances" (Habermas, 1996) are disruptions to distributed arguments, marking concerns that warrant more public attention and public dialogue across difference; (2) these disturbances often mark disruptions in previously stable experiences of rationalities and reasonabilities; (3) people going public about these disruptions are often raising questions about polity and the commons in order to re-negotiate both; and (4) recognizing and constructing polity and the commons with others is an increasingly difficult thing to do.

Before I turn to life-world disturbances that mark potential concerns for public dialogue across difference, I first unpack some contemporary conditions complicating the concerns people recognize as public and undercutting the ways people see themselves "stuck together" with others. In particular, I focus on the ways neoliberal discourses and strategies bear down on youth lives and simultaneously erode the means by which youth might call others to share their concerns. Understanding contemporary threats to public life is especially important for contextualizing argument in the social practices of deliberative publics because these threats frame compelling rationalities and reasonabilities underlying both the need for public life and the need to regularly re-invent public life.

Conceptualizing Public Life Under Contemporary Conditions

Conceptions of public life have long been tied to state governance, including who governs—a king or a set of nobles or the poor—and how those who govern are kept in check, or if, indeed, there are mechanisms to hold them in check. As I mentioned in the introduction and in Chapter 1, commonly held contemporary notions of public life and of democracy are based on an Enlightenment era ideal that theorizes public life as a deliberative democracy of the middle class—separate from both the state and the market—but capable of influencing the state, often to support the needs of the market in relation to propertied interests. This construction of relationships among the state, the economy, and the people obscured many of the ways people experienced life under capitalism—"hiding stark inequalities of wealth and power" as well as how those were distributed unevenly across sex, race, class, nationality, and sexuality

(Duggan, 2003, p. 5). Historically, under economic liberalism, these inequalities have routinely been rendered "private" or "personal" and bracketed away from consideration in "public" life (Duggan, 2003; Fraser, 1990). That is to say, some people's interests—primarily those of White propertied men—were considered "public" while other people's interests were considered "private" and, thus, "inappropriate" for public attention or dialogue. However, this bracketing is not simply an occurrence of the past. It persists now in similar and equally elusive forms.

Of course, the language of economic liberalism that cleanly separates these economic, state, public, and private spheres does not account for the real and complex ways they interrelate, but it does suggest something about the ways people come to conceptualize how their own individual lives connect with the lives of others. In the U.S., "personal" issues involving marriage rights or domestic abuse have only relatively recently been recognized as public concerns. Other concerns, like those about fair pay, are often still seen as personal or private concerns, primarily affecting a lone individual or family despite the persistent, patterned, and pervasive wage gaps that still exist for a large swath of the U.S. working population. For example, consider U.S. wage gaps reported in 2014. Overall, women working full-time earned 83% of the wages men did. But then take a look at intersectional identities: the median earnings per week for Asian women was $841; for White women, $703; for Black women, $611; and for Latinas, $548 (Bureau of Labor Statistics, 2014). The disparities widen within some groups if nationality or age or sexuality or marital status are taken into account. Millions of people across the U.S.—especially marginalized people—are affected and yet wages or salaries are often still considered too "private"—not public enough, which is to say, not in people's collective interests enough—for people to discuss with others, even at the dinner table. The flip side is that economic liberalism aims to contain and constrain public and state interests so that they do not regulate or interfere in the "private" property of those who pay wages, historically, and still primarily, White men.

This is significant for considering some of the questions raised in the introduction regarding engaging youth in public literacies, most notably those related to conceptualizing and constructing public life with others: *How do we co-construct what needs to be deliberated with others? How do we construct shared concerns? How do we learn to listen for concerns that deserve more public attention?* Youth who would attend to their own and others' lived lives for public and yet-to-be-public concerns must also consider how particular concerns and particular people are discursively positioned in relation to public life. Indeed, calling others to attend to and share a concern, whether or not they've experienced it themselves, may involve enticing them to consider what they previously thought of as "private" as a matter of public interest. Certainly, this was some of the significant cultural work of African American youth in the Civil Rights Movement when they aimed to extend racial equality into "private" employment practices, customer bases, and civil institutions. "Personal" experiences at water fountains, public buses, public schools, and lunch counters all became important sites of public attention and public dialogue.

As you likely recall, prior to the Civil Rights Movement in the U.S., the New Deal also expanded notions of public and state interests to what were previously "private" economic matters. The Civil Conservation Corps was one such effort. Together, these efforts to expand the state and public life were seen by some as efforts to reduce freedoms of "private" economic and family life. In response, some people aimed to reprivatize as much as possible, *except* concerns related to family and sexual life, like birth control, abortion, or gay marriage (Duggan, 2003, p. 8). Some people, thus, argued for *more privacy* in economic and civil society and *less privacy* (and more state governance) in their non-favored forms of family life (Duggan, 2003, p. 8).

Neoliberalism and the Erosion of Polity

This new version of economic liberalism, now coined *neoliberalism*, characterizes much of contemporary U.S. public life (Alexander, 2010; Clifton, 2016; Dingo, 2012; Duggan, 2003; Long, Fye, & Jarvis, 2012). Operationally, neoliberalism, despite being tied to a particular set of interests, functions "as a kind of non-politics—*a way of being reasonable*" (Duggan, 2003, p. 10, emphasis added), without interrogating or being open to public deliberation about the particular ways neoliberalism plays out in particular people's lived lives. Overall, the primary strategy of neoliberalism is *privatization*—"the transfer of wealth and decision-making from public, more or less accountable decision-making bodies to individual or corporate, unaccountable hands" (Duggan, 2003, p. 12).

In the U.S. and around the globe, as public resources, like water and food, and public institutions, like schools and prisons, are bought and run by corporations, they are effectively removed from public domain and accountability; they are off limits as public concerns. These moves systematically erase resources previously shared as a commons—something I'll discuss more later in this chapter—and simultaneously re-figure and constrain relations among strangers, focusing them on capital and wealth rather than polity, while also removing the practical and moral means by which strangers can collectively appeal to one another and reason together.

2.1 Eliciting Alternative Rationalities and Reasonabilities

One of the primary strategies of neoliberalism is to separate economic conditions from systems that bear down unevenly on people, to instead, blame poor economic conditions on a lack of "personal responsibility" (Dingo, 2012; Duggan, 2003). Neoliberal systems produce people who think it is natural to blame individuals when systems fail; indeed, these systems produce people who cannot see or believe that a system failure is anything other than an individual failure. The real catch is that neoliberal strategies blame system failures for some people on systems (which is typically the case when those the systems were designed to benefit and who have benefitted from the systems most often and most reliably experience difficulties) and system failures for others on individuals (typically those the systems were not designed to benefit). But systems don't work equally well for all people, and they bear down on people differently, unevenly. In other words, systems—educational systems, employment systems, health systems, etc.—will often catch someone with an intersectional identity of a Latina single mother from Mexico or a Black Queer youth in rural Georgia differently than they will catch someone with a different intersectional identity.

Public literacies attend most of all to where systems we share don't work for people and to where relationships with strangers indicate that distributed rationalities and reasonabilities are inequitable and unjust. These disturbances are, after all, where we most need argument and public life to effect some change. Neoliberalism is particularly dangerous for democratic public life precisely because it denies that the concerns the most marginalized would raise are *public* concerns at all. Here, I offer two possible tools to help youth learn to attend differently to people's concerns in order to consider alternatives to blame/guilt models of self–other relations.

Understanding the Story-Behind-the-Story

The *story-behind-the-story* is a practice that deliberately positions typically marginalized speakers and writers as active decision-makers in their own lives. Asking youth to tell the *story-behind-the-story* of an encounter invites them to "revea[l] the hidden logics and interpretative reasoning" behind their actions, an important step toward recognizing their often under-acknowledged agency (Flower, 2008, p. 56), rivaling dominating ideologies and practices. It is a practice that elicits the *hidden transcript* (see Chapter 3), asking, "What's really going on?" The practice of eliciting the *story-behind-the-story* is a direct counter to prevailing myths that often undergird neoliberalism, including myths of the representative man or model citizen, of the need for assimilation, of bootstrap mentalities, of Aid-to-Africa discourse, among others. Instead, the *story-behind-the-story* replaces abstractions of "Others" and untested claims with detailed accounts of particular individuals with specialized expertise making their way under particular conditions—"valued-but-not-privileged understandings and interpretations that a deliberative democracy needs to consider" (Higgins, Long, & Flower, 2006, p. 30). In particular, the *story-behind-the-story* attends to unspoken logics in the *public transcript* (see Chapter 3): *Who gets cast as an agent, an actor, a decision-maker? Who is harmed in this encounter? Who gains in this encounter? What's at stake for the most vulnerable person? What's at stake for the least vulnerable person?*

Seeing Others as Decision-Makers

Rather than invoking people as victims or problems when systems aren't working, public literacies ask youth to consider what a person is up to on their own terms. The following questions can be useful for re-seeing people in particular situations as they navigate systems:

- *Goals and Desires.* What goals does a person have in this instance? What does she need or hope to accomplish? How does this person need this system to work for her?
- *The Struggle: Problems, Concerns, Limitations.* How does this person see the struggle? What questions, problems, concerns, or limitations is this person concerned with? What concerns is she raising?
- *The Tools: Strategies, Logics, Stances, Actions.* What strategies and tools does she leverage in a difficult encounter to try to get a system to work for her? What situated logics make this make sense to her? What kind of stance does she take, or what action does she take? What is this person hoping to do through that stance or action?
- *Taking Stock.* What is this person trying to account for? What is she trying to protect? What does she say is at stake, or what seems to be at stake? What does she name as losses and gains?
- *Cultural Work.* What aspects of a particular culture or local public does this person see himself speaking to, for, with, or against (*Flower, 2008*)? What (*or whom*) is this person trying to change?

This erasure of public life is not, however, aimed at the erasure of government; instead, it is aimed at capitalizing on government. These privatized services often rely on lower-paid workers, lower-quality materials, and at times, direct government subsidies. The public and state expansion of welfare resisted in the New Deal is, thus, redistributed not to the marginalized, who experience wage inequality, among other difficulties, but to "job creators" and "capital creators" (Duggan, 2003, p. 15). Lisa Duggan summarizes the language game of neoliberalism this way:

> When the state acts to support "private" business interests—providing subsidies and bailouts, for instance—that can be good. But when the state acts in the "public" interest—providing housing for the poor or protection for the environment or raising minimum wages—that can be intrusive, coercive, and bad.
> (*p. 13*)

Neoliberalism is so dangerous in part because it shames those whom the market harms, blaming individuals for system failures, while removing any public means of correcting those systems.

Constructing polity and public life with others has become increasingly difficult as private troubles have been largely cut off from larger social, economic, and political considerations; as moral principles of mutual caring, respect, and compassion for others have both been relegated to personal and family spheres; and as moral principles guiding public life have been both cast off by privatized interests and co-opted for purposes of branding and profitability.

Youth Lives and Neoliberalism

The difficulties of neoliberalism are not merely "adult" difficulties. Neoliberalism also positions youth and their lived lives in terms of the market—as portfolios, as niche consumers, or as problems that marketable services can address—rather than as people under public trust and public care. Many youth experience these pressures as stress (Flower, 2008; Peck, Flower, & Higgins, 1995; Pope, 2003). While neoliberalism casts these pressures as individual concerns, we might consider what it might mean to engage youth in taking up these concerns first and foremost as shared, public concerns.

Youth Selves as Portfolios

Students applying for college or otherwise thinking about their futures are pressured to see themselves in terms of their marketability; increasingly, youth must "package" themselves primarily as entrepreneurs—as "free agents" managing their selves as business portfolios (Gee, 2004, p. 105). On college applications and job applications, they must be "ready and able to re-arrange the[ir] skills, experiences, and achievements creatively (that is, to shape-shift into different identities)" in order to define and portray themselves as competent and worthy for a new niche need as the market shifts. As literacy scholar James Gee (2004) explains,

> If I am now an 'X' and the economy no longer needs 'X's, or 'X's are no longer the right thing to be in society, but now 'Y's are called for, then I have to be able to shape-shift quickly into a 'Y.'
>
> *(p. 105)*

Youth often experience these pressures as stress and anxiety, motivating them to do community service, make straight A's, cultivate a "niche" skill, attempt to "go viral" on social media, participate in student government, participate in an internship, and so on, in order to create a distinct, marketable self.

Youth as Niche Consumers

The pressure youth experience to commodify their selves (Duits & van Romondt Vis, 2009) requires constant innovation and continual self-invention. This pressure coincides with the ways corporations market to youth, appealing to the "need" to craft an "authentic" identity on the market and among peers, thus creating "one's own celebrity brand" (Griffin, 2014, p. 34). Gaining increased access to youth through smart phones, computers, television, and other electronic devices, multinational corporations address youth as consumers, branding products around relationships and identities, and relying on the neoliberal pressures youth experience to engage in a continual project of "(self)surveillance, transformation, and improvement" (Griffin, 2014, p. 33) as if it were their own "free" choice. The pressures of neoliberalism are negatively impacting the mental health of young people, contributing to depression, anxiety, and stress as they try "to construct and display themselves as distinctive, authentic and discerning selves through consumption and as ethical, responsible moral subjects" (Griffin, 2014, p. 33). These pressures put youth with the "right" cultural and financial resources in a position to be upheld as moral pillars while those without are viewed as moral failures. As Griffin (2014) puts it, "If young people behave or appear in ways that are perceived as excessive, unhealthy, irresponsible, undisciplined, then this is constituted as a *moral* failure of the self (Croghan et al., 2006; Griffin et al., 2009)" (p. 33).

Youth as Problems

The youth in Callie's eighth grade class certainly were aware of being positioned as problems because of their language, their clothes, their presence, or their skin. Privatization of social care—for youth, for the elderly, for the poor, for people who are mentally or physically ill or challenged in some way—is often promoted through language of *personal responsibility*, shifting costs from state agencies to individuals and families (Duggan, 2003, p. 14). However, for youth—especially poor youth and youth of color—"'responsibility' is more often a form of repression—and 'success' is achieved when a particular subject shows obedience to the rules laid down by a facility or staff member" (Meyers & Schept, 2015, p. 4). In practice the disciplining and punishment of youth ranges from posters prominently placed next to pencil sharpeners or by entryways, shouting in bold letters, "The attitude STOPS here!" (Dean, 2016) or "NO EXCUSES!" (Pinnow, 2013), to metal detectors and School Resource Officers embedded in schools, to policing youth clothing (Pinnow, 2013), to enforcing curfews (Flower, 2008), to high stakes standardized testing, to "correcting" heritage languages (Alim, 2004), to zero-tolerance policies that closely resemble the culture of prisons.

Re-imagining Polity Under Contemporary Conditions

The rhetorical work of constructing shared concerns and cultivating dialogue across difference involves not only considering how public (or not) others see a concern but also considering who else does, or should, share that concern, and on what grounds. This is a question of polity: *Whose lives are interdependently intertwined around this concern? Who is "stuck together"?*

Historically, polity has been tied to geography and economics, most often in relation to a single governing body like a city, a state, or a nation-state. However, as neoliberal strategies shift to global processes and global markets, resources and systems are broadly distributed and intricately linked; decisions are networked and often made behind closed doors; and power structures of the market and the state are increasingly tangled.

This is especially troublesome because, as you'll see in an upcoming description of the Bolivia water wars, corporate-state interests often destroy or privatize the resources people share in common, and erase and/or render insufficient local deliberative processes tied to an individual nation-state. Historically, deliberative democracy has most often been situated within the legal system, representative government and institutional arrangements of national state boundaries (Fischer, 2004). However, many scholars consider this conceptualization of public life inadequate to sustain a vibrant democracy (Dryzek, 2000). Under contemporary conditions, deliberative democracy that is limited to functioning within the mechanisms of the nation-state and electoral democracy is increasingly limiting and insufficient for bringing about more just systems and relationships for everyday people.

For this reason, deliberative democracy, John Dryzek (2000) argues, needs to recapture its critical bent and re-figure itself to work within as well as transcend the constraints of the nation-state (Rosenberg, 2003). Further, and more to the point of this book, public deliberation must be a pedagogical project as well as a political one, "fostering the capacity of personal autonomy and constructive interpersonal relations that the governance of the lives of real people require" (Rosenberg, 2003, p. 15). The goal, contextualized in ELA and FYC classrooms, is to assist young people in their efforts to better understand, communicate, and negotiate their own ideas and interests, as well as those they share with near and distant others, in the face of power and opposition and competing discourses (Fischer, 2009, p. 24). Conceptualizing deliberative publics around polity and the commons in a world increasingly interconnected beyond local and even national bounds is an important step toward re-figuring argument as dialogue across difference capable of supporting an inclusive and pluralistic public life in a world simultaneously connected and fragmented.

Re-imagining the Commons Under Contemporary Conditions

Young people—all of us, really—experience pressures and anxieties about the ways global forces impact their day-to-day lives and possible futures. Importantly, this also means that merely local understandings and *a priori* claims are often insufficient to make sense of, let alone address, many shared concerns, even many of those that are first understood as local concerns. This anxiety points to a need to contextualize polity and the commons to include and move beyond the local as globalization complicates the ways people's lives are intertwined.

Consider, for example, Bolivia's water wars at the turn of the 21st century. Rhetorician Darin Payne (2012) explains:

> Thirty years prior, right next door in Brazil, Freire was outlining problem-posing education as a means of helping peasant students understand how their lives are subjugated by a ruling class and, importantly, how they might work to create local changes, how they might organize and agitate for, say, clean drinking water in specific communities. All well and good, but by 2000, the relations of production and consumption had shifted, as evidenced in Bolivia: San Francisco's Bechtel Corporation is part of a transnational consortium that had gained ownership over that country's drinking water. Bechtel's acquisition of such a fundamental local resource was the outcome of neoliberalizing loan terms dictated by the [World Bank], which insisted on privatization when Bolivia sought loans to rebuild their water systems (Shiva).
>
> *(p. 7)*

Thus, a local public resource—a *commons*—became a globalized and private resource as the "relations of production and consumption . . . shifted" (Payne, 2012, p. 7). When a young person's family, able to access water the week before, suddenly cannot access water because they cannot pay the new exorbitant rates, argument as a claim-driven text form is insufficient. Who would the young person make her case to anyway? Often, that's not even clear when these kinds of globalizing neoliberal practices and policies suddenly impact water quality or access. Equally worrisome is that the loss of a resource of the commons is nearly always accompanied by a loss of rights to the relations of the commons.

This struggle over water is, after all, not merely a struggle over resources; it is fundamentally a struggle related to the intersection of argument and public life. The struggle over resources is a struggle over the nature of public life, over who we see ourselves interdependently connected to, how we characterize the nature of that connection, and what that means for how we will be together, how we will do argument together—if and how we will listen and learn from one another, see our own well-being tied up in the well-being of others, create to-some-degree shared values, allow for productive dissensus, and so on.

Attending to commons and where they are violated is an important part of public life, for "the best measure of how a democracy functions is how it distributes the goods of the land: the air, waters, wandering animals, fisheries, and public lands, otherwise known as the 'public trust' or the 'commons'" (Midkiff, 2010, p. ix). A *commons* is essentially a resource held "in common," something valuable and un-owned, and, thus, free for all. A commons does not require anyone else's permission to use, or if permission is needed because the resource is limited, then the resource is shared in an equitable way and permission granted in a neutral way. The essence of a commons is that it is not a possession, and so no one owner has "the exclusive right to choose whether the resource is made available to others" (Lessig, 2001, p. 20).

Some *commons*, like water or the Boston Common, are limited in a way that "my use of it competes with your use of it"; others, like language or Einstein's theories, are not rivalrous in that "my use of it does not inhibit yours" (Lessig, 2001, p. 21). Whether or not a resource is limited is not what determines a commons. Instead, Lessig (2001) explains: "What has determined the commons is the *character of the resource* and *how it relates to a community*. In theory, any resource might be held in common" (Lessig, 2001, p. 21). This value-oriented determination reflects an important and central aspect of public life: strangers determining if and how they see themselves interdependently stuck together (Young, 1997), as well as how they will relate with one another—what they will share, how they will share, and with whom.

This is less complicated for a resource that cannot be exhausted. However, with a limited resource, like potable water, how we share that resource matters immensely. Of course, there is risk in sharing resources. A person can diminish the commons by taking excess resources out of the commons or by abusing what is held in common. This is what is known as "The Tragedy of the Commons" (Hardin, 1968). Treating a commons as individual property erodes the commons as a commons *and* erodes the ways strangers see and relate to one another. That is, treating a commons as something that can be bought, sold, and owned changes the nature of relationships among strangers, shifting them from one of interdependent citizens who at times need to deliberate together and regulate resources for the good of all to those of sellers and consumers whose primary interest is their own individual gain, an interest rendered "private."

In Bolivia, water that had previously been a commons shared with everyone in Bolivia, but belonging to no one as property, was sold as property. The commons was, thus, eroded as people were stripped both of their access to clean drinking water (it then belonged to a distant ruling elite) and also of their right to any political or public process (since water was no longer part of the commons, the private corporation—and not any local polity—made decisions about "the *character of the resource* and *how it relates to a community*" and determined how those decisions would be made). The people most in need of clean drinking water in Bolivia became even more distanced from any public process that might improve the conditions of the most basic resource needed for human life.

Where previously there had been a public right to water *and* a public right to deliberate about water rights and access, privatizing water re-shaped public life, denying the right to and possibility of productive dialogue across difference. This denial, however, did not erase the need for deliberation, for argument, for navigating uncertainty, conflict, and difference. Instead, this denial reconstructed uncertainty, conflict, and difference not as sites for social practices of argument but as sites of violence. Payne (2012) continues:

> When local citizens protested the immediate and massive rate hikes that occurred within weeks of transnational privatization, they suffered police brutality (including tear gas and rubber bullets, leading to numerous casualties and five deaths) in a series of skirmishes that eventually led to the

undoing of the contract (which had been set to last an astonishing forty years). The turning point in the water wars, it could be argued, came with the global media coverage of teenager Victor Hugo Daza being shot in the face, and thus killed, by state police.

(p. 7)

Boutrous Boutros-Ghali, former secretary general of the United Nations, predicted in 1996 that a struggle over the world's water resources would be the defining struggle of the 21st century. A 2006 *New York Times* headline proclaimed, "There's Money in Thirst." The article stated, "Everyone knows there is a lot of money to be made in oil. But a fresh group of big businesses is discovering there may be even greater profit in a more prosaic liquid: water" (Deutsch, 2006). A handful of multinational corporations are, quite literally, banking on a pending global water crisis (Piper, 2014). Many youth in the U.S.—from Huron, California, to Flint, Michigan—are already experiencing the effects of treating the commons as private property.

2.2   Mapping Recurrence and Variation

It can be difficult for any of us to understand the impact of routinized practices on people's life-worlds (Habermas, 1996), even our own. Juxtaposing rival perspectives of the same system(s) can be one way of understanding the rationalities and reasonabilities that are operating in the most mundane but consequential ways. It is equally important that youth have tools for making sense of these accounts beyond merely personal interpretations—"now I see that these are people just like me" (Herzberg, 1994, p. 139). To leave it at that is to engage in a kind of temporary band-aiding that leaves the systems that reproduce these structural conditions unaddressed and that continues to teach youth to construct their connections to others in public life primarily in relation to their own feelings and experiences. Juxtaposing rival perspectives can help youth to attend to the "networked arguments" (Dingo, 2012) circulating across systems and to listen for the structural conditions that constrain and shape what is possible for particular people. Importantly, this means seeing that *this one person* related to *this one area of concern* is, in fact, linked to larger, networked social arrangements.

Valuing Multiple Perspectives

To invite young people into considering and responding to a range of possible perspectives—from those perhaps most familiar to those least familiar—you might include poems, short stories, TED talks, documentaries, audio essays, songs, editorials, academic articles, newspaper blogs, and so on that demonstrate a range of thinking that overlaps, contradicts, raises questions, surprises, and complicates students' (and your) ideas. Reading and viewing shorter works that include a range of different experiences with strangers and institutions can help *stir up the dust* and raise questions about those differences.

Mapping Recurrence and Variation

By juxtaposing a range of rival experiences, perspectives, and terms operating in tangible ways in and across systems, teachers can begin to make visible to students the ways discourses connect and diverge, take shape and shift across systems—and especially the ways they differently "catch" different people. Visibly and collaboratively juxtaposing, mapping, and dramatizing these in relation to one another and unpacking what's at stake in these perspectives—the differences that make a difference—can begin to reveal a complex dialogue already in motion and can set the stage for students unpacking their own hidden logics in relation to the ideas they're brushing up against in class through texts and with their peers. By juxtaposing rival experiences, perspectives, and the language used to name different people's experiences, students can start to recognize systems at work (see Figure 2.3).

Capitalism, Creativity, and the Commons	
Texts	**Perspectives**
Unilever's Dove "Real Beauty" campaign Unilever's Axe Body Spray ads Unilever's Fair & Lovely ads for skin-whitening cream	Multinational corporation creating socially conscientious ads for U.S. women; raunchy ads that cast women as oversexed animals for young men in the U.S.; and skin-whitening ads for women in Asia and Africa
Capitalism : A Love Story	Family videoing themselves being evicted
	Workers on strike
	Sully, a "hero" airplane pilot talking to Congress about pilot wages; another pilot talking about being on food stamps
	An African American woman asking a White carpenter not to board up a neighbor's house
	"Condo Vulture" in Florida buying houses after 2008 crash
The Moral Underground: How Everyday Americans Subvert an Unfair Economy	Bea, a middle manager, who "messes up" paperwork at a box store to give a prom dress to a low wage worker who can't afford to buy one for her daughter
	Bosses: "I'm not running a social program"
	Parents who can't make a living
The New Work Order excerpt	The language of fast capitalism: corporate bosses motivating low wage workers with titles and responsibility, but not pay
Documentary of Jean-Michel Basquiat	Urban graffiti artist whose art critiqued the sociopolitical consequences of capitalism on black bodies
YouTube interview with Muhammed Yunus	Social entrepreneur who first lent microloans to poor women in Bangladesh to alleviate poverty and "empower" women
Excerpts from Dead Aid	The impact on small villages when well-meaning Westerners send "aid" (i.e., bulk items like mosquito nets)
Dave Eggar's The Circle	Fictional account of a worker wearing a headset, hearing corporate info all day long and being held accountable for perfect scores on online surveys
"The Story of Stuff"	Animation of global processes of production and their impacts on different people

FIGURE 2.3 Texts to Support Juxtaposing Multiple Perspectives at the Intersection of Capitalism, Creativity, and the Commons

Tensions between shared benefit and individual benefit, between the ideal and the actual are also the very things that necessitate the shared use of reason and the safeguarding of public life. Neoliberal strategies erode public life and leave sick publics in their wake, blaming any differences on individuals' moral failings. "Sick publics" do not allow for dissensus, for critique, for difference (Bruner, 2010). They insist that there is little, if any, difference between people's understandings of the ideal and people's experiences of material realities. "Healthy publics" instead cultivate backtalk "to critique the distance between our ideational and material economies as best we can" (Bruner, 2010, p. 59). That is, healthy publics cultivate argument as dialogue across difference to expose the sometimes "deep distance" (Bruner, 2010, p. 63) between what publics profess about themselves and what people actually experience of those publics. M. Lane Bruner (2010) describes this as "limit work" in which publics expand their outer limits by attending to dissensus in order to leverage available means "to productively transform sick publics and states into healthy publics and states" (p. 61). However, when a public persists in telling people to get in line rather than attending to and negotiating new meaning and/or practices in light of dissensus—when it "suppress[es] critical thought" in any number of ways (p. 63), including through privatizing, and thus erasing, the commons and public spheres—a public contributes to its own ill health as it constructs the use of language among superiors and inferiors and constructs the purposes of language around dominance.

The most important point here with regard to engaging youth in public literacies, is that social practices of argument—where argument is deeply connected to navigating uncertainty, conflict, and difference with others—are essential for sustaining healthy public life. Casting argument primarily in terms of persuasion or win-loss, and limiting, or worse, erasing deliberative public life are markers of ill health. And yet, in our classrooms, argument persists primarily in terms of persuasion; in recent U.S. democratic processes, the violence and the suppression of difference has marked discourse more than the shared use of reason; and around the globe, more and more private-public partnerships re-figure and constrain or erase public life when public resources, like water and food, and public institutions, like schools and prisons, are bought and run by corporations.

Distributed Arguments, Life-World Disturbances, and the Beginnings of Public Life

Putting rationalities and reasonabilities—as well as the activities, texts, technologies, and relationships they are distributed across—to use for our individual purposes and for building a world together requires (1) that we become aware of the "structuring structures"—as Pierre Bourdieu (2000) calls them—of distributed arguments, and (2) that we respond to the distributed arguments we encounter, positioning ourselves and our ways with words in relation to others, their ideas, and their ways with words. Significantly, attending not only to arguments but also to their distribution, which is increasingly global as well as local, also has implications for how we see our lives intertwined with others and, thus, for how we attend to public or yet-to-be public concerns.

As public sphere theorists tend to cast publicity, public life begins when an idea is framed, launched, and circulated within what Nathan Crick and Joseph Gabriel (2010) call the "arc of controversy" (p. 212). Public world-making, according to Michael Warner (2005), is a matter of "[r]unning it up the flagpole and see[ing] who salutes" (p. 114). As Higgins, Long, and Flower (2006) put it, you know you're onto a public idea when the buzz around it escalates to an undeniable din (p. 13). These markers all indicate something to cultivate further argument about. But how do we get to this point? In particular, how do any of us recognize concerns embodied in the situated knowledge of others so that these concerns might receive the public attention they deserve?

In his scholarship on the ethics of life writing, Paul Lauritzen (2004) suggests that there is an ethical imperative for us to include situated knowledge in our deliberation:

> All serious moral reflection must involve a dialectical movement between general principles and concrete cases and that proper moral deliberation involves attending both to rules and to the affective responses of particular moral agents facing particular decisions.
>
> *(p. 19)*

As a "concrete case" of the ways individuals have experienced firsthand how a given institution, its policies, and its practices play out in day-to-day life (Lauritzen, 2004, p. 19), situated knowledge serves as a rich, experientially based resource for interpreting and problematizing familiar abstractions and stock solutions to problems that have not yet been fully understood (Clifton, Long, & Roen, 2012). Think about the water crisis in Flint, Michigan. City officials indicated that there might be an increased risk of using local tap water, warning that sick and elderly people might need to take extra precaution but the water was otherwise safe to drink. However, LeeAnne Walters's experience with Flint water indicated something far more devastating:

> It was the summer of 2014 when Walters first realized something was very wrong: Each time she bathed the three-year-olds, they would break out in tiny red bumps. Sometimes, when Gavin had soaked in the tub for a while, scaly red skin would form across his chest at the water line. That November, after brown water started flowing from her taps, Walters decided it was time to stock up on bottled water.
>
> The family developed a routine: For toothbrushing, a gallon of water was left by the bathroom sink. Crates of water for drinking and cooking crowded the kitchen. The adults and teenagers showered whenever

possible at friends' houses outside Flint; when they had to do it at home, they flushed out the taps first and limited showers to five minutes. Gavin and Garrett got weekly baths in bottled water and sponge baths with baby wipes on the other days. Slowly, the acute symptoms began to wane.

(Lurie, 2016)

In the following months, Gavin and Garrett experienced rashes and stunted growth, 14-year-old JD suffered abdominal pains so severe that Walters took him to the hospital, LeeAnne's eyelashes all fell out, and the entire family lost large clumps of hair (Lurie, 2016).

Clearly, the claims city officials circulated about water in Flint did not match Walters' own situated knowledge of the water crisis. It is often the case that everyday people have something to say about public institutions' forms, regulations, and procedures, as they may know something about the gaps between the professed intent of specific policies on the one hand and how they play out in lived experience on the other. Families living in apartments know a lot about how landlord-tenant policies play out. High school seniors can tell you about how off-campus lunch actually works. Transgender youth know a lot about how gender is regulated in their schools. However, an individual's situated knowledge isn't usually accessible to others as part of the collective public knowledge, even about a public resource like water. And yet, it is clearly important for public health and, at times, an important site for the shared use of reason—for argument as dialogue across difference.

People's encounters with dynamic, mostly stable distributed arguments in everyday activities and relationships inform and/or produce their situated knowledge—what they know, sometimes confusedly (Bourdieu, 2000), as they recognize, tweak, resist, and/or reproduce distributed arguments *in situ* and among systems. The stability of those encounters, not to mention the perpetuation of distributed arguments, relies on rationalization (Flyvbjerg, 1998) and on some degree of ongoing agreement or consensus about what is rational and especially reasonable. Stability, of course, as I mentioned earlier, does not necessarily indicate justice or effectiveness or equality. However, "life-world disturbances" (Habermas, 1996) that suddenly render a visible rupture between a person's life-world and the systems a person finds himself part of up-end the rationalities and reasonabilities that a person previously experienced as stable. They create "wobble" (Fecho, 2011) and doubt. Habermas (1985) explains that doubt arises "in situations over which we are not in control; they are something which objectively happens to us" (p. 198).

Doubt does not arise until "situational conditions change to such a degree that habitual behavior is disrupted and needs and desires are thwarted" (Crick & Gabriel, 2010, p. 209). Doubt emerges when rationalities and reasonabilities we've come to rely on (and not think about) are disturbed:

As soon as a behavioral habit is rendered uncertain by the resistance of reality, doubt arises with regard to the orientation that guides behavior. The undermining of habits awakens doubt in the validity of the corresponding beliefs. And this doubt motivates efforts to find new beliefs that will restabilize the disturbed behavior

(Habermas, 1968, p. 120).

In response to life-world disturbances, like the ones LeeAnne Walters or Nate or the eighth graders described in Chapter 1 experienced, we suddenly sit upright and pay attention; what had previously gone mostly unnoticed is suddenly an object of inquiry and action. As Fecho (2011) explains,

> When something wobbles—a wheel on a car, a glass of wine on a waiter's tray, a child's top, the Earth on its axis—we notice. It causes us to stare and consider. Wobble taps us on the shoulder and *induces us to ask why. It nudges us toward action. It suggests we get out of our chair and do something.*
>
> (p. 53, emphasis added)

Life-world disturbances prompt us not only "to ask why," but also to *explain why*—to consider what kinds of reasons might explain a change in terms of cooperation, and thus, to account for shifts or violations in rationalities and reasonabilities. These explanatory accounts are "shaped at the point of utterance" (Britton, 1980, p. 147), *before* a person has a sense of understanding what has happened to them, or why. James Britton explains this inventive work:

> When we start to speak, we push the boat out and trust it will come to shore somewhere—not *anywhere*, which would be tantamount to losing our way, but somewhere that constitutes a stage on a purposeful journey. To embark on a conversational utterance is to take on a certain responsibility, *to stake a claim that calls for justification*: and perhaps it is the social pressure on the speaker to justify his claim that gives talk an edge over silent brooding *as a problem-solving procedure.*
>
> (p. 147, emphasis added)

Importantly, this sense-making is a collaborative process. You likely do this when you call your mom or your partner or a friend or colleague after something strange and unexpected happened at work. Maybe you'd followed procedures as best you knew how and somehow a supervisor or colleague corrected or reprimanded you for what you thought was the right thing to do. If it's troubling enough and confusing enough, you'll likely tell someone what happened and begin to tell them why you think it happened, what was really going on. Perhaps, you say something like, "I followed all the directions on the document. I got their permission ahead of time. Then, after I turn things in, they say it's all wrong. I have no idea why they would do that. The only thing I can think is that . . ." and you offer an explanation. You are generating and shaping accounts of rationalities and reasonabilities as you utter them. You do this to consider as best you can what might have been reasonable to others. You likely do this in large part, initially, to gain a more full understanding of the situation. You are starting a dialogue across difference.

In venturing explanations of life-world disturbances, people are also often testing and constructing polity and the commons. In tentative explanations, we engage in a "moment by moment interpretative process by which we make sense of what is happening around us," (Britton, 1980, p. 149), recognize and construct patterns (Leonardo, 2005), and in *sharing* these explanations, raise implicit questions that set up a demand for further shaping and justification (Britton, 1980, p. 149):

- Is this just me?
- Is this something to work out with my boss?
- Does this concern other people here, too?
- Is this a broader concern for people—workers, bosses, African Americans, people of color, women, mothers—in other workplaces too?
- Should this concern others, if it doesn't yet?
- Who else should this concern?
- What relationships should I reasonably be able to rely on in making sense of and rectifying this life-world disturbance?

These are questions of polity. Sometimes, talking with an elder or friend or co-worker is enough to make sense of a situation and what to do next. We may realize that a situation doesn't necessarily need more public attention or dialogue. However, as a person experiences a life-world disturbance as more urgent, more confusing, and more complex, more extended dialogue among strangers might be needed to gain a more full understanding of what's going on. In this iterative process of attending to life-world disturbances and of offering and considering explanatory accounts, people construct polity as they search for and construct patterns by making claims about what happened and why and why it matters and who should care. In doing this, they are also constructing the commons—what they should be able to hold in common with others as a public good.

Of course, explanatory accounts of life-world disturbances are tentative, con-flicting, and perspectival. The account LeAnne Walters offers will be different than that of the mayor or a city council member or a worker at a water treatment plant or a scientist or environmentalist or doctor or a water meter reader. And yet, these varying perspectives are necessary for a more full understanding of a complex situation. This is the nature of the public use of reason, of argument in deliberative publics where free and equal people reason together about the public good—what public good to pursue and how to pursue it together. In considering explanatory accounts they must consider what kinds of reasons they may reason-ably give themselves and one another in the face of pressing questions and doubts about the public good. Attending to life-world disturbances as sites of inquiry and knowledge-building is important for making distributed arguments visible and for cultivating further argument about the public good and how best to pursue it going forward.

If we are going to deliberate with the fullest range of facts available, these kinds of experiential and explanatory accounts are indispensable (Lauritzen, 2004, p. 24). However, the reason for attending to life-world disturbances and situated knowledge isn't merely to glean information to inform adjustments so that an institution can run more efficiently; far more significantly, eliciting and circulating people's situated knowledge of how distributed arguments impact their lives are matters of social justice (Branch, 2007; Cushman, 1998; Long, 2009; Sauer, 2003). As Cornel West (1993) argues, the dignity and efficacy of everyday people often hinge on their ability "to attenuate the institutional constraints on their life-chances for surviving and thriving" (p. 4). It is to this work that I turn next.

References

Alexander, M. (2010). *The new Jim Crow*. New York: The New Press.

Alim, H. S. (2004). Hearing what's not said and missing what is: Black English in White public space. In C. Paulston & S. Keisling (Eds.), *Discourse and intercultural communication: The essential readings* (pp. 180–197). Malden, MA: Blackwell Publishers.

Appadurai, A. (2006). The right to research. *Globalisation, Societies, and Education*, 4(2), 167–177. London: Routledge.

Bakhtin, M. (1981). *The dialogic imagination: Four essays by M. M. Bakhtin*. Trans. C. Emerson & M. Holquist. Austin, TX: University of Texas Press. (Original work published 1975).

Barfield, C., Glassman, J., & Naím, M. (2008). A conversation about globalization. Available online at http://iipdigital.usembassy.gov/st/english/publication/2008/08/200808 21172457xjyrrep0.1554376.html

Bazerman, C. (2002). Genre and identity: Citizenship in the age of the internet and the age of global capitalism. In R. M. Coe, L. Lindgard, & T. Teslenko (Eds.), *The rhetoric and ideology of genre* (pp. 13–37). New York: Hampton Press.

Berlin, J. (1987). *Rhetoric and reality: Writing instruction in American colleges, 1900–1985*. Carbondale, IL: Southern Illinois University Press.

Bourdieu, P. (2000). *Pascalian meditations*. Trans. Richard Nice. Stanford, CA: Stanford University Press.

Branch, K. (2007). *Eyes on the ought to be: What we teach when we teach about literacy*. Cresskill: Hampton Press.

Britton, J. (1980). Shaping at the point of utterance. In R. Young & Y. Liu (Eds.), *Landmark essays on rhetorical invention in writing* (pp. 147–152). New York: Routledge.

Bruner, M. L. (2010). The public work of critical political communication. In J. Ackerman & D. Coogen (Eds.), *The public work of rhetoric* (pp. 56–75). Columbia, SC: University of South Carolina Press.

Bureau of Labor Statistics. (2014). Highlights of women's earnings in 2014. [Data file]. Available online at http://www.bls.gov/opub/reports/cps/highlights-of-womens-earnings-in-2014.pdf

Charney, D. H. & Newirth, C. M., with Kaufer, D. S. & Geisler, C. (2006). *Having your say: Reading and writing public arguments*. New York: Pearson/Longman.

Clifton, J. (2016). Feminist collaboratives and intercultural inquiry: Constructing an alternative to the (not so) hidden logics and practices of university outreach and microlending. *Feminist Teacher*, 24(1–2), 110–137.

Clifton, J., Long, E., & Roen, D. (2012). Accessing private knowledge for public conversations: Attending to shared, yet-to-be-public concerns in the deaf and hard-of-hearing DALN interviews. In S. L. Dewitt, C. Selfe, & L. U. Logan (Eds.), *Stories that speak to us: Exhibits from the digital archive of literacy narratives*. Boulder, CO: Computers and Composition Digital Press. Available online at http://ccdigitalpress.org/stories/chapters/roenlongclifton/

Clifton, J., Loveridge, J., & Long, E. (2016). Healthy infrastructure: A Constructive approach to conflict. *Community Literacy Journal*, 11(1),

Clifton, J. & Sigoloff, J. (2013). Writing as dialogue across difference: Inventing genres to support deliberative democracy. *English Journal*, 103(2), 73–84.

Crick, N. (2010). *Democracy & rhetoric: John Dewey on the arts of becoming*. Columbia, SC: University of South Carolina Press.

Crick, N. & Gabriel, J. (2010). The conduit between lifeworld and system: Habermas and the rhetoric of public scientific controversies. *Rhetoric Society Quarterly*, 40(3), 201–223.

Crusius, T. W. & Channell, C. E. (2009). *The aims of argument: A brief guide*. 6th ed. Boston: McGraw.

Cushman, E. (1998). *The struggle and the tools: Oral and literate strategies in an inner city community*. Albany, NY: SUNY Press.

Dean, A. (2016). Angela's story. In B. Fecho, M. Falter, & X. Hong (Eds.), *Teaching outside the box but inside the standards: Making room for dialogue* (pp. 65–84). New York: Teachers College Press.

Deutsch, C. H. (2006). There's money in thirst. *New York Times*. Available online at http://www.nytimes.com/2006/08/10/business/worldbusiness/10water.html

Dewey, J. (1998). *Experience and education*. New York: Free Press.

Dingo, R. (2012). *Networking arguments: Rhetoric, transnational feminism, and public policy writing*. Pittsburgh, PA: University of Pittsburgh Press.

Dryer, D. (2008). Taking up space: On genre systems as geographies of the possible. *Journal of Advanced Composition*, 28(3), 503–534.

Dryzek, J. (2000). *Deliberative democracy and beyond: Liberals, critics, contestations*. Oxford: Oxford University Press.

Duggan, L. (2003). *The twilight of equality? Neoliberalism, cultural politics, and the attack on democracy*. Boston, MA: Beacon Press.

Duits, L. & van Romondt Vis, P. (2009). Girls make sense: Girls, celebrities, and identities. *European Journal of Cultural Studies*, 12(1), 41–58.

Erdely, S. (2012). One town's war on gay teens. *Rolling Stone*. Available online at http://www.rollingstone.com/politics/news/one-towns-war-on-gay-teens-20120202

Fecho, B. (2011). *Teaching for the students: Habits of heart, mind, and practice in the engaged classroom*. New York: Teachers College Press.

Fischer, F. (2004). Professional expertise in a deliberative democracy. *The Good Society*, 13(1), 21–27.

Fischer, F. (2009). *Democracy and expertise: Reorienting policy inquiry*. Oxford: Oxford University Press.

Fleming, D. (2010). Finding a place for school in rhetoric's public turn. In J. Ackerman & D. Coogan (Eds.), *The public work of rhetoric* (pp. 211–228). Columbia, SC: University of South Carolina Press.

Flower, L. (2008). *Community literacy and the rhetoric of public engagement.* Carbondale, IL: Southern Illinois University Press.

Flyvbjerg, B. (1998). *Rationality and power: Democracy in practice.* Chicago: University of Chicago Press.

Foss, S. K. & Griffin. C. L. (1995). Beyond persuasion: A proposal for an invitational rhetoric. *Communication Monographs,* 62, 2–18.

Fraser, N. (1989). *Unruly practices: Power, discourse, and gender in contemporary social theory.* Minneapolis, MN: University of Minnesota Press.

Fraser, N. (1990). Rethinking the public sphere: A contribution to the critique of actually existing democracy. *Social Text,* 25/26, 56–80.

Freedman, A. & Smart, G. (1997). Navigating the current of economic policy: Written genres and the distribution of cognitive work at a financial institution. *Mind, Culture, and Activity,* 4(4), 238–255.

Gage, J. T. (1983). Teaching the enthymeme: Invention and arrangement. *Rhetoric Review,* 2(1), 38–50.

Gee, J. (2004). *Situated language and learning: A critique of traditional schooling.* New York: Psychology Press.

Giroux, H. (2014). *Protesting youth in the age of neoliberal cruelty.* Available online at http://www.truth-out.org/news/item/24437-protesting-youth-in-the-age-of-neoliberal-cruelty

Griffin, C. (2014). What time is now? Research youth and culture beyond the "Birmingham School". In D. Buckingham, S. Bragg, & M. Kehily (Eds.), *Youth cultures in the age of global media* (pp. 21–36). London: Palgrave Macmillan.

Habermas, J. (1968). *Knowledge and human interests.* Trans. Jeremy Shapiro. Boston: Beacon Press.

Habermas, J. (1985). Questions and counter-questions. In James Bohman (Trans.), Richard J. Bernstein (Ed.), *Habermas and modernity* (pp. 192–216). Cambridge, MA: MIT Press.

Habermas, J. (1996). *Between facts and norms.* Trans. W. Rehg. Cambridge, UK: Polity Press.

Hardin, G. (1968). The tragedy of the commons. *Science,* 162(3859), 1243–1248.

Herzberg, B. (1994). Community service and critical teaching. *College Composition and Communication,* 45(3), 307–319.

Higgins, L., Long, E., & Flower, L. (2006). Community literacy: A rhetorical model for personal and public inquiry. *Community Literacy,* 1(1), 9–43.

Higgins, L. D. & Brush, L. D. (2006). Personal experience narrative and public debate: Writing the wrongs of welfare. *College Composition and Communication,* 57(4), 694–729.

Hillocks, G. (2011). *The teaching of argument writing, grades 6–12: Supporting claims with relevant evidence and clear reasoning.* Portsmouth, NH: Heinemann.

Horton, M. (1961). Myles Horton's Talk at Experimental Citizenship School Workshop, February 19–21. Highlander Archives, Box 40, folder 4, n.p. Monteagle, TN: Highlander Folk School.

Johnson, N. (2012). Information infrastructure as rhetoric: Tools for analysis. *Poroi: An Interdisciplinary Journal of Rhetorical Analysis and Invention,* 8(21), n.p.

Knoblauch, A. A. (2011). A textbook argument: Definitions of argument in leading composition textbooks. *College Communication and Composition,* 63(2), 244–268.

Lauritzen, P. (2004). Arguing with life stories: The case of Rigoberta Menchu. In P. J. Eakin (Ed.), *The Ethics of Life Writing* (pp. 19–39). Ithaca, NY: Cornell University Press.

Leonardo, Z. (2005). The color of supremacy: Beyond the discourse of White privilege. In Zeus Leonardo (Ed.), *Critical pedagogy and race* (pp. 37–52). Boston: Blackwell Publishing.

Leopold, D. (2015). The shocking reality of Donald Trump's plan to deport millions. Available online at http://www.msnbc.com/msnbc/donald-trump-shocking-reality-deportation-plan. New York: MSNBC.

Lessig, L. (2001). The future of ideas: The fate of the commons in a connected world. Available online at http://www.the-future-of-ideas.com/download/lessig_FOI.pdf. New York: Random House.

Long, E. (2009). Rhetorical techne, local knowledge, and challenges in contemporary activism. In Peter Goggin (Ed.), *Sustainability: Rhetorics, literacies, and narratives* (pp. 13–38). New York: Routledge/Taylor & Francis Press.

Long, E. Fye & Jarvis. J. (2012). Gambian-American college writers flip the script on Aid-to-Africa discourse. *Writing Democracy: Special Issue of Community Literacy Journal*, 6(1), 53–76.

Lunsford, A., Ruszkiewicz, J., & Walters, K. (2010). *Everything's an argument: With readings*. 5th ed. Boston: Bedford/St. Martin's.

Lurie, J. (2016). Meet the mom who helped expose Flint's toxic water nightmare. *Mother Jones*. Available online at http://www.motherjones.com/politics/2016/01/mother-exposed-flint-lead-contamination-water-crisis

Meyers, R. & Schept, J. (2015). Editor's introduction. Youth under control: Punishment and "reform" in the neoliberal state. *Social Justice*, 41(4), 1–7.

Midkiff, K. (2010). *Not a drop to drink: America's water crisis and what you can do about it*. San Francisco, CA: New World Library.

Miller, C. (1994). Rhetorical community: The cultural basis of genre. In A. Freedman & P. Medway (Eds.), *Genre and the new rhetoric* (pp. 67–78). London: Taylor & Francis.

Miller, C. R. (1984). Genres as social action. *Quarterly Journal of Speech*, 70(2), 151–167.

Newell, G. E., Bloome, D., & Hirvela. A. (2015). *Teaching and learning argumentative writing in high school English language arts classrooms*. New York: Routledge.

Palmer, W. (2009). *Discovering arguments: An introduction to critical thinking and writing with readings*. 3rd ed. Upper Saddle River, NJ: Prentice Hall.

Payne, D. (2012). Pedagogy of the globalized: Education as a practice of intervention. In D. Payne & D. Desser (Eds.), *Teaching writing in globalization: Remapping disciplinary work* (pp. 1–16). Lanham, MD: Lexington Books.

Peck, W. C., Flower, L., & Higgins, L. (1995). Community literacy. *College Composition and Communication*, 46, 199–222.

Pinnow, R. (2013). An ecology of fear: Examining the contradictory surveillance terrain navigated by Mexican youth in a U.S. middle school. *Anthropology & Education*, 44(3), 253–268.

Piper, K. (2014). *The price of thirst: Global water inequality and the coming chaos*. Minneapolis, MN: University of Minnesota Press.

Pope, D. (2003). *Doing school: How we are creating a generation of stressed out, materialistic, miseducated students*. Grand Rapids, MI: Integrated Publishing Solutions.

Ramage, J., Bean, J., & Johnson, J. (2010). *Writing arguments: A rhetoric with readings*. 8th ed. New York: Pearson/Longman.

Reznitskaya, A. & Anderson, R. C. (2002). The argument schema and learning to reason. In C. C. Block & M. Pressley (Eds.), *Comprehension instruction* (pp. 319–334). New York: Guilford.

Rosenberg, S. W. (2003). "Restructuring the concept of deliberation." Paper delivered at the Annual Meeting of the American Political Science Association, Philadelphia, August 2003.

Sauer, B. A. (2003). *The rhetoric of risk: Technical documentation in hazardous environments*. New York: Taylor & Francis.

Spinuzzi, C. (2004). Describing assemblages: Genre sets, systems, repertoires, and ecologies. *Computers Writing and Research Lab.* White Paper Series #040505–2.

Spinuzzi, C. (2008). *Network: Theorizing knowledge work in telecommunications.* Cambridge, UK: Cambridge University Press.

Spinuzzi, C. & Zachry, M. (2000). Genre ecologies: An open-system approach to understanding and constructing documentation. *Journal of Computer Documentation,* 24(3), 169–181.

Strauss, V. (2012). How standardized tests are affecting public schools. *The Washington Post.* Available online at https://www.washingtonpost.com/blogs/answer-sheet/post/2012/05/17/gIQABH1NXU-blog.html

Warner, M. (2005). *Publics and counterpublics.* New York, NY: Zone Books.

West, C. (1993). *Keeping faith: Philosophy and race in America.* New York: Routledge.

Witte, S. P. (1992). Context, text, intertext: Toward a constructivist semiotic of writing. *Written Communication,* 9(2), 237–308.

Wood, N. V. (2006). *Essentials of argument.* Upper Saddle River, NJ: Pearson/Prentice Hall.

Yancey, K. B. (1999). Looking back as we look forward: Historicizing writing assessment. *College Composition and Communication,* 50, 483–503.

Young, I. M. (1997). *Intersecting voices.* Princeton, NJ: Princeton University Press.

3

CONSTRUCTING SHARED CONCERNS AND ALTERNATIVE PRACTICES OF ARGUMENT IN PUBLIC LIFE

Attending to disturbances that might warrant more public attention—like Lee-Anne Walters' experiences, suicides of gay youth across the country, school policies for dealing with bullies, or the range of concerns eighth graders raised—would fashion writing instruction as a "context[t] of discovery" (Crick & Gabriel, 2010, p. 212) where young people might identify problem situations that arise in people's everyday lives, including their own. And yet, Applebee and Langer (2011) note that "writing as a way to study, learn and go beyond—as a way to construct knowledge or generate new networks of understanding—is rare" (p. 27). Where writing classes do engage students in inquiry, they often create a "context of discovery" related to generalizable issues or conceptual themes, like heroes, adulthood, or change. Inquiry related to questions that are existentially perplexing are certainly worthwhile; however, deliberation that remains hypothetical remains distant from the goals of deliberative publics, which consider "how particular cases, not general issues, can be dealt with effectively" (Danisch, 2015, p. 413).

As important is that much inquiry in ELA classrooms leans toward individual rather than shared inquiry and knowledge building; deliberative publics foster both. After all, we deliberate not simply because we disagree, but rather because some experience has disrupted our sense of stability to such a degree that we are compelled into inquiry and action (Crick & Gabriel, 2010, p. 209). There's something we've got to figure out, something in our experiences that's got to change, and we need others to help us do both. Deliberation is not about universal reasoning about all possible scenarios, but about situated reasoning about this particular scenario that we are facing now. To do the work of situated reasoning together—of argument as dialogue across difference—we need the grounded details of lived experiences "if we are going to deliberate with the fullest range of facts available to us" (Lauritzen, 2004, p. 24). After all, it is within the actual lives of citizens that the impacts of distributed arguments can be perceived most sensitively (Habermas, 1996, pp. 307–308). If we are to create "contexts of discovery" for cultivating deliberative publics, our writing classrooms must engage youth in attending to lived lives—their own and others.

In this chapter, I call on two metaphors to suggest something of the well-tooled performative nature of public literacies needed to attend to impacts of distributed arguments: one is critical bifocality (Weis & Fine, 2012); the second is public listening for three kinds of critical incidents (Clifton, Long, & Roen, 2012; Clifton & Sigoloff, 2013; Flanagan, 1954; Flower, 2008; Higgins, Long, & Flower, 2006). Both are aimed at attending to people-in-systems and especially the uneven ways distributed arguments bear down on people and, at times, disrupt their capacity for thriving. Following the section on public listening, I theorize the capacity of hybridized, inventive texts, like critical incidents, to engage youth in critically re-imagining and enacting inclusive and generative social practices of argument and public life.

Critical Bifocality

As someone who has recently turned 40, I can tell you people turn to bifocals when something about their sight on its own is limited or failing in some way. They need an artful tool for helping them see *both* near and far at once. Bifocals are something more than simple reading glasses. They are not an end in themselves, designed for one activity. Instead, they aim to coordinate seeing what's right in front of a person with seeing the broader context at a distance so that the full range of a person's activities are well-informed by all that they see. Bifocals support a broader range of more fluid movement than, say, reading glasses do. I won't extend the metaphor further, but I linger over it in part to highlight the ways it points to the possibilities of well-designed tools to afford quick, precise, well-informed movements. We need artful tools precisely where we experience our own limitations. This is true of our physical limitations; it is also true of discursive limitations, where our current discourses—always historical, cultural, and ideological—limit what they permit us to see and do and understand and build with others.

Cultivating public deliberation about the ways distributed arguments impact people's lives requires developing what Lois Weis and Michelle Fine (2012) describe as *critical bifocality*—practices for critically attending to the ways "structures produce lives at the same time as lives across the social class spectrum produce, reproduce, and at times, contest these same social/economic structures" (p. 175). The metaphor of *bifocality* suggests something of the need for this kind of sight. Rather than seeing critical bifocality as an inquiry unto itself, the work of deliberative publics would lean critical bifocality toward the pragmatic, which would entail leveraging critical bifocality toward deliberation over goal-oriented action as well as values, which inherently includes relations with others in order to transform limitations into "new paths in order to reach—or better yet—to produce—an alternative destination" (Atwill, 2010, p. 69).

And yet, ethicist Alisdair MacIntyre (1984) would offer caution in determining courses of action: "I can only answer the question 'What am I to do?' if I can answer the prior question 'Of what story or stories do I find myself a part?'" (p. 216). However, for young people—any of us, really—determining "what story or stories do I find myself a part?" is an increasingly difficult thing to do. As public life is increasingly limited, co-opted and complicated by globalizing forces, deliberative publics call on critical bifocality to attend to people's localized experiences and to "trac[e] circuits [of privilege] by connecting global flows of capital, bodies, ideas, and power with local practices and effects" (Weis & Fine, 2012, p. 196). For example, critical bifocality might involve situating LeeAnne Walter's experiences in Flint, Michigan, in relation to the Bolivia Water Wars as well as neoliberal strategies and global flows described in the *New York Times's* "There's Money in Thirst" (Deutsch, 2006); in Ken Midkiff's (2010) *Not a Drop to Drink,* and in Karen Piper's (2014) *The Price of Thirst: Global Water Equality and the Coming Chaos.*

As an artful tool of public literacies, critical bifocality engages youth in developing a creative and critical stance toward stabilizing forces and distributed arguments in people's everyday lives as a means of attending to public and yet-to-be-public concerns that warrant further attention and deliberation. However, we don't often attend to the structures first. Instead, it is often the wobble (Fecho, 2011) of a life-world disturbance (Habermas, 1996) that points to an urgent need to frame our individual stories in terms of public life with others and to make sense of the systems and the rationalities and reasonabilities that have disrupted the life-world; in other words, life-world disturbances create an exigency for attending to the structures that produce and, at times, disrupt lives. While people tend to recognize more quickly when their own life-worlds are disrupted, attending to the lives and concerns of others requires developing productive and generative stances and tools for public listening.

3.1   Unpacking Self–Other Relations

The systems we're part of bear down in particular ways. To scaffold in-class deliberation capable of moving beyond scripted ways of relating and thinking, it can be helpful both to recognize familiar patterns of relating and to construct alternatives.

Mapping Situated Accounts

Doing a kind of discursive mapping of critical incidents can help youth come to see the ways different people are positioning themselves and others. For example, in looking at one particular dramatized situation that may mark a public concern, students might discuss the *Seeing Others as*

Decision-makers questions (see *Engaging Youth in Public Literacies 2.1*) in Chapter 2 for each of the stakeholders involved. This helps students begin to see how each person positions himself or herself, as well as how they might position one another.

Generating and Testing Grounded Possibilities

With more robust understandings of a complex situation, it may be possible to imagine alternative actionable options and outcomes (Flower, 2008; Higgins, Long, & Flower, 2006). Drawing on situated accounts in readings and viewings as case studies for in-class deliberation, teachers and youth can together unpack self–other relations and consider alternative options and outcomes for a given situation. The following example indicates both the importance and difficulty of this kind of thinking as well as how engrained and hidden (to us) particular rationalities and reasonabilities can become. In one of my own classes, we read "Gonna Work It Out: Peace and Rebellion in Los Angeles" a chapter in the iconic Hip Hop text *Can't Stop, Won't Stop* in which Jeff Chang (2005) offers a journalistic account of the days leading up to and including the Rodney King trial and subsequent L.A. riots of 1992. From Chang's text, I pieced together an excerpt:

> Daude Sherrills added a Unified Black Community Code, a code of conduct for gang members. It began, 'I accept the duty to honor, uphold and defend the spirit of the red, blue and purple, to teach the black family its legacy and protracted struggle for freedom and justice.' It warned against alcohol and drug abuse and use of the 'N-word and B-word,' and even laid down rules of etiquette for flagging and sign-throwing. It called for literacy, school attendance, voter registration programs for community investment . . .
>
> Against all odds, they had built an infrastructure of communication for peace. But for peace to last, it would take more than talk. There would need to be jobs, services, and support. So on April 28, as the party went down at Nickerson Gardens, the peacemakers marched with 250 Crips and Bloods from seven different neighborhoods to City Hall to announce the truce at a Los Angeles City Council meeting.
>
> "We made a presentation to the City Council, telling them that we was coming together to bring an end to all the violence in the 'hood,'" says Aqeela. "We told them we would like to have access to funding."
>
> "But Council members didn't exactly jump out of their chairs. One suggested applying for a $500 grant," Aqeela recalls, "And they were like, 'Thank you very much,' and ushered us out of there as quickly as they possibly could.'"
>
> *(pp. 366–368)*

I asked students to work in groups to imagine alternative responses for both groups:

> Discuss: How might Council members have experienced this scene? How might gang members have experienced this? What alternative options for the Council members can you imagine? What alternative options for the gang members can you imagine?
>
> Then: Create several *What if . . . then . . .* statements for Council members' possible responses and several for gang members' possible responses.

Despite explicit directions to consider alternative options for council members and to generate a list of options and outcomes in the form of *if . . . then . . .* statements, most groups, in a primarily White class, only named alternative options and *if . . . then . . .* statements for gang members. They laid all the responsibility on the gangs: "They shouldn't have worn colors. They shouldn't have marched down there. They shouldn't have come in such numbers. They scared the Council."

Most of the groups seemed unaware, or perhaps aware and un-phased, that they had put all the responsibility on the gangs. I pointed out that they had not assigned any responsibility to the Council. The conversation stalled. I asked, "The Council has no responsibility in this? Apply for a grant? That was their only and best course of action in this moment?" I wish I had handled this in a more dialogical way; this was one of my "Nate moments." Perhaps I might have revisited some of our earlier questions, inviting them to see the African American men and women as decision-makers. Perhaps I might have asked, "So, tell me about the other folks involved. How might the Council members have responded differently? Based on what you know about the gangs' intentions, do you think the Council was in danger? What do you think the gang members hoped would happen? How might they have wanted the Council to respond?" But I didn't. Of course, they kept working in their groups and could then come up with some alternatives, but still largely voiced that the responsibility lay with the gang members.

I share this example to mark how persistent these scripted ways of thinking and being and relating are, for students and for teachers—for me. It is also important to note the limitations of simply attending to these encounters as part of contained classroom discussion. With regard to cultivating public literacies, there is only so much preparation we can do through historical or hypothetical or fictional accounts; we need to *experience* the limitations of the ways we operationalize and produce these scripts—and we need to *experience them as limitations* in real time with real people. Unless they are felt as limitations, there is no exigency for inventing alternatives.

Attending to Public and Yet-to-Be-Public Concerns

In listening for the ways distributed arguments impact people's lives in disturbing and uneven ways, attending to narratives of life-world disturbances and initial explanatory accounts can be especially helpful. In particular, listening for what John C. Flanagan (1954) refers to as a *critical incident*—a technique often used to better understand problems in high-order performances like landing an airplane or making a medical diagnosis—can focus attention on what precisely goes wrong in moments when policies and practices, and their underlying rationalities and reasonabilities, are operationalized in ways that disrupt the life-world. Lorraine Higgins, Elenore Long, and Linda Flower (2006) describe the critical incident as a resource for subsequent joint inquiry and deliberation among people who otherwise have few occasions to listen and to learn from one another: "Yet personal stories alone don't necessarily support intercultural inquiry. The challenge is harnessing narrative's capacity to dramatize the reasons behind the teller's values and priorities (Young, 1997, p. 72) and to illustrate the rich contextual background and social conditions in which problems play themselves out" (p. 21).

In listening for critical incidents, we are attempting to hear where the private, localized knowledge of an individual or group might be reflective of or indicative of a more public issue of shared concern. Part of the test of a critical incident is its ability to elicit resonance with a listener, to evoke meaningful response, stir a relevant memory, or connect to another's prior knowledge, experience, or understanding in some way. Thus, when we are listening for critical incidents, we are listening for the places where someone else's story gets traction or raises tensions with our own or with someone else's story we've heard (Clifton, Long, & Roen, 2012). That is, we are listening-rhetors, or those who are actively pattern matching. As we recognize patterns that are in some way compelling and yet still elusive, we often respond by offering narratives and explanatory accounts we see as connected. We engage again in building a more full understanding, jointly shaping a more full account at the point of utterance. This is, perhaps, easy enough to imagine when others have had experiences that are in some way familiar and recognizable to you. But how do we pattern match when the experiences of others are unfamiliar or when they directly contradict or contrast our own experiences?

Listening Across Difference

Listening across difference is a rhetorical and political activity—essential for doing and teaching argument as dialogue across difference. It is also a way of performing reasonability with others. Again, it's helpful to distinguish rationality from reasonability. As you likely already know, "reasonable people often have crazy ideas" (Young, 2000, p. 24). What makes them reasonable is their openness toward others and their willingness to listen and learn from people who may want to interrogate their ideas and to explain why their ideas are inaccurate or off base, limited or harmful. If our understandings of the world are always partial and perspectival, limited in some way, and if inclusive and just public life would have us consider how our ideas and actions impact others, then listening and learning from others is not only a reasonable thing to do, it is also a rational thing to do *if* our aims are to construct inclusive public life with others. And yet, people are sometimes too quick to label the assertions or experiences of others as wrong or irrational—and to label the people wrong or immoral or worse—in order to avoid having to engage with them at all, dismissing the people and the ideas in one fell swoop; underneath these dismissals are often unspoken assumptions of knowing better or being better, distributed arguments that are often the legacy of painful, colonizing histories and ongoing power relations that inform and reproduce who a person will or will not dismiss out of hand. Since reasonable people often disagree and because reasonability involves a moral responsibility to consider our lives in relation to others, *dismissive moves*, like judging too quickly, are themselves often symptoms of unreasonableness and uneven power relations.

Consider this classroom exchange in a class I taught in the aftermath of Arizona's "ethnic studies ban." I projected the following paragraph on the screen:

> In April 2010, the Arizona Legislature passed SB1070, which makes it a state crime to be undocumented and requires police to check for documents if they have "reasonable suspicion" a person is in Arizona without such documents. Weeks later, HB2281 was signed into law, banning ethnic studies in K–12 schools. A law is currently being written that would deny U.S. citizenship to children born in Arizona of undocumented parents. In addition, the State Department of Education has introduced the English Fluency Initiative, banning teachers with "heavily accented" English from working with English Language Learners. English Only classes have been mandated for learners of English as a Second Language.
>
> *(excerpt from Django Paris's AERA 2011 proposal)*

A White young woman in the class said, "Okay, maybe that happens here [in Arizona], but not at this school." An African American young woman responded with her own experience at school:

> Everywhere here is segregated. You can see it in the cafeteria. All the Black people sit together; there's nowhere else for us to sit. Even the teachers here know it. As school starts in the fall, the African American teachers pull all the Black students together and warn us that we're more visible here. We stick out and teachers will notice us more. [They tell us to] sit in the front of the classroom, be on time, dress conservatively, speak up in class. Other [White] students can get by without doing those things 'cause they blend in. Not us.

The same White young woman replied definitively as if to end the conversation, "No, there's no segregation." And the class grew quiet. Her response worked in that moment to silence the local knowledge and experience of the African American young woman who had just spoken. I asked other students what they thought about what had just been said by these two young women. No one spoke. I turned on the moment and asked students, "So, what do we do in spaces where one person's local knowledge is laid side-by-side with someone else's?" Then I asked students to write down their responses and reactions.

In dialogue around life-world disturbances, where divergent experiences come into contact with each other, people often enact familiar but unproductive stances. As is clear in the classroom conversation just described or in the Day of Remembrance discussion in Nate's classroom in Chapter 1, stances that refuse reasonability also refuse to recognize a concern as a *shared* concern that deserves more public attention and public dialogue. In cultivating public deliberation about the ways distributed arguments impact people's lives, it is not enough, then, simply to support youth in documenting life-world disturbances although this is important and necessary work I'll turn to later in this chapter. Indeed, documenting the ways people's lives are disrupted without engaging youth in constructing more just reasonabilities is perhaps irresponsible, potentially perpetuating the very rationalities and reasonabilities that were problematic in the first place. It is necessary, then, to support well-tooled ways of attending to public and yet-to-be-public concerns.

In common vernacular, you've probably heard someone talk about the importance of "walking in someone else's shoes." This is one way people talk about attending to the experiences of others, especially those that seem unfamiliar. It's also a way of invoking reasonability around the principle of reciprocity. While the sentiment is well-intentioned, it is also limited in the ways it invites us to see each other's differences and attend to each other's experiences. Take my friend who was a child soldier in South Sudan. Or the people of Bolivia who had no access to water. There is no way I can "walk in their shoes." Neither can I walk in the shoes of Tamir Rice or Trayvon Martin or Sandra Bland. Nor can I walk in the shoes of others whose lives may in some ways seem more familiar and similar to mine. How, then, might we position ourselves, our stories, in relation to others? And how might we attend to others' lives and experiences without insisting that they closely resemble our own?

Rather than invoking a reciprocity that is mirror-like, where we can see ourselves in someone else's experiences, Iris Marion Young (1997) calls for "asymmetrical reciprocity," recognizing that it is neither possible nor desirable "to walk in someone else's shoes." Reciprocity, Young asserts, expresses moral respect, enlarged thought, and wonder, and asymmetry arises from people's greatly varying life histories and social positions. Asymmetrical reciprocity "start[s with] the assumption that one cannot see things from the other's perspective and [must] *wait to learn by listening to the other person*" (Young, 1997, p. 49, emphasis added). This requires adopting a stance that includes "openness as well as being able to see one's own position, assumptions, perspective as strange, because it has been put in relations to others" (Young, 1997, p. 56). Attending to public and yet-to-be-public concerns requires that we "distinguish between taking the perspectives of other people into account, on the one hand, and imaginatively taking their positions, on the other hand. Through dialogue people can sometimes understand each other across difference without reversing perspectives or identifying with each other" (Young, 1997, p. 39).

Listening for Public and Yet-to-Be-Public Concerns

As a metaphor, listening, like critical bifocality, is instructive about the kind of stances, tools, and practices young people need for inclusive public life. As an activity, listening invokes something performative, enacted with others in the moment. It suggests attention outward and inward, and if you think about those charged moments or long meetings when it is perhaps most difficult to "hear someone out," it suggests active engagement, intentional waiting, and open-handed perseverance (Brayboy, 2005)—a deliberate orienting of the self in relation to others and to context. Royster (1994) posits that while listening can be leveraged as an important "code of cross-cultural conduct" (as qtd. in Ratcliffe, 1999) at various points in the work of deliberative publics, it has a distinct role in attending to public and yet-to-be public concerns.

As a trope for interpretive invention and the co-construction of new understandings, listening suggests altogether different orientations to dialogue and difference. In *The Other Side of Language: A Philosophy of Listening*, Gemma Corradi Fiumara (1996) suggests that a philosophy of listening might allow for "truer forms of dialogue" (p. 13). Rather than establishing point and counterpoint and listening for what might be immediately agreed with or dismissed in someone else's account, we may instead become "apprentices of listening rather than masters of discourse" (Fiumara, 1996, p. 57). In this version of listening, a listening-rhetor would attend to what is silenced or unsaid or cast out—for what is exiled in some way—and consider its relation to cultures, contexts, and selves. Rhetorician Krista Ratcliffe (1999) explains that this is not a relativistic "anything goes" stance, nor a naïve one; instead, listening in this way presumes "an ethical responsibility to argue for what we deem fair and just while simultaneously questioning that which we deem fair and just" (p. 203). She contends that listening in this way "may help us invent, interpret, and ultimately judge differently in that perhaps we can *hear* things we cannot *see*" (p. 203, original emphasis).

Noticing how little and how poorly people listen to one another, Ratcliffe (1999) raises questions about the difficulty of listening:

> Why is it so hard to listen to one another? Why is it so hard to resist a guilt/blame logic when we do listen? Why is it so hard to identify with one another when we feel excluded? Why is it so hard to focus simultaneously

on commonalities and differences among ourselves? And how do the powerful differentials of our particular standpoints influence our ability to listen?

(p. 198)

Community literacy scholars, likewise, note "[T]he most difficult and fragile task
[is] to figure out where and how to listen" (Simmons & Grabill, 2007, p. 445).
Similarly, when community meetings fail, community residents often characterize the failures as failures in listening (Higgins, Long, & Flower, 2006, p. 15);
by extension, when residents express a leeriness to invest in public inquiry and
deliberation, that skepticism often turns on whether others—whether adults or
Suits—"in fact, will listen" (Higgins, Long, & Flower, 2006, p. 25). Such scholarship makes clear: acts of public listening are as tenuous as they are valuable.

Just as recurring social situations and their distributed arguments cue and
produce familiar texts and social interactions, so, too, do they cue and produce
familiar and normalized ways of listening and understanding. That is, our ways
of listening—and rationalities and reasonabilities that would signal *who* to listen
to (or not) and *how* to listen to them—are also distributed across genre ecologies. Reasonabilities and rationalities are, then, not only connected to activities,
texts, and technologies, but they are also attached to particular bodies. Consider
the range of ways people are talking about gender-neutral bathrooms. In large
part, this is a conversation about what is rational and reasonable—what is possible and desirable—for trans bodies (and who gets to decide). The embodiment
of rationalities and reasonabilities is also reflected in particular ways people with
particular bodies learn to listen.

To see how this is so, it is instructive to take in turn a set of examples Ratcliffe
(1999) offers. She begins with Deborah Tannen's (1990) astute claim that men
and women learn to listen differently: men often listen in a way that will help
them position themselves as one up while they resist being put in a one-down
position by others; women invoke a rapport dynamic with encouraging non-
verbal and verbal cues (p. 142). In other words, notes Ratcliffe (1999), "men are
socialized to play the listening game via the questions 'Have I won?' and 'Do you
respect me?' while women are socialized to play it via the questions 'Have I been
helpful?' and 'Do you like me?'" (p. 203). While I am not trying to reify gen-
dered norms Tannen (1990) observed of men and women back in the 1980s, I
am suggesting that reasonabilities and rationalities distributed across a range of
activities in genre ecologies produce people in particular and recognizable ways
that often become familiar in their recurrence and in some way naturalized and
uninterrogated.

Listening is, thus, informed by the precise ways institutions bear down on identities, particular intersections of identities—for example, Queer + Latina or African
American + working class + man or White + Deaf + woman[1]—perpetuating and
conditioning particular ways of being.[2] To drive home this point, Ratcliffe (1999)
cites a fictional scenario by Nikki Giovanni (1994), a poet's internal dialogue with

herself while composing a talk for the 372nd Annual Convention of Black and White Women in America:

> I suppose we shouldn't even talk about how the women's movement wouldn't listen to the Black women when we tried to say that the average white woman didn't understand her maid. I mean, [in the movie *An Imitation of Life*] when Lana Turner said to Annie, "I didn't know you belonged to a lodge," Juanita Moore replied, "Well, Miss Laura [*sic*], you never asked." There was no women's movement; there was a white women's movement and Black women never were, nor felt, included. It's all been an imitation of life to us, and the long walk home won't change that.
>
> *(pp. 85–86)*

In this scenario, familiar and resonant and true despite being in some ways fictional, Giovanni (1994) points out the ways that some privileged people, in this case White privileged women, do not listen to others, in this case Black women. This is not simply a matter of *not listening*; it does not even occur to Lana that listening to her maid, Annie, might be a possible or worthwhile thing to do, despite the ways Lana would have attended to some of the most intimate details of Annie's life. Together, Giovanni (1994) and Tannen (1990) reflect part of why public listening is so hard. Recurring social situations cue people to be "caught up" in particular ways. When people "take up" these cues, they reproduce recognizable patterns, including patterned ways of listening or not listening, proving Bazerman's (2002) point: "If you hang around a certain place long enough you will become the kind of person who hangs around that kind of place" (p. 14).

These scripted ways of listening and relating play out in everyday encounters. Of course, people are often quite savvy at negotiating these encounters. And yet everyday encounters over housing, water, food, and employment, like the ones described next, show that people's lives are often disturbed in ways that others might not recognize as disturbances *unless* they learn to engage in public listening. Consider a woman in an industrial town in the northeastern U.S., who asks Ellen Cushman (1998) to help her produce a phone script for calling to ask about available apartment buildings. Flipping through the newspaper, Mirena tells Cushman (1998):

> "None of these landlords will let me rent when they hear me on the phone. They probably won't even show me the place or tell me where it is."
>
> "Why's that?"
>
> "The way I talk. They'll know I'm Black. You want to help me practice what I'm gonna say on the phone?" I agreed. She said my talking with her would "help [her] sound more respectable, you know White."

Afterward, Mirena told Cushman (1998) "'*That's what landlords want to hear.* They want to rent to someone they recognize.' [Another neighborhood woman] said that 'It ain't that *I* think White is more respectable than Black. But I think they gonna think that way'" (p. 85). In this case, predictable ways others will or won't listen condition what Mirena and other neighborhood women will or won't say and how they say it. They don't agree, but experience tells them they won't be listened to otherwise. Further, they connect *listening* to *recognition*. Identification with a person—"someone they recognize"—frames reciprocity and polity; difference threatens it. Thus, in this case and many others, material well-being is tied to ways of listening.

Equally perplexing is the connection between listening and power. Cushman (1998) documents another scenario in which Raejone, a 24-year-old mother of two, is talking with a social worker about welfare and housing. The housing office representative, Kathy Oaks, tells Raejone that she will read to Raejone the Section 8 housing application "'because some of the words are tricky'" (Cushman, 1998, p. 157) to which Raejone thinks to herself "What? 'Cause I'm poor, I can't read, you f—ing bitch?" Raejone reads ahead, noticing that the fine print stated that providing information about race was optional, and then asked Oaks why she filled in the optional information about race without either reading the fine print to her or asking if she wanted her ethnicity disclosed. Raejone was careful not to alienate herself from the gatekeeper entirely. She recalls, "I could say, 'yo' what's your problem? Gimme my benefits" (pp. 158–159). But in Raejone's estimation, such an approach would have only confirmed Oaks' negative attitude about her, letting her think, "'Oh, another lazy nigger'" (p. 159). Raejone figured: "'I ain't gonna give them that satisfaction'" (p. 159). Raejone points out that Oaks had no right to make decisions on her own about the ways they interacted over the form or what Raejone chose to disclose on the form. And yet Raejone must be careful in pointing out the ways Oaks is not listening to her—not even constructing a space in which listening to Raejone is an option—because of the power relations at play already informing and shaping the ways reasonabilities are enacted through listening.

Cross-cultural, and especially gatekeeping, encounters, require that we listen differently to "hear what's really going on" (Long, 2008, p. 100). Long (2008) explains "we'd need a special audio recorder that could simultaneously record two frequencies: one broadcasting the signal for the *public transcript*; the other, the *hidden transcript*" (p. 100). Hidden transcripts challenge the superiority of the public transcript, calling into question the rationalizations that allow recurring situations to recur in the particular ways they recur. Using hidden transcripts to call public transcripts up short, residents were able "to both mollify and rebuke, play into and off of, adopt and adapt, placate and challenge, conform and undermine, accommodate and resist" (Cushman, 1998, pp. 227–228). These tensions and clashes often point to places where institutions are not working for people's lives. Attending to the "dualing dualities" (Cushman, 1998, p. 139) can point to the unspoken ways people experience rationalities and reasonabilities as coming up short, opening up space, not only for "critique, question[ing], seek[ing] paths around, and attempt[ing] to subvert the racist and classist ways these institutions work" (Cushman, 1998, p. 96), but also for public dialogue across difference.

Gaining understanding through public listening, then, entails more than simply listening for a speaker/writer's intent. It also involves more than simply listening for our own self-interested intent, which may range from "appropriation (employing [what we hear] for one's own ends), to identification (smoothing over differences), to agreement (only affirming one's own view of reality)" (Ratcliffe, 1999, p. 203). Instead, understanding means listening to the world around us and the ways others name and describe their experiences "not *for* intent but *with* intent" (Ratcliffe, 1999, p. 203)—with the intent to understand not just the claims or the rationalities and reasonabilities within which the claims function, but the complex negotiations people engage in as competing rationalities and reasonabilities clash in real time in public and hidden ways. To clarify this process of understanding, Ratcliffe (1999) recommends inverting the term and defining understanding as *standing under*—consciously standing under discourses that surround us and produce us and others, while consciously acknowledging "all our particular and fluid standpoints" (p. 205).

With regard to public literacies, standing under our own discourses means identifying the various distributed arguments we encounter across genre ecologies, noting what we "take up" and learn is possible or not (Dryer, 2008; Miller, 1994) for us and others as we are "caught up" (Bazerman, 2002) in recurrent social situations. Recognizing that the rationalities and reasonabilities of these arguments cue and produce ways of listening and arguing and imagining with others—ways that can become so naturalized for us that they are no longer visible to us (Ratcliffe, 1999, p. 203)—points to the need for explicitly teaching artful stances and tools for public listening and dialogue across difference.

Taken together, these accounts suggest that public listening is

- *A stance born of moral humility*: Listening in public life invokes what Michael Warner (2005) would call a unique "stranger relationality" (p. 74–76) predicated on openness (Middleton, 2011, p. 170), particularly an awareness that despite one's best effort, one simply cannot imagine what it's like to walk in another's shoes, but, instead "with careful listening" one "can learn to understand important aspects of . . . lives and perspectives" different from one's own (Young, 1997, p. 42). Quoting Gemma Corradi Fiumara (1996), Ratcliffe (1999) writes that such openness exposes the "'fragility of our [own] doctrines'" (p. 105). This is especially significant for attending to the ways distributed arguments may disrupt others' lives while leaving our own intact, exposing the limitations and injustices of our own rationalities and reasonabilities.

- *A performative rhetorical practice*: The point here, then, is not to mete out by some calculus distinct ways that reading, writing, speaking, and listening each affect public engagement. Instead, it is to recognize listening as part of performative public literacies to emphasize and attend to the range of expertise and knowledges that are purposefully called on and orchestrated within public life.

- *Epistemic.* Public listening claims cultural difference as a site of learning. Even more to the point, such sites allow for precise knowledge to be constructed that may well not be constructed otherwise or elsewhere. The knowledge-building is a co-constructed interpretation, a more fully elaborated account of shared concerns, made possible by collaborative inquiry in which participants listen and learn from one another across difference.

- *Supported by artful stances, tools, and practices.* Practices affiliated with public listening can be scaffolded through non-normative artful tools stable enough to be taught, yet flexible enough to be relevant and adaptable across contexts (Atwill, 2010). These artful tools—like *public transcripts* and *hidden transcripts*—work to expose hypocrisies and life-world disturbances and rectify injustices of the system world perpetuated by distributed arguments. As such, tools for public listening assume a transgressive spirit that defies domestication and, thus, supports the transformative visions of critical publics (Bruner, 2010).

- *Temporal.* Different practices of listening support different dimensions of public life within the rhetorical "life-cycle" of a given deliberative public. Some practices of listening are more attuned to the emergent work of constructing shared concerns with others. Some support the behind-the-scenes "design" work that helps call a public into being and focus and frame subsequent inquiry and deliberation. Other tools help scaffold inquiry and deliberation in an opportune moment of public engagement.

- *Intersectional.* Because "patterned treatments" (Leonardo, 2009, p. 77) of distributed arguments do not bear down on a singular identity in isolation, public listening is attentive to particular intersections of oppression and privilege that point to sites of life-world disturbances and condition the ways people listen and learn from others, or don't.

- *A way of performing reasonability.* As a moral practice, public listening attends to the ways people name and describe their experiences of systems and practices and the distributed arguments they perpetuate. Tools and practices of public listening scaffold particular attention to the ways distributed arguments bear down unevenly in people's lives and to the ways people's lives are disrupted by unjust systems and practices that are out-of-sync with their own goals and needs. Equally important, public listening works as an inventive practice for co-constructing more just grounds for relating with others across difference.

- *Asymmetrical.* Public listening does not demand recognition or familiarity as a prerequisite for attending to others' lives and concerns, hopes and desires. Instead, public listening assumes and values difference and is patient, attentive to the wonder and self-determination of others.

- *Critically attentive to distributed arguments.* Rationalization is a primary strategy in the exercise of power, and deliberative publics aim to condition and leverage power toward common good. As power is often more interested in maintaining power than in pursuing the common good, public listening is critically attentive to the ways power might neglect or side-step or falsify deliberation in normalizing and naturalizing distributed rationalities and reasonabilities in everyday activities.
- *Crucial to recognizing and constructing polity.* Tools and practices of public listening scaffold a stance of asymmetrical reciprocity capable of recognizing the ways people's lives are intertwined locally and globally with near and distant strangers and capable of at times constructing shared interdependence with others where previously a sense of polity had been limited or nonexistent.

Our listening and interpretation of what we are hearing are always constructions, always highly contextual, and always highly dependent on our own particular lives, histories, experiences, and knowledge. What resonates with one person or group may not resonate at all or in the same way with someone else. Further, our understandings are always provisional. It is not necessary, therefore, for teacher- or student-rhetors engaged in this kind of listening to be (or to become) experts or insiders in a given D/discourse. Listening for and listening to and interrogating life-world disturbances is not about gaining mastery or accruing status (Young, 1997). Rather, listener-rhetors assume "[a] respectful stance of wonder toward other people [that] is one of openness across, awaiting new insight about their needs, interests, perceptions, or values" (Young, 1997, p. 56). Public listening is thus grounded in "attentive and interested questioning" where answers are always regarded with wonder as gifts and where listeners recognize that the other person may choose, for reasons of his or her own, to remain silent or offer only part of a story (Young, 1997, p. 56).

As listening and understanding and seeing newly is the goal, neither teachers nor students necessarily need to be experts to spark conversations that invite others to attempt to recognize or construct critical incidents (Clifton, Long, & Roen, 2012; Clifton & Sigoloff, 2013; Flanagan, 1954; Flower, 2008; Higgins, Long, & Flower, 2006) and interpret/understand them. However, as Higgins, Long, and Flower (2006) note in their work in community literacy with problem narratives, some background knowledge may be helpful, even necessary, serving not only to inform our own expertise, but also to call it into question by juxtaposing it with the expertise of others (p. 23). The more nodes we have to inform our tentative schemas, the more we can appreciate the nuances within a critical incident.

Because tapping into localized knowledge can reveal the ways distributed arguments play out in people's lives and offer insight into problems that we hadn't previously recognized or understood or seen in the same way, conversations that attempt to elicit this situated knowledge are worth having. Further, as critical incidents may be tied to issues of social justice and related to the material world and to people's dignity, the more conversations, the better, and ELA and FYC classes are sites where these might also have disciplinary value in teaching argument as dialogue across difference.

Public Listening for Critical Incidents

Institutions, their practices, and their distributed reasonabilities and rationalities can change only as we—stakeholders, teachers, youth, customers, service professionals, citizens, patients, tenants, managers, owners—change. As Porter, Sullivan, Blythe, Grabill, and Miles (2000) put it: "Institutions R Us. We made 'em. We can change 'em." (p. 611) But this is far easier said than done. In part, this is because of the ways public and private are conceptualized. For example, the phrase "public policy" implies that such policy is more public than private. But there's much about public policy that is often hidden from view. For instance, as Crick and Gabriel (2010) note, enacting public policy is not usually a decision point in itself, but rather the reflection of decisions already made—and ones perhaps more private and less publicly available than the text or daily enactment of the official policy. Policies that are made public by government organizations or other institutions monitor, govern, and regulate the spaces and terms under which our private lives intersect with institutions. Remember Raejan's experience, for example, or LeAnne Walter's. Public policies stem from our interactions with other individuals—even ones we might consider private—where some part of our interaction falls under the perceived jurisdiction of an institution (Cushman, 1999, p. 47). This is true whether we're talking about the use of public parks or tenant–landlord agreements or public restroom rights or the use of phones in class. Public spheres theorists have most often framed public life starting from the point that an idea moves from private to public, but tensions between private and public knowledge exist at every point within the arc of a controversy (Crick & Gabriel, 2010), and we need different kinds of private knowledge to inform public conversations at different points within the trajectory.

However, when life-worlds are disturbed, simply explaining that a practice is limited or ineffective or harmful is rarely enough to bring about a change in policy, practice, or self–other relations. Martha Nussbaum (1995) has noted that "an ethics of impartial respect for human dignity will fail to engage real human beings unless they are made capable of entering imaginatively into the lives of distant others and to have emotions related to that participation" (p. xvi). Rules and propositions do not often move us, especially, on behalf of those who are not like us. It is a difficulty of imagination.

But narratives have the power to implicate readers, to draw us out of the narcissistic enclosure of the ego in ways that more conventional point-driven explanation does not. Richard Kearney (1996) cites the importance of Holocaust narratives. Holocaust survivors felt an ethical imperative to make others participate so that the horrors of the Holocaust wouldn't be repeated.

Certain injustices appeal to narrative imagination to plead their case lest they slip irrevocably into oblivion. Ethical experiences of good and evil, as Nussbaum (1995) says, need to be felt upon the pulse of shared emotions. Or as Paul Ricoeur (1988) says, commenting on narratives of the Holocaust, the horrible must strike the audience as horrible (p. 43). The examples that Kearney (1996) draws upon make clear the ability of an experiential narrative to allow us to be impacted by a distant other. But that premise holds true whether we're talking about something with the gravity of the Holocaust or—as Cornel West (1993) reminds us—the way that an institution or public policy plays out in daily life.

Equally important for deliberative publics is that general principles and platitudes are inadequate both for comprehending the total spectrum of human activities and for becoming expert rhetors and virtuoso social actors in public life (Flyvbjerg, 2001, p. 22). Rule-based deliberation founded on formal logic "focuses on those properties of human activity by which humans most resemble machines or Weberian bureaucrats" (p. 22). While logic and analysis are important, this model—often enacted in ELA and FYC classrooms using the Toulmin model—exaggerates the importance of mathematical rationality and analysis based on platitudes, "allowing them to dominate our view of human activity: so much so that other equally important modes of human understanding and behavior are made invisible" (Flyvbjerg, 2001, p. 23).

To transcend the "insufficient [critical-]rational perspective," we also need "context, judgment, practice, trial and error, experience, common sense, intuition, and bodily sensation" (Flyvbjerg, 2001, p. 23). These only come to us through experience with concrete cases. Generalizable rules are inadequate in the face of contingency and uncertainty, the very domains in which rhetorical pragmatism—and the events of our lives—demand we take wise action. Specific case knowledge is, thus, crucial "to control and order the decision-making process so that contingency, uncertainty, and probability [do] not prevent action" (Danisch, 2015, p. 55).

However, personal stories alone are not enough to foster public deliberation. Instead, carefully culled and crafted dramatizations are needed that make visible conflicting rationalities and reasonabilities that are, to some stakeholders, otherwise hidden. As Higgins, Long, and Flower (2006) explain:

> Narratives that elaborate on stakeholders' reasoning, social positioning, and life contexts generate new information and propel discussion that can move people beyond personal expression to public problem solving. When narrative is elaborated in this way and focused around the causes of and responses to problems, it can be used for case analysis. In the context of public deliberative inquiry, critical incidents elicit carefully contextualized accounts of how people actually experience problems involving, for instance, landlord–tenant relations, gang violence, school suspension policies, or welfare reform.
>
> *(p. 21)*

In public listening for critical incidents, we attend to life experiences that we and/or others experience as urgent, disruptive, and problematic in some way; that warrant attention, resources, problem-solving, and/or action that on our own we cannot bring about; and that, even when quite personal interests or circumstances are involved—restroom practices, sexual orientations, house hunting for a place to live, accessing water for personal use, buying groceries for your family—the attention, dialogue, and action needed requires involving near and distant strangers.

Conceptualizing Critical Incidents

Certainly, literary works of all kinds are full of rich critical incidents where people experience tension with the rationalities and reasonabilities of particular times and places playing out in real time and with high stakes. These can be a helpful way of introducing young people to the idea of critical incidents or life-world disturbances. It is especially helpful to select relatable incidents that may create "wobble" (Fecho, 2011, p. 53) and to take on the role of provocateur, engaging youth in the work of public listening. In my own teaching, I aim to draw students into dialogue about a felt difficulty that as yet has no satisfying resolution, such as a spliced excerpt (below) from a text Pittsburgh youth Mark Howard (1992) created about suspension policies.

The purpose of this rap is to tell what really happens in school between students, teachers, and vice principals, and what causes suspension.

It started with two students in the class talking out of place
The boy starts getting rude and got all up in the girl's face
The girl didn't like it so she got up and yelled back. . . .
The teacher turned around just as the girl broke out in tears
The teacher kicked her out and said, *Go straight to the VP* . . .
She talked and talked and tried to tell him what's going on . . .
The VP said, *You're lying 'cause that's not what I heard*
The teacher wouldn't lie so I'm going with the teacher's word . . .
She said, *It's hopeless, every time I tell you, you say I lied*
The VP didn't listen and slowly the girl cried
The VP said, *You're going home for about three days* . . .
The point of this story—nobody pays attention
To a student 'cause they young

This critical incident invites students to name other incidents and encounters related to their lives at school and in their communities. Together, we begin to pay attention to each others' worlds, calling each other to attend to encounters that intrigue, perplex, confuse, or disturb us. I and my students bring in photographs of a Maricopa County Sheriff's Office van with a large "Do Not (Illegally) Enter" sign plastered on the back (see Figure 3.1), pictures of signs in front of a young

FIGURE 3.1 Maricopa County Sheriff's Office Van

Photo by J. Clifton

adult clothing boutique that state, "No one under 16 allowed without an adult" (Figure 3.2), or signs from a "safe sex" campaign touting, "I always get consent."

These encounters come from every domain of our lives—from the personal (being bullied) to the institutional (loud Black girls getting sent to the school office) to the public (incidents at protests, rallies, or forums; signs circulating in public spheres). In public listening for life-world disturbances, listening for different kinds of critical incidents can help to make visible a range of ways people's life-worlds are disturbed, some more immediately urgent and apparent, others more slow and recurrent over time. In the text that follows, I outline three kinds of critical incidents: (1) personal constructions of critical incidents; (2) composite critical incidents; and (3) co-constructed critical incidents.

Here it is important to distinguish between a critical incident as a "life-world disturbance"—which is the focus of public listening and this next section—and a critical incident as a *rendering* of a complex scenario capable of calling a deliberative public into being and scaffolding a collaborative problem-solving dialogue—which I will take up later in this chapter. Public listening for a critical incident as a "life-world disturbance" invites attending to the data of people's lived lives, our own

FIGURE 3.2 Poster Outside a Shop in Downtown Columbia, Missouri

Photo by J. Clifton

and others. Sometimes data that indicates a disturbance is immediately obvious, as in LeAnne Walters's case or in students' responses to the Day of Remembrance. Sometimes, however, it is the accumulation and juxtaposition of data points culled from experience, interviews, observations, documents, and so on, that converts what might have been a frustration or curiosity or felt difficulty (Dewey, 1998) into a possible shared concern that needs to be tested with others. Attending to these distributed data points is especially important for making sense of the ways power works through distributed arguments enacted in everyday activities of genre ecologies. Going along with "confusedly knowing" what is "for us" and "not for us" often depends on not quite being able to name a singular occurrence as *the* life-world disturbance. Distributing rationalizations—and any disruptions—across genre ecologies can aid in constructing confusion that is confusing enough to make deliberation elusive but not so confusing that people don't recognize that something is askew. The recurrence of materials, activities, texts, and so on cue and produce normalized rationalities, reasonabilities, and ways of being; however, an intricate dance between the familiarly recurring and the not-quite-predictable keep those who encounter out-of-sync rationalities and reasonabilities on their toes—guessing and second-guessing where they will next experience disruptions. In the confusion—and to avoid the experience of confusedly knowing—people often begin to construct and circulate underground approaches, in the process surveilling themselves without necessarily making public the concern that needs to be addressed.

The three kinds of critical incidents described next are about public listening for public and yet-to-be-public concerns as a matter of justice and as a deliberate stance of moral reasonability with others who, like us, need their lives to work. Simply recognizing or constructing a mental model of a possible shared concern is not, however, enough to call others to deliberate over that concern. That rhetorical work requires carefully crafting complex details of situated knowledge in a way that a range of stakeholders who may reasonably disagree might both find the concern compelling and recognizable and have sufficient details and perspectives to be able to come to well-informed conclusions with others. This careful crafting will be a focus later in this chapter; for now, I turn to critical incidents as data points that indicate possible sites of public inquiry and dialogue across difference.

In my own classes, I often offer examples of the ways I continue to attend to public and yet-to-be-public concerns. Here, much as I would in class, I offer examples for each of the three kinds of critical incidents—not as ideal texts or paradigmatic incidents but as ways of conceptualizing these disturbances that otherwise pass us by. This conceptualizing is important for orienting youth to the rhetorical and inventive work of public literacies and public life and, specifically, for teaching youth to attend to their own lives and the lives of others in ways that might support public deliberation. Later in this chapter, in the section "Valuing Multiple Perspectives: Reframing Points of Stasis," I relay a transcript of a classroom discussion related to particular critical incidents; first, I offer examples in order to point out several kinds of critical incidents youth might listen for.

Personal Constructions of Critical Incidents

In Higgins, Long, and Flower's (2006) rhetorical model of community literacy, these incidents are described as "problem narratives" when they reenact a situation that a person found particularly troubling, demanding, or otherwise challenging (p. 21). Because of the fine-grained detail, hidden logics, experiential knowledge, and contextual cues that they convey, such critical incidents ask listeners to question and test common sense or even personal pet theories against more operational dramatizations of distributed arguments playing out in mundane and commonly recognizable ways. These readily apparent critical incidents often take the shape of anecdotal responses to questions like: "Can you recount a situation where . . . ?" or "Do you have a memory of . . . ?" or "Can you tell me about a time when . . . ?"

I wrote a critical incident (Figure 3.3) dramatizing a cross-racial encounter at a local bookstore that took place at a state-sponsored public event to commemorate Arizona's bicentennial celebration of statehood. The incident was intriguing because of the ways different people's perspectives and experiences intersected and competed with each other in a given moment. The event took place while Arizona's anti-immigration legislation was receiving national attention at the same time that Arizona celebrated its statehood, a legacy marked by historical and ongoing conflict with people of color. During the event at a local bookstore, a Black producer omitted or downplayed stories of racial conflict in a state-sponsored documentary about a Black neighborhood during the Civil Rights Movement, one of the most turbulent and well-known eras of racial conflict in U.S. history. Even after hearing details of racial violence, White audience members chose to side-step the historical violence and dominance that the producer was naming and tried to read those details in terms of their own experiences of nostalgia.

Sample Critical Incident: "People Don't Want to Hear That"

Background

At a local bookstore, Bruce Nelson, a black actor and producer, read several short stories and showed a short film about growing up in Washington Park, a historically black neighborhood in Mesa, Arizona. After the film, Bruce opened up the floor for questions and comments. A mostly White audience asked questions about street names, which high school he attended, how he completed the filming, but they avoided questions about the content of his stories. Several times, Bruce mentioned that there were parts he left out of his stories "because people don't want to hear that."

Incident

Jennifer: Can you say more about your choices to leave out certain details? It sounds like you're leaving out parts that might be painful or controversial. But as a member of the audience, especially a White audience member, I need to hear those stories. And given the political climate in Arizona right now, I think you have a lot to offer through these stories by showing how you and others were affected day-to-day.

Bruce: Well, I mean it's painful. Some things I'm not sure I could read, you know, because it was hard. And it makes me angry.

I remember a paper route I had through the White part of town. Well, there were only a couple of blocks that were the Black part of town. If you left that part, ventured past

FIGURE 3.3 Personal Construction of a Critical Incident

those streets at all, you immediately felt uncomfortable. But I had this paper route—I was keen on making money—and boys would hide my papers or beat me up.

Sometimes it was pretty bad. And I remember going to a man's house and ringing the doorbell, and he said, "C'mon around back, boy, and I'll pay you." And I did. And right away I knew something wasn't right. And he opened the door and sicked his dog on me. That kind of thing was common.

White woman: Did you go to McClintock High School? Because I went there when it was integrated and we were nice to them. I didn't see any problems like that with Black people at our school.

Bruce: Well, have you heard of [this part of town]? That was another Black part of town and it was much worse. White people would come with guns and knives. Black people would call the cops and they wouldn't come.

It's hard to tell these stories. Some guys didn't make it. Some died. Some got taken away. Some chose other paths. A lot of guys didn't make it.

And it doesn't make sense. I mean, we cut the 'fro, we put on a suit. And that's not enough. We do what they tell us and that's still not enough.

I can remember picking cotton and then going to sell it with my dad. The White man was clearly not weighing it right. I told him he wasn't. I knew my numbers and I knew that didn't add up. The White man told my dad, "You better get your boy outta here." And my dad told me to be quiet. But it clearly wasn't right.

White man: I remember picking cotton over in the fields near [that part of town].

White woman: Me, too, we picked cotton growing up too.

Bruce: But you see picking cotton means something different for me, for my people. People say, "Oh, I picked cotton growing up," and I think, "Man, you still don't get it. You still don't get it."

FIGURE 3.3 (Continued)

Sometimes these incidents are disturbing enough and/or shared enough to mark an issue of collective concern that needs further deliberation. At other times, concerns may emerge—as they did in early conversations with eighth graders about their roles and concerns in their school or community—with only a vague sense of how that concern often plays out in real time or who else shares, or should share, that concern. In that case, it can be helpful to pursue additional data; in particular, it can be helpful to interview likely stakeholders and cull across interviews to construct a mental model of a composite critical incident.

Composite Critical Incident

Sometimes interviews reveal personal constructions of critical incidents; they often also circulate other, less elaborated forms of situated knowledge, and the relevance of this knowledge to a potentially public issue of shared concern becomes especially apparent in relation to other interviews. In that case, a critical incident is co-constructed by a listener-rhetor drawing illustrative details from across several interviews and embedding these details in a carefully constructed composite scenario whose truth-value would be its capacity to reflect the dynamics if not the specific details of a shared experience. For example, interviews with Deaf students and teachers consistently speak to the need for advocates who will intentionally provide them access to a technology, discourse, or social network (Clifton, Long, & Roen, 2012). The goal of public listening for composite critical incidents is to highlight how the situated knowledge encoded in the interviews inform and shape problem narratives that merit more and more sustained public attention.

This approach is similar to Linda Flower's (2002) approach to critical incident interviews described in "Intercultural Knowledge Building." In preparation for a public dialogue on workplace and work life issues, Flower (2002) and a team of researchers (including students) interviewed various stakeholders who had experienced changes in welfare-to-work legislation in various ways, given their unique perspectives, for instance, as human resource managers, union leaders, new hires entering the workforce from welfare, and the new hires' co-workers. To develop catalysts for discussion at deliberative sessions among concerned community members participating in the Think Tank's sequence of events, Flower's (2002) team crafted a set of written scenarios. These scenarios consolidated insights and details from the interviews into a set of dramatizations of what some of the most prominent recurring welfare-to-work issues look like, not in policy institutes' white pages, but down on the ground and in real time—as experienced by those with firsthand knowledge of the policy changes. Circulated in a *Briefing Book* mailed to Think Tank participants' homes, these scenarios were read by participants prior to and in preparation for their roundtable discussions. As Flower explains, as the basis for written or performed problem narratives, details from critical incident interviews can replace participants' generalities and untested pet theories with observations of specific behaviors, logics, and beliefs. This new knowledge can, in turn, lead to both more realistic understandings of complex problems and to more informed—and, thus, wiser—plans of action.

By way of example, consider the richly detailed, strategic, actionable knowledge made available through interviews in The Ohio State University online Digital Archive of Literacy Narratives. For instance, in the Deaf and Hard of Hearing collection, references to mothers' roles in their children's literacy learning seem to indicate a difficulty with public schooling that led parents to compensate for school's insufficiency to support their children's education. The compensation seems to indicate a concern that is significant and urgent and without any other means of being addressed. The relaying of these experiences could be culled from across the interviews and consolidated into a single composite to inform richer and more grounded understandings of access and Discourse.

While this composite critical incident has not yet been crafted for a deliberative public, it does raise the possibility of a shared concern warranting more public dialogue:

- Jane Fernandes explains in her literacy narrative that her mother was deaf. All the same, she wanted her deaf children to have access to the social capital—encoded in Discourse—that the Hearing world afforded her hearing children. Fernandes credits specific strategies of her mother's with her own literacy learning—strategies ranging from taping written words and definitions to their corresponding objects around the house to reading aloud to her deaf children to staging informal advocacy meetings with teachers on playground duty (part 1, 04:12; 5:08–12; 15:22–60).
- Warren Francis describes his mother's efforts to revise his Individualized Educational Plan (IEP)—revisions that moved him from the special education room to advanced English classes to address that he was gifted as well as hard of hearing (part 1, 16:08; 16:50–17:08; part 2, 00:34–55).
- Christopher Driscoll recounts his mother's active concern for his well-being, for instance, by researching cochlear implants when he was very young and networking through a deaf woman in their small rural community to access "the sign language community . . . and the Deaf community even there in [his] small hometown" (part 1, 5:34–69) (Clifton, Long, & Roen, 2012).

On their own, each of these scenarios may or may not form a critical incident; taken together, they begin to crystallize around the seemingly consistent need of the deaf and hard of hearing, at least as far as these interviewees are concerned, for advocates who intentionally provide them access to technology, discourse, or social networks. The patterns that emerge for listener-rhetors may be an indication of a concern that merits more public attention and dialogue.

Co-constructions of Critical Incidents

At its most perplexing, situated knowledge invites listeners to co-construct the critical incident itself. Rather than seeing this as a colonizing move to stabilize meaning, I contend that this is also an act of public listening. The test of such a construct is whether it resonates for other readers/listeners, not unlike Michael Warner's (2005) understanding of how any public discourse works: "raise it up the flagpole and see who salutes" (p. 114). In such a situation, the listener is drawn to something perplexing about the experience that the contributor recounts. With the intent of honoring the complexity and nuances of that experience, a listener (say, a writing teacher preparing for a class discussion or a student researcher designing materials for an upcoming community dialogue) might deliberately transform loosely connected details and observations from an interview into a critical incident in an effort to draw other members of that local public into joint inquiry regarding the incident's implications for informed action.

For example, in listening to Christopher Driscoll's interviews (part I, 17:30) in the DALN, I found the following strands perplexing:

- Driscoll consistently noted resistance to reading and writing. He spoke of not knowing what the point was of writing/typing stories and of being forced to read.
- He recalled reading mystery books by R. L. Stein, the author of the popular *Goosebumps* series that I remember some of my sixth-grade students enjoyed.
- I recalled reading that "as the literature on literacy and deafness has often reported, when they are judged by Hearing English literacy standards, deaf high school seniors in the United States have an average reading ability at the 3.6 grade level" (Brueggemann, 2004).
- Driscoll remembered reading the R. L. Stein books and signing to himself as he read before signing to his teacher to demonstrate his comprehension. He said his teacher would tell him that his understanding of the book was not what the book was about at all. Motivated by pizza as an incentive, Driscoll would re-read and re-sign until he ascertained the meaning to his teacher's satisfaction.
- I recalled a scene in the memoir *Train Go Sorry* where teachers at a deaf residential school had adapted a fairy tale for a senior class play, "spending more than twenty hours over a two-week period cutting, reordering sentences, and making the dialogue easier to translate into sign language" (Cohen, 1994, pp. 36–37), bearing witness to the difficulties of translating written English to ASL (Clifton, Long, & Roen, 2012).

These strands construct a critical incident that wonders if Driscoll's resistance to reading and writing is related to difficulties of moving between English—the language of the dominant Discourse but a language he only has access to through text—and ASL—the language of his Primary Discourse. Other constructions are, of course, possible and perhaps more plausible, especially where they are better grounded in an Insider Discourse. That there are other possible constructions is, in part, the value of these co-constructed critical incidents. Far from being stable constructions, they invite testing; they move away from what Ratcliffe (2005) calls dysfunctional silence (p. 88) and toward dialogue across difference. The point, of course, of public listening for critical incidents is (a) to attend to where privately held situated knowledge might indicate a concern we and others should attend to and (b) to help to circulate, as appropriate, such situated knowledge to support shared understanding, inquiry, and communicative deliberation. It is to this second aim that I turn next.

Public literacies join public listening with imagining, anticipating, and calling into being a deliberative public. This requires considering how to make critical incidents *as happenings* visible and compelling to others, especially to those who might play a significant role but nonetheless are far removed in some way—geographically, relationally, experientially, or politically. Thinking about a situation as it plays out and considering near and distant stakeholder-audience-rhetors, background information about the critical incident, a range of perspectives informing and shaping a given incident, public and hidden transcripts, genre ecologies connected to this incident, and distributed arguments producing the incident invite young people to begin constructing a critical bifocality—looking simultaneously at this one incident *and* at the systems and arguments it contributes to and is produced by.

In the coming sections, I describe what this process has looked like with students, but I do so with a caveat. While I think some of these practices and tools are worthwhile, I am not holding them up as *the* things to do to teach public literacies. Instead, I offer them as a way of casting imagination for possibilities you might invent and co-construct with your students. This caveat is significant because the role of invention and the rhetorical work of *critical re-imagining* are also central to enacting public literacies.

Critical Re-imagining

Our ways of imagining and what any of us are able to imagine as possible are not universal; rather, they are an effect of discourse, materials, and relations producing and teaching us what is for us and not for us (Dryer, 2008). It is a "stretching of our imagination" (hooks, 1997, p. 165) and a "decoloniz[ing of] our minds" (hooks, 1997, p. 178) that is most needed when what is in place is ineffective, inhospitable, unjust. We need artful well-tooled ways of re-seeing public life; in particular we need to re-imagine reasonabilities, which include the ways we imagine ourselves and others—and the ways we imagine them imagining us—as well as rationalities, with their pragmatic, goal-oriented bent. The work of seeing newly, of imagining is a critical project. bell hooks (1997) quotes Michael Taussig (1987) describing his work exploring colonialism and healing:

> I am trying to reproduce a mode of perception—a way of seeing through a way of talking—figuring the world through dialogue that comes alive with sudden transformative force in the crannies of everyday life's pauses and juxtapositions. . . . It is always a way of representing the world in the round-about "speech" of the collage of things. . . . It is a mode of perception that catches on the debris of history.
>
> *(as qtd. in hooks, 1997, p. 166)*

Public literacies call on the debris of both long and recent histories and the crannies of everyday life to remember what has been shared and to see again through dialogue possibilities for transformation—leveraging literacies to represent the world, to imagine it newly, and to re-figure it. To imagine, hooks (1991) notes, is "a way to begin the process of transforming reality. All that we cannot imagine will never come into being" (p. 55). Imagination—the inventive capacity to produce images of what's not present or has not yet been experienced—is fostered in current experiences of limitations, in the "crannies of everyday life's pauses and juxtapositions," like the ones I've outlined so far, and "is the hard pragmatic centre" (Egan & Nadaner, 1988, p. ix) of building a world "as it ought to be" with others (Branch, 2007; Horton, 1961).

Imagining can offer a way of negotiating desire and contradiction (Golden, 1996)—disturbances and disruptions—as well as ethics and power. In the face of desire and contradiction, relations of power are revealed. In deliberative democracy, the legitimacy, rationality, and reasonability of collective decision-making processes in a polity rely on the condition that institutions, policies, practices, and relationships are arranged in such a way that what is considered common interest has been determined from shared deliberation conducted fairly and freely among free and equal individuals (Benhabib, 1981, p. 69). What is put in place is "legitimate" as long as it does reflect and continues to reflect the reasonability—the moral principles—agreed to by all those affected by its consequences. As disruptions reveal or bring about uneven consequences or unanticipated consequences, what is put in place and the means by which it was put in place are "subjected to increased legitimation demands" (Benhabib, 1981, p. 50). That is, what or who has been legitimized is questioned as are the grounds—the underlying values and rationalities—and the processes—who decided and in what way—that rendered certain practices, institutions, policies, and people legitimate and others not legitimate or less legitimate. These increased legitimation demands open an opportunity to join crisis and critique—not only about the issue at hand but about public life itself. Of course, critique alone is not enough to open the door to "new modes of interaction, experience and cognition, new forms of life and experimental institutional structures" (Benhabib, 1981, p. 58) around argument and public life. Instead, if we are to use critique for reconstruction, we must join critique with imagination.

It is necessary, then, to do more than listen for public or yet-to-be-public concerns; this is, in many ways, a form of critique. If young people would aim at re-figuring the world in more just ways, they must also aim at re-figuring public life. Moving from public listening for critical incidents to the work of crafting critical incidents invites young people to engage in the work of critical re-imagining at just this intersection.

In my own classes, as I ask students to look at different critical incidents, I also introduce my own writing, like the dramatization of the critical incident in the bookstore, which draws on the conventions of multiple more conventional text types, to construct a critical incident in a way that might lend itself to public deliberation and that might re-figure public life itself, something I'll return to later in this chapter. With regard to conventions, for example, you might look back at the Day of Remembrance critical incident that opens Chapter 1 and see that it draws on conventions of a feature article, or Mark Howard's (1992) dramatization of a critical incident employing conventions of a rap or poem earlier in this chapter, or the critical incident describing the bookstore encounter, which more closely resembles a screenplay. Reading critical incidents across a range of text types helps to focus on what's critical about a critical incident, on the construction of an inventive genre,[3] and on the rhetorical work of a critical incident in a deliberative public rather than focusing on a critical incident as a text type.

Valuing Multiple Perspectives: Reframing Points of Stasis

Early on, students and I linger in our discussions about these critical incidents. Often, I start discussions with a simple, "What's going on? And how do you know?" Soon, we turn to considering different people's experiences and understandings of an encounter—a move that performs public listening for public and hidden transcripts *and* also begins to invite students to develop their own critical bifocality as they attend to the ways structures and histories might shape a person's perspectives and experiences. For example, in discussing the "Miscommunication" rap, I ask each student to consider one stakeholder and to give a one- or two-word response to "The problem is . . ." Rather than talking about the critical incident along binary lines that suppose there is a singular point of stasis, a clear impasse—an oversimplification that often impedes dialogue, we instead consider how different stakeholders might *construct* points of stasis, a "point

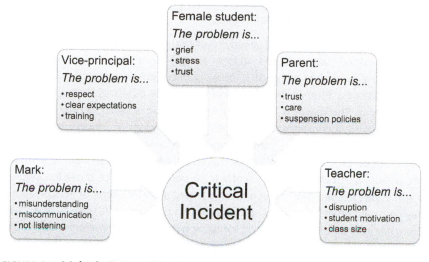

FIGURE 3.4 Multiple Points of Stasis

Created by J. Clifton

at which discourse *ought* to begin" (Foster, 2005). As students read the sentence they've written aloud, I post their responses on the board. The juxtaposition of the range of ways one individual might read this situation alongside a range of readings across these stakeholders sheds some light on how complex these "life-world disturbances" (Habermas, 1996, p. 173) can be (see Figure 3.4) and on the limitations of dominant understandings of argument. Perceiving the limitations of argument opens the possibility—and a desire—for more productive ways of doing argument in public life.

The discussions we have in class around critical incidents do important work on at least two fronts: (1) Students start to see the limitations of familiar models of deliberation that cast argument as a right-wrong, win-loss, zero-sum endeavor; and (2) they begin to experience their writing as a purposeful, audience-centered endeavor capable of constructing a participatory relationship with stakeholder-audience-rhetors. If the critical incidents they write are to call people with competing perspectives into deliberation, the ways they dramatize an incident must reveal conflict that matters to the stakeholders involved, must be recognizable and compelling for multiple stakeholders, and must not villainize or glorify any stakeholders. In their writing, then, students are engaged in the work of critical re-imagining. They begin to consider what might be required for a complex, charged deliberation to be productive without bracketing or silencing differences, and they begin to consider what choices they might make in their writing to cue and invite a range of stakeholders to argue differently.

3.2 Cultivating Dialogical Selves

Determining stakeholders—who already cares or should care about this concern, or who has a vested stake of some kind in a concern—is an important part of calling a deliberative public into being. So is the work of considering multiple experiences and perspectives. Sometimes, youth tend to imagine others as singular selves in singular roles: The mayor is only the mayor, not also a father, a pharmacist, an investor in land, a conservationist, a golfer, a descendant of a founding family of a small town. And yet these various I-positions (Hermans & Hermans-Konopka, 2010) suggest different kinds of concerns, different kinds of relationships he might care about—and care about differently if he considers one of those I-positions, or some intersection, primary in a given context. Further, some of his I-positions may constrain others; his mayor-self interested in the economic viability of a small town may influence him to say or do something that his conservationist-self would otherwise oppose. The opposite is also true. He may show up at a school function, seeing himself primarily as a father, but if someone says something about the price of medicine, he might also experience other I-positions—that of an aging man, a pharmacist, or perhaps even mayor—as salient.

Of course, youth, too, will care differently and respond differently in relation to ever-changing contexts. Working with youth to cultivate their own dialogical selves, to value others' dialogical selves (Fecho & Clifton, 2017), and to rhetorically invoke their own and others' dialogical selves can be helpful in calling a deliberative public into being and in navigating difference in dialogical ways.

Cultivating Selves-in-Dialogue

Freeze-framing complex situations and dramatizing critical incidents can foster dialogical reflection within and among multiple stakeholders. Individual students might read the text of a critical incident they've written or watch the juxtaposed performances of multiple monologues they've created Anna Deveare Smith–style and then reflect on their selves-in-dialogue:

- Which of my I-positions are most salient in this situation? How does that change as the incident unfolds?
- What experiences or ways of thinking do each of these I-positions raise to the surface for me? *As a _____ (student, daughter, teammate, friend, photographer, activist, citizen, scholar . . .), I am most concerned about . . . I find myself thinking about . . . I wonder . . . I hope . . .*
- Which of my I-positions seem to be in dialogue with one another? In what way? In which moments, and how, do I experience self-conflict, self-critique, self-agreement, self-consultancy?
- What seems to be most resolved to me? Where is there tension or something unresolved among my I-positions?

Valuing Others' Dialogical Selves

Students might consider one other stakeholder in the freeze-framed situation:

- Which I-positions seem most salient to that person in this situation? How does that change as the situation unfolds?
- What does that person see as the "problem" here?
- What would that person most want me to care about as a _____ (*student, daughter, teammate, friend, photographer, activist, citizen, scholar . . .*)? Would that person ask me to foreground a different I-position than the ones I have so far?

Invoking Others' Dialogical Selves

In writing and in conversation, youth might consider how they might cue others to approach a situation, a concern, people, dialogue, and possibilities.

- What is the range of I-positions I might cue this person to invoke? How might cuing a person's other I-positions (or intersections of I-positions) also shift the rationalities and reasonabilities this person calls on or enacts?
- How might cuing another I-position change the ways this person sees the "problem" here? How might it change what this person thinks is possible, or not possible?
- What do I want this person to care about as a _____ (*student, daughter, teammate, friend, photographer, activist, citizen, scholar . . .*)? How might I signal to this person or invite this person to foreground a different I-position than the ones he or she has so far?

The impasse that Nate experienced with students on the Day of Remembrance underscores the need for calling people with divergent perspectives into dialogue with each other. Through reading and writing critical incidents, students begin to use writing as a means toward productive public engagement that opens up dialogue across difference, expands our understandings, and invents alternative, networked courses of action stemming from jointly constructed understandings and values. And these are the purposes we discuss together as we think about genres generally and about the critical incident as a specific kind of inventive genre aimed at coordinating particular kinds of public activities with others.

Writing and Invention: Constructing and Coordinating Social Practices of Argument

Conventional text types, like the résumé, for example, emerged as people engaged in certain practices with each other. As the practices continued, often across different social contexts or organizations, some conventions were fostered while others were downplayed or abandoned. Over time, those conventions crystallized through wide use and recognition (Bazerman, 2012, p. 228). As arguments distributed across genre ecologies are called into question, they indicate sites where the conventions, the activities, and the rationalities and reasonabilities may need more public attention and public dialogue. While the recurrence of materials, tools, texts, and activities stabilizes conventions, where social practices are just emerging or where they are ineffective or unjust, writers are in the unique position of constructing conventions for emergent and revisable texts that can fuel the desired social practices.

As I introduce students to a range of critical incidents, I help students imagine and construct the social contexts in which they're writing, the purposes for which they're writing, and the people to whom they're writing. Below, I describe ways I've used Mark Howard's (1992) critical incident about suspension policies as an incubation site for students' thinking about their own writing. After students name possible points of stasis among stakeholders who might be invested in the concern Howard (1992) names in his rap, we return to the discussion about suspension policies and ask what *work* they think Howard's critical incident has to do to call together these people with different perspectives.

It is clear that students sense the drama inherent in these incidents. One group says they see a critical incident as a "hinge place" or a "turning point," evoking moments of tension and drama. Likewise, another student, Mandy, explains that a critical incident shows "how other people were missing that this was AN ISSUE to the writer." Students wonder aloud about the intent of the critical incident. Kelly asks, "Should it teach a lesson?" I pose another question: "If we're saying that the purpose is to draw us into dialogue, what would 'teaching a lesson' do to that dialogue?" Across the room, Jessica responds that using a critical incident to teach someone a lesson would "shut *dialogue* down . . . teaching a lesson shows people what to do so they don't need to talk together or figure anything out . . . or the lesson pisses them off and they don't want to talk with you about that." As the dialogue progresses, students begin to see that the decisions they make in rendering a critical incident will have an impact on the work a critical incident is able to do and especially on the ways it might scaffold or limit argument as dialogue across difference. To pull our thinking together, we generate a list:

Prompt:	*The critical incident needs to . . .*
Jerome:	Expose consequences of each person's perspective.
Sam:	Hear what people have to say.
Alice:	Be specific. Give lots of details.
Mandy:	Leave things open. There can't be a solution already. That's what they're [the stakeholders] trying to figure out.
Angie:	Show different reactions.
Art:	Be about something that affects a lot of people, but something that can narrow to show how just a few people experience it.
Kelly:	See perspectives in relation to each other.

Candace:	Name lots of factors involved.
Angie:	Invent guidelines that people would actually follow.
Jake:	Tell a clear story, show some kind of familiar conflict.
Liz:	Make it come alive, where people can see what's happening.
Carl:	Make you, the reader, question your position on something.
James:	Make you open your eyes.
Ely:	Connect with readers. They should see themselves in it.
Liza:	Inspire change. Something, someone needs to change.

(class discussion, September 13, 2012)

As students note, taking other people's perspectives seriously is important along-side the more pragmatic possibility of "inventing guidelines that people would actually follow." In our lives, these aren't ever separated. In this inventive genre of the critical incident that aims to call people with radically different life-world experiences together, these problem narratives embody lived experiences where relationships, policies, and motives are intertwined.

3.3 Critically Re-imagining and Rhetorically Re-inventing the Social Practices of Argument

Cultivating public subjectivities, constructing public exigencies

One classroom teacher who'd been working with middle school students to craft critical incidents observed:

> Students' initial "What the Heck?" moments were not doing the work a critical incident needs to do: call others into dialogue about a concern that warrants more public attention and dialogue. Some wanted to write about grandpa's war stories, the day the hog got loose, or basketball injuries; these did not open up inquiry, critique, and dialogue. We tried to narrow what makes a critical incident so critical, and in doing so, revisited an insightful purpose set forth by a student: people need a reason to come together and dialogue.

This teacher's observation marks the difficult time young people—maybe many of us—have conceptualizing the possibility that writing might do some work in the world beyond self-expression. Writing teachers often tell writers to write about what they care about, what they know most about; however, there are dangers in holding this up as the primary motivation for writing in public life. If self-expression and self-interest are the motivation and the substance of writing, they may also become the basis and substance for the ways we read or attend to others' experiences. This is particularly worrisome in public life where we need to be able to call strangers, who may very well have quite different experiences and interests than our own, to attend to our concerns, and where those strangers also need to be able to call us to attend to theirs. *Stranger* relationality and difference—*dis*-identification—mark public life more than identification. Self-expression and interest, or as Jenny Rice (2012) frames it, personal feelings, should not "serve as the primary connective tissue to our public spaces" (p. 6). The "fallout from such feelingful relationality" (p. 6) is that a common way people come to measure their connection to concerns others raise for public deliberation is in terms of whether they are personally "affected" or "unaffected" (p. 6). The danger there is that this binary lends itself to re-inscribing power relations and/or to perpetuating enclaves. In public listening and in dramatizing critical incidents, young people learn alternative ways of reading themselves into public life (Rice, 2012), alternative ways to see themselves in relation to others' concerns.

This teacher's observation also points to an old critique of writing instruction: that student writing is only for the teacher and not for any real-world purpose. Indeed, students at first could not imagine that what they wrote about or the way they wrote might call other people to *do something*. Even more significantly for public literacies is that they could not imagine that their writing had the capacity to shape realities—not only the ways others see and understand the world but also the activities they do with others. Some of the most important work of this kind of writing is that it focuses on constructing realities: *What stakeholders are involved? How do they need to be able to see themselves and each other? What ways of relating will be destructive? What ways of relating might be useful? How can you cue reader-rhetors and cue the folks you hope will talk with you to approach this situation, each other, and the dialogue in a particular way (and not in other more familiar ways)?*

Focusing on the Self–Other Relations and the Social Practices of Argument

One of my undergraduate classes came up with a list of conditions for writing critical incidents in light of the social practices of argument a writer might be trying to coordinate through his or her writing:

You've got a compelling critical incident when

- it dramatizes a typical or recognizable moment or situation;
- there's a high "so what" factor;
- it's clearly important and/or urgent and something we should talk about, understand better, and figure out how to change;
- it gives people who don't typically talk together a reason to talk together;
- it features a situation that has no easy resolution, no easy answer;
- it features several people who don't necessarily agree: they have different perspectives on what happened and why it matters;
- it gets specific and freeze-frames a moment or extended scene for people who will be part of the dialogue (we hear the words of the people involved

in the incident, see who is doing what, care about the people and about what happens next);

- it slows down to dramatize usually unspoken, fast-moving moments in which people are making decisions;
- it doesn't vilify or glorify any one of the participants;
- all of the people who would need to come together to talk about this see something they care about in the critical incident; or
- the situation ends, but there is clear unresolved conflict.

To imagine the social contexts in which they are crafting a critical incident, I return to Howard's (1992) rap about suspension policies to consider the range of people who might have a vested interest in the concerns he raises—people whose attention he needs to capture. Drawing on the community literacy metaphor of "people at your table," I show students an image representing people around a table, with each larger circle representing a different stakeholder in this immediate situation. The smaller circles represent additional voices and perspectives some of us bring to the table, contextualizing this immediate dialogue in relation to a still broader dialogue among a constellation of people committed to this shared concern—people, who may, in addition to caring about suspension policies also care about school push-out, youth rights, and the school to prison pipeline, for example (see Figure 3.5). These people, with their conflicting perspectives

FIGURE 3.5 People at Your Table

Adapted from Flower (1998, p. 436)

and experiences, instantiate the mixed and complex audiences students need to imagine as they construct their own critical incidents.

Co-constructing Textual Conventions for Inventive Social Practices

When I turn to teaching students the craft of writing a critical incident, I focus on the broad work of this inventive genre—to call a deliberative public into being and to generate dialogue across difference—as the test of our writing. In light of this purpose, I ask students to consider conventions that might help them achieve this goal through their writing. First, I ask students to read several critical incidents, some of which I've crafted from encounters in my own life, for example: (1) a version of Nate Boswell's account at the beginning of this book; (2) Mark Howard's (1992) rap; (3) an account of racial tensions between a Black film producer and White audience members as the producer recounts scenes from his childhood growing up in Mesa, Arizona; and (4) a dramatization of a classroom conversation where a Black student relays her experience of modern-day segregation in school and a White student says "that doesn't happen here."

In small groups, I ask students to discuss (a) *which* critical incident is best and why (b) *what* they think a critical incident is (c) *what work* a critical incident should do, and (d) *four key features* of a generative critical incident. In these discussions, students are not trying to "uncover" the "correct" features. Rather I tell them that they are trying to build together our own sense of what makes for compelling data from our lives and what makes for compelling writing of life observations.

Thinking more carefully about the potential public work of a critical incident turns students' attention to how they might actually craft one of their own. In doing this, they are critically re-imagining public life and the ways their words and design choices might construct a version of public life they have not necessarily seen before. A student says that a critical incident should "force you to think . . . *challenge* your assumptions," but wonders how this is actually done. She asks, "Are critical incidents supposed to be reported as just-the-facts or include the author's thoughts and feelings?" Another student astutely asks if "critical incidents are a type of journalism or something else entirely?" Looking back across the examples, they see interview excerpts, screenplay features, memoir-like reflective moments, and inner monologue, among other textual conventions. Together, we begin to create a chart of key features and possible conventions (see Figure 3.6) they might draw on in their writing, and connect each feature back to an example from the texts.

I continually draw the conversation back to the *rhetorical work* that this type of writing is trying to do. For example, if part of the work of a critical incident is to show how an issue typically plays out, then readers need enough details to clearly picture the event in their minds, including what happened and how those involved reacted. Focusing on the purpose of a critical incident—to open up dialogue across difference—helps me talk with student writers as they make decisions about where

Features of a Generative Critical Incident	Conventions to Call On	Examples
Background info / context	Phrases or other cues to signal timing (month, year, season)	(Day of Remembrance CI) • In the fall of 2010 . . .
	Briefly narrate relevant current events (news headlines or quote from a relevant news story)	(Day of Remembrance CI) • Day of Remembrance • 15 gay youth killed themselves
	Describe the scene and setting • time period, place, environment • movement, action, atmosphere	(People don't want to hear that) • Arizona bicentennial • Anti-immigration legislation in national headlines • in the morning, when the bell rang for class • Phoenix-area high school • students gather in purple shirts at the flagpole • when the bell rang for class, students in the hallway saying . . .
	Briefly narrate relevant current events (news headlines or quote from a relevant news story)	(Day of Remembrance CI) • Day of Remembrance • 15 gay youth killed themselves (People don't want to hear that CI) • Arizona bicentennial • Anti-immigration legislation in national headlines
	Briefly narrate relevant broader contexts	(People don't want to hear that CI) • Civil Rights Movement
	Phrases or cues to contrast international, national, regional, local contexts	(People don't want to hear that CI) • AZ bicentennial celebration and national anti-immigration protests
	Dialogue or inner monologue to show stakeholders' perspectives on local situations, events, or contexts	(Day of Remembrance CI) • "it's about gay pride" • "that's not what the purple was there for at all. It wasn't gay pride in any way" (People don't want to hear that CI) • "people don't want to hear that" • "I didn't see any problems like that" • "We picked cotton, too" • "Man, you still don't get it"

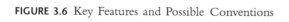

FIGURE 3.6 Key Features and Possible Conventions

Multiple perspectives	Block quotes from interviews	(Day of Remembrance CI) Nate's quote explaining conflict and why it matters
	Screenplay dialogue to show differing perspectives on an event, situation, or context	(People don't want to hear that CI) • "people don't want to hear that" • "I didn't see any problems like that" • "We picked cotton, too" • "Man, you still don't get it"
	Screenplay dialogue or italics to show differing perspectives of each other	(People don't want to hear that CI) • "Man, you still don't get it" (Miscommunication) • "You're lying" • "The teacher wouldn't lie" • "You're guilty"
	Inner thoughts (from an interview) in block quotes or in italics	(Day of Remembrance CI) • "that's not what the purple was there for at all. It wasn't gay pride in any way" • "It was really upsetting"
Dramatizing unresolved conflict	Concrete details show where and how this issue or conflict plays out	(Day of Remembrance CI) • in the morning, when the bell rang for class, students in the hallway saying . . . • Phoenix-area high school, students gather in purple shirts at the flagpole (Miscommunication) shows who does/says what in the classroom, in the office
	Journalistic details (who, what, where, when, why)	(People don't want to hear that CI) • background
	Quote where stakeholders name the conflict	(People don't want to hear that CI) • "people don't want to hear that" • "Man, you still don't get it" (Day of Remembrance CI) • "it's about gay pride" • "that's not what the purple was there for at all. It wasn't gay pride in any way"

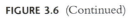

FIGURE 3.6 (Continued)

		(Miscommunication) • The point of this story is lost communication. • The point of this story—nobody pays attention / To a student 'cause they young
	Ends with lack of resolution	(Day of Remembrance CI) • "Some students were wearing purple and didn't even know why." (People don't want to hear that CI) • "Man, you still don't get it"

FIGURE 3.6 (Continued)

they might economize details and where they might need to linger to show someone's reaction or to make visible someone's hidden logic for making a particular decision or to reveal an important detail that some stakeholders are well aware of, but that others will be surprised to learn.

But Is This Argument?

Absolutely! In crafting their writing with possible social practices of argument in mind, students are doing and theorizing argument; they are making decisions to critically re-imagine and rhetorically invent a compelling alternative to familiar and scripted ways of addressing uncertainty, conflict, and difference. Through their choices of content and conventions, they are considering the reasonabilities they hope to invoke with others and *how* they might cue stakeholder-reader-audience-rhetors to take up those self–other relations in their collaborative problem-solving. They are recognizing and theorizing how to navigate multiple rationalities and, by coordinating social practices of argument, they are, in effect making a claim about how a deliberative public might negotiate new, shared rationalities and reasonabilities.

On the one hand this might seem like a radically new understanding of argument, but I would contend that this reflects the dynamism and liveliness that John Dewey understood to make argument matter. As Nathan Crick (2010) explains:

> For [Dewey] argument functions to place some object within a universe of discourse and thereby demonstrate its relationship between propositions and consequences. . . . Argumentativeness helps develop something "small" into something "big" by tracing out its associations with other meanings, objects, and events. Without the potential for growth, argumentativeness is mere belligerence; without cultivation and care, an embro[nic idea] dies

in utero. The instrumental arts bring our potential ideas and actions to term by facilitating behavior and judgment within a problematic situation.

(p. 150)

In their decision-making within a problematic situation, youth are also imagining and operationalizing the pragmatics, constructing and coordinating the experiences of argument:

- What information will each stakeholder need?
- How should I frame the sticking points?
- How do I honor each stakeholder's (possibly conflicting) situated knowledge while creating a text that is brief and easy to read at a glance, allowing stakeholders to get on with the dialogue rather than linger over the text as a thing on its own?
- What public and hidden transcripts need to part of this incident and this dialogue?
- What power dynamics might threaten a productive dialogue, and in the texts I create, how do I invoke a range of expertise and construct processes for arguing differently?
- What other texts, materials, activities, and relations inform and shape the incident at hand? How might different stakeholders see those connections, and how might I put those in conversation?

By constructing and crafting a public issue through an inventive genre such as the critical incident, student writers come to experience genres of writing as situated social action and as rhetorical tools for perspective taking—two primary functions of human language (Gee, 2001, p. 715). In other words, students come to see their writing as rhetorical because they are making decisions about the work they want their writing to do with particular people rather than about a particular form the writing must fit. They also come to see their writing as "public world-making" (Warner, 2005, p. 14) as they critically re-imagine and aim to re-figure public argument as dialogue across difference. In Figure 3.7, a student-writer, Jackie, explains the work she hopes her critical incident does and briefly describes the kinds of data she included to represent multiple perspectives and to call people with divergent experiences and perspectives into dialogue with each other. The critical incident she wrote follows the headnote she created.

Jackie plans this critical incident with action in mind—she plans for this incident to ground discussions about workplace practices in class, at the restaurant where she works, and in other workplaces. In other words, she aims to call together a local and networked deliberative public around an issue of shared concern. As she gathered data, crafted a critical incident, and planned for ways she might use the critical incident with others, Jackie was engaged in productive knowledge-making and what Michael Warner (2005) calls "poetic public world-making" (p. 114).

The student writer explains:

> I wrote this critical incident because I was confused and uncomfortable with the racist comments the White workers would announce aloud at the restaurant. I didn't want to have to choose sides. I included details from my day-to-day observations during my first week at work so that I could write a critical incident that would show what typically happens at work. I tried to show the ways different people experience these interactions—the White girls grouping together, the Mexican girl off on her own, the manager nowhere to be found, the Mexican men frustrated and cursing. I think it's important to talk about the backgrounds we bring into situations like this and to think about what's going on with someone else. Mostly, I hope this critical incident would help people at my restaurant and people in similar situations to talk together about what's going on, about what different people need, and about how they might treat each other with respect.

Sample Critical Incident: "Speak My Language"

In the fall of 2010, the state of Arizona implemented a series of laws banning ethnic studies in schools and requiring police to ask anyone who looks "suspicious" to show their papers documenting citizenship or appropriate visas. These laws gained national attention and also provoked local tensions in already charged situations.

Day 1

After school lets out, Jackie, a student-worker, arrives at a local restaurant for her first day of work. She's nervous, not knowing what to expect. A coworker, a girl from a rival high school, introduces Jackie to one of the managers. The manager is friendly and tries to put Jackie at ease by joking with her and then giving her simple tasks to complete on her first day. Jackie notices that the girls who work in the front of the restaurant and the boys who are delivery drivers are mostly White while the "fryers" in the kitchen are all Latinos. As Jackie washes dishes and later prepares salads, she sees two of the girls working in the front of the restaurant arguing with an older Latino fryer.

A few days later

After working a few days at a new job, Jackie realizes that the conflicts between White student-workers and undocumented Latino/Latina immigrant-workers are an everyday occurrence. Jackie works in the front of

---

FIGURE 3.7 Student Critical Incident: "Speak My Language"

the restaurant with three other girls who are white, young, pretty, high school students and with one Mexican girl who works instead of going to school. One of the girls' responsibilities is to listen to the "fryers" in the back of the restaurant; when the fryers put up the orders, the girls in the front of the restaurant have to make sure they get to the right person or in the right bag.

A Mexican "fryer" in his thirties calls to the girls in the front of the restaurant in Spanish, the only language he knows, letting them know the next order is ready. Angry, one of the White girls in the front of the restaurant calls back, "Speak my language, or I won't talk to you."

Jackie is surprised and uncomfortable. She sees how hard the Mexican men work in their 120 hours per week, and she wants to speak up for this man but doesn't say anything. The Mexican girl working the front of the restaurant translates for the other girls and then goes to get the order. The fryer curses the other girl in Spanish under his breath.

The girl who scolded the Mexican man walks over to Jackie and the other White girls, leaving the Mexican girl on her own to wipe counters across the restaurant. The girl vents, "That's ridiculous. I'm supposed to understand what he's saying? Can't he at least learn to say what's on the menu? I mean, I have no idea what he's talking about."

Another girl from Jackie's high school says, "Seriously. Why do we have to do things their way? It's not right. I mean, they're making like $10 an hour, and they don't even speak English."

The third girl chimes in, "Yeah, right? I'm making $8. It sucks working this shift, too. I'm always tired. I work hard, I'm legal. *AND*, I'm smarter and have more skills. No way they should get more hours *and* more pay."

Frustrated with the tensions this creates, Jackie wonders about her role at the restaurant.

FIGURE 3.7 (Continued)

Certainly, inventive genres like the critical incident can use data from our lives to render experience (Romano, 2000, p. 68) by inviting others to pay attention to perspectives and experiences they don't typically attend to. As important—arguably more important—the critical incident, and other emergent genres, can also call us to *do something* with the data from our lives, like Jackie did as she planned public forums in and beyond the classroom. With regard to public concerns, this involves constructing polity with others and cultivating further collaborative problem-solving.

Where students experience violated interests and hope deferred in immediate and/or sustained, mundane ways, we can help them leverage writing to do significant work in local and networked contexts, where we all must perform "actually existing democracy" (Fraser, 1990, p. 56). In the face of felt difficulties and life-world disturbances, pedagogy framed around democratic deliberation would develop and leverage inventive argument and writing to:

- Re-see a situation or a rhetor
- Make the personal shared
- Construct shared concerns
- Construct more complex understandings of localized issues
- Engage others' ideas and experiences
- Network arguments in, out, and among institutions
- Create public forums
- Listen across difference
- Analyze, evaluate, imagine/invent alternatives
- Generate public dialogue
- Construct intercultural inquiry
- Engage in productive problem-solving
- Construct wise action in uncertain circumstances

Rather than avoiding spaces of difficulty in the name of "safety," I contend that our writing classrooms might instead engage youth in the work of knowledge-building, critically re-imagining, and rhetorically inventing precisely where they experience the limits of distributed arguments, adversarial models of situated argument, and public life.

Notes

1. Debates about whether to use "Deaf" or "deaf" are as contested as any of the issues raised in the critical incidents mentioned in this book. Some scholars use "Deaf" as a way of recognizing the unique culture and shared language of deaf people and "deaf" as a way of referring merely to a medical/audiological condition. In deaf and disability studies, many authors and scholars indicate their preference and distinctions in opening footnotes, but as Brenda Brueggemann acknowledges ("Introduction: Reframing" 1) and deals with more extensively in her essay, "Think-Between: A Deaf Studies Commonplace Book," making the distinction doesn't lessen the confusion for writers or readers. I am aware, too, of the further and inherent complications I face as a hearing writer making this distinction. Still, while I understand that many who are designated as medically deaf are not necessarily Deaf culturally and that there are a host of people with hearing loss who may fall in, out, or between Deaf and Hearing cultures at any one time, I use "Deaf" (capitalized) to indicate Deaf culture and identity. In doing that, I am distinguishing "Hearing" or "Deaf" (capitalized) as cultures from "hearing" or "deaf" (lowercase) as audiological acts or conditions. This is an attempt to counter the invisible nature of the dominant Hearing culture and to help myself and readers, especially hearing ones, become more aware of the ways our hearing may restrict our understanding of issues raised by those who are culturally Deaf or medically deaf.
2. It may seem odd—downright insensitive, even—to celebrate listening while highlighting the Deaf and Hard-of-Hearing. But I do so in light of the attention listening has received of late as an under-theorized and under-taught means for exposing unearned

privilege and for fostering cross-cultural engagement—that is, for cultivating authentic learning across differences that tend to divide us.

3. Here, an "inventive genre" refers to the creative invention of alternative social situations, responses, practices, and tools-in-use; to artfully craft the text of the critical incident requires critically re-imagining the social practices of argument that text aims to invite as well as the practices and distributed arguments it aims to interrogate.

References

Applebee, A. and J. Langer. (2011) A snapshot of writing instruction in middle schools and high schools. *English Journal* 100.6: 14–27.

Atwill, J. M. (2010). *Rhetoric reclaimed: Aristotle and the liberal arts tradition.* Ithaca, NY: Cornell University Press.

Bazerman, C. (2002). Genre and identity: Citizenship in the age of the internet and the age of global capitalism. In R. M. Coe, L. Lindgard, & T. Teslenko (Eds.), *The rhetoric and ideology of genre* (pp. 13–37). New York: Hampton Press.

Bazerman, C. (2012). Genre as social action. In P. G. James & H. Michael (Eds.), *The Routledge handbook of discourse analysis* (pp. 226–238). New York: Routledge.

Benhabib, S. (1981). Modernity and the aporias of critical theory. *Telos*, 49(Fall), 39–59.

Branch, K. (2007). *Eyes on the ought to be: What we teach when we teach about literacy.* Cresskill: Hampton Press.

Brayboy, B. (2005). Toward a tribal critical race theory in education. *Urban Review*, 37(5), 425–446.

Brueggemann, B. (2004). Introduction: Reframing deaf people's literacy. In B. Brueggemann (Ed.), *Literacy and deaf people: Cultural and contextual perspectives* (pp. 1–28). Washington, DC: Gallaudet University Press.

Bruner, M. L. (2010). The public work of critical political communication. In J. Ackerman & D. Coogen (Eds.), *The public work of rhetoric* (pp. 56–75). Columbia, SC: University of South Carolina Press

Bureau of Labor Statistics. (2014). Highlights of women's earnings in 2014. [Data file]. Available online at http://www.bls.gov/opub/reports/cps/highlights-of-womens-earnings-in-2014.pdf

Chang, J. (2005). *Can't stop, won't stop.* New York: Picador.

Clifton, J., Long, E., & Roen, D. (2012). Accessing private knowledge for public conversations: Attending to shared, yet-to-be-public concerns in the deaf and hard-of-hearing DALN interviews. In S. L. Dewitt, C. Selfe, & L. U. Logan (Eds.), *Stories that speak to us: Exhibits from the digital archive of literacy narratives.* Boulder, CO: Computers and Composition Digital Press. Available online at http://ccdigitalpress.org/stories/chapters/roenlongclifton/

Clifton, J. & Sigoloff, J. (2013). Writing as dialogue across difference: Inventing genres to support deliberative democracy. *English Journal*, 103(2), 73–84.

Cohen, L. H. (1994). *Train go sorry: Inside a deaf world.* New York: Vintage Books.

Crick, N. (2010). *Democracy & rhetoric: John Dewey on the arts of becoming.* Columbia, SC: University of South Carolina Press.

Crick, N. & Gabriel, J. (2010). The conduit between lifeworld and system: Habermas and the rhetoric of public scientific controversies. *Rhetoric Society Quarterly*, 40(3), 201–223.

Cushman, E. (1998). *The struggle and the tools: Oral and literate strategies in an inner city community.* Albany, NY: State University of New York Press.

Cushman, E. (1999). The public intellectual, service learning, and activist research. *College English,* 61(3), 328–336.

Danisch, R. (2015). *Building a social democracy: The promise of rhetorical pragmatism.* Lanham, MD: Lexington Books.

Deutsch, C. H. (2006). There's money in thirst. *New York Times.* Available online at http://www.nytimes.com/2006/08/10/business/worldbusiness/10water.html

Dewey, J. (1998). *Experience and education.* New York: Free Press.

Dryer, D. (2008). Taking up space: On genre systems as geographies of the possible. *Journal of Advanced Composition,* 28(3), 503–534.

Egan, K. & Nadaner, D. (Eds.). (1988). *Imagination and education.* New York: Teachers College Press.

Fecho, B. (2011). *Teaching for the students: Habits of heart, mind, and practice in the engaged classroom.* New York: Teachers College Press.

Fecho, B. & Clifton, J. (2017). *Dialoguing across cultures, identities, and learning: Crosscurrents and complexities in literacy classrooms.* New York: Routledge.

Fiumara, G. C. (1996). *The other side of language: A philosophy of listening.* New York: Routledge.

Flanagan, J. C. (1954). The critical incident technique. *Psychological Bulletin,* 51(4), 327–358.

Flower, L. (1998). *Problem-solving strategies for writing in college and community.* Fort Worth: Harcourt.

Flower, L. (2008). *Community literacy and the rhetoric of public engagement.* Carbondale, IL: Southern Illinois University Press.

Flower, L. (2002). Intercultural knowledge building: The literate action of a community think tank. In B. Charles & R. David (Eds.), *Writing selves, writing societies: Research from activity perspectives* (pp. 239–270). Web. Fort Collins: WAC Clearinghouse. Available online at http://wac.colostate.edu/books/selves_societies/

Flyvbjerg, B. (2001). *Making social science matter: Why social inquiry fails and how it can succeed again.* New York: Cambridge University Press.

Foster, H. (2005). Kairos and stasis revisited: Heuristics for the critically informed composition classroom. *Composition Forum.* 14.2. Available online at http://compositionforum.com/issue/14.2/foster-kairos-stasis.php

Fraser, N. (1990). Rethinking the public sphere: A contribution to the critique of actually existing democracy. *Social Text,* 25/26, 56–80.

Gee, J. P. (2001). Reading as situated language: A sociocognitive perspective. *Journal of Adolescent and Adult Literacy,* 44(8), 714–725.

Giovanni, N. (1994). *Annual conventions of everyday subjects: Racism 101* (pp. 83–89). New York: William Morrow.

Golden, J. (1996). Critical imagination: Serious play with narrative and gender. *Gender and Education,* 8(3), 323–336.

Golden, J. (1996). *Between facts and norms.* Trans. W. Rehg. Cambridge, UK: Polity Press.

Hermans, H. & Hermans-Konopka, A. (2010). *Dialogical self theory: Positioning and counter-positioning in a globalizing society.* Cambridge, UK: Cambridge University Press.

Higgins, L., Long, E., & Flower, L. (2006). Community literacy: A rhetorical model for personal and public inquiry. *Community Literacy Journal,* 1(1), 9–43.

hooks, b. (1991). Narratives of struggle. In P. Mariani (Ed.), *Critical fictions: The politics of imaginative writing* (pp. 53–61). New York: The New Press.

hooks, b. (1997). Representing blackness in the White imagination. In R. Frankenberg (Ed.), *Displacing whiteness: Essays in social and cultural criticism* (pp. 165–179). Durham, NC: Duke University Press.

Howard, M. (1992). Excerpts from "Whassup with Suspension, Fall 1992". In Peck, Flower, and Higgins, "Community Literacy." From the back files of the Community Literacy Center. Available online at http://english.cmu.edu/research/clc

Kearney, R. (1996). Narrative and ethics. Proceedings of *The Aristotelian Society,* Vol. 70, pp. 29–46. Bristol: Longdunn Press.

Lauritzen, P. (2004). Arguing with life stories: The case of Rigoberta Menchu. In P. J. Eakin (Ed.), *The Ethics of Life Writing* (pp. 19–39). Ithaca, NY: Cornell University Press.

Leonardo, Z. (2009). *Race, whiteness, and education.* New York: Routledge.

Long, E. (2008). *Community literacy and the rhetoric of local publics.* West Lafayette, IN: Parlor Press.

MacIntyre, A. (1984). *After virtue: A study in moral theory.* 2nd ed. Notre Dame, IN: University of Notre Dame Press.

Middleton, J. I. (2011). Finding democracy in our argument culture: Listening to Spike Lee's jazz funeral on the levees. In K. Ratcliffe & C. Glenn (Eds.), *Silence and listening as rhetorical acts* (pp. 163–180). Carbondale, IL: Southern Illinois University Press.

Midkiff, K. (2010). *Not a drop to drink: America's water crisis and what you can do about it.* San Francisco, CA: New World Library.

Miller, C. (1994). Rhetorical community: The cultural basis of genre. In A. Freedman & P. Medway (Eds.), *Genre and the new rhetoric* (pp. 67–78). London: Taylor & Francis.

Nussbaum, M. C. (1995). *Poetic justice: The literary imagination and public life.* Boston: Beacon Press.

Piper, K. (2014). *The price of thirst: Global water inequality and the coming chaos.* Minneapolis, MN: University of Minnesota Press.

Porter, J. Sullivan, P., Blythe, S., Grabill, J. T., & Miles, L.(2000). Institutional critique: A rhetorical methodology for change. *College Composition and Communication*, 51(4), 610–642.

Ratcliffe, K. (1999). Rhetorical listening: A trope for interpretive invention and a "code of cross-cultural conduct." *College Composition and Communication*, 51(2), 195–224.

Ratcliffe, K. (2005). *Rhetorical listening: Identification, gender, whiteness.* Carbondale, IL: Southern Illinois University Press.

Ricoeur, P. (1988). *Time and narrative.* Trans. Kathleen Blamey and David Pellaeur. Vol. 3. Chicago: University of Chicago Press.

Romano, T. (2000). *Blending genre, altering styles: Writing multigenre papers.* Portsmouth: Boynton/Cook.

Royster, J. (1994). When the first voice you hear is not your own. *College Composition and Communication,* 47(1), 29–40.

Simmons, M. W. & Grabill, J. T. (2007). Toward a civic rhetoric for technologically and scientifically complex places: Invention, performance, and participation. *College Composition and Communication*, 58(3), 419–448.

Tannen, D. (1990). *You just don't understand: Women and men in conversation.* New York: Ballantine.

Taussig, M. (1987). *Shamanism, colonialism, and the wild man.* Chicago: University of Chicago Press.

Warner, M. (2005). *Publics and counterpublics.* Brooklyn: Zone.

Weis, L. & Fine, M. (2012). Critical bifocality and circuits of privilege: Expanding critical ethnographic theory and design. *Harvard Educational Review*, 82(2), 173–201.

West, C. (1993). *Keeping faith: Philosophy and race in America.* New York: Routledge.

Young, I. (2000). *Inclusion and democracy.* Oxford: Oxford University Press.

Young, I. M. (1997). *Intersecting voices.* Princeton, NJ: Princeton University Press.

4

ARGUMENT AS DIALOGUE ACROSS DIFFERENCE

The *Praxis* of Public Life

While inventive texts like the critical incident aim to coordinate activity of deliberative publics where previously there had been no public attention—or limited, perhaps even unproductive attention—the particular deliberative work that young people will need to critically re-imagine and attempt to rhetorically invent will depend on the particular exigency they aim to address. With regard to public life, this is often connected to what Crick and Gabriel (2010) call "the arc of the controversy"—how others see this particular concern in relation to a "life-cycle" of public deliberation (Long, 2009). Those of us who teach, or have taught, literature are familiar with "plot charts" that aim to visualize the dramatic structure of a narrative. These plot charts tend to take the shape of arcs or mountains to show the ways conflict emerges, rises, culminates, and perhaps is in some way, to some degree resolved within the cover of a novel or epic poem. A similar dramatic reading of public controversies (Crick & Gabriel, 2010; Gross, 2006; Habermas, 1996) can help young people think of shared concerns—conflicts and disturbances—in terms of rhetorical action rather than storehousing and circulating knowledge.

The significance of this distinction for argument in public life is illustrated in the following exchange cited by Crick and Gabriel (2010, p. 201) in their discussion of public scientific controversies. The exchange took place at a symposium in 1972 between two climatologists who were discussing what to do in the face of rising CO_2 levels:

> "I guess I am rather conservative," one expert remarked. "I really would like to see a better integration of knowledge and better data before I would personally be willing to play a role in saying something political about

this." A colleague replied: "To do nothing when the situation is changing very rapidly is not a conservative thing to do."

(as qtd. in Weart, 2008, p. 86)

As Crick and Gabriel point out, the second scientist's response is especially notable for its recognition that the situation calls out for practical judgment (Paroske, 2009, p. 151) in the face of contingency. Rather than demanding certainty of a "right way" to proceed or demanding certainty in terms of "knowing enough" or gaining a full and complete understanding, the scientist points to the nature of argument in public life. Rather than using uncertainty as a means to preclude action, as Crick and Gabriel (2010) note: "He posits the rhetorical principle that in the face of shared 'imperfection marked by urgency,' something must be done (Bitzer 6)" (p. 202). Argument in public life, thus, moves fluidly between contexts of discovery and contexts of judgment.

Life-world disturbances that construct a political exigency mark more than a dispassionate intellectual disagreement, reflected in visualizing argument as intellectual fencing; instead, these disturbances mark an urgency in which "participants are always highly aware of the situation and act from it" (Brante, 1993, p. 181). After all, public deliberation requires "the actual experience of collective doubt" (Crick & Gabriel, 2010, p. 217), or as Habermas (1987) notes, it often "takes an earthquake to make us aware that we had regarded the ground on which we stand everyday as unshakable" (p. 400). Even more importantly, constructing a life-world disturbance as a political exigency that will create a sense of collective doubt is a *"situated* affair" (Crick & Gabriel, 2010, p. 202) that "creates *interaction*; thus it signifies convergent as well as divergent tendencies between groups of antagonists regarding a common concern" (Brante, 1993, p. 181).

This understanding supports seeing public or yet-to-be-public concerns as "social dramas" that involve "real-life sequences of events that share a common underlying dramatic structure" (Gross, 2006, p. 153). The core commitments instantiated in a framework for public literacies—(1) accessing and attending to public and yet-to-be-public concerns; (2) fostering inclusive public dialogue across difference; (3) embracing a productive rhetorical pragmatism; (4) becoming agile performers in contemporary public life; and (5) generating conditions, forums, tools, and practices for contemporary public life—align closely with this kind of dramatic reading of "life-world disturbances" (Habermas, 1996). Adapting Alan Gross's (2006) work related to stages of scientific controversy, we might think of the commitments of public literacies in terms of dramatic acts of "social dramas" (p. 153). As summarized by Crick & Gabriel (2010, p. 217), in the first act, the Breach, people bring an "underlying social conflict vividly to public attention" (p. 153); in the second act, Crisis, a conflict is leveraged to create and coordinate deliberative publics. And in the third act, Redressive Action, deliberative publics "adjudicat[e] rival claims" and determine informed and just courses of action (p. 153). A dramatic approach "demand[s] that resolution not merely be an 'intellectual' affair of expert consensus" (Crick & Gabriel, 2010, p. 217), but must be resolved by enacting possibilities in view of the deliberative public and must be made publicly accountable by ongoing deliberation over the effectiveness and justice of the courses of action that were pursued (Gross, 2006, p. 46). Thus, deliberative publics cultivating argument about life-world disturbances do not aim at "fractured consensus about an abstract intellectual matter that is publicized over the mass media" (Crick & Gabriel, 2010, p. 217); rather, they aim to dramatize shared concerns in order to redress them by negotiated shared understandings and making collective judgments that inform a range of individual and shared actions.

The role that situational context plays in public literacies cannot be overstated. Distributed arguments—rationalities and reasonabilities distributed, often tacitly, across genre ecologies—often go through what Baumgartner (2006) calls "punctuated equilibrium," long periods of stability punctuated by moments of dramatic change. While the stability of these recurring distributed arguments also reproduce power relations, Crick and Gabriel (2010) comfort us with the observation that, as in the case of climate change, life-world disturbances causing individuals to experience doubt in beliefs and "behavioral rules" (Habermas, 1968, p. 120) are not often so "immediately and irrevocably catastrophic" (p. 212) that they preclude all action or response or hope of remediation. Instead, disruptions are often slow and cumulative, "providing time necessary for public engagement" (ibid) even while requiring us to act and respond with partial knowledge in the face of "constraints we cannot control and outcomes we cannot predict" (Clifton, 2013). This observation is also good news for English Language Arts and First-Year Composition classrooms as these disruptions to a world that is "first and foremost a world we care about" (McGuire & Tuchanska, 2000, p. 26) of necessity put us in a space of inquiry and invention where our "doubt motivates efforts to find new beliefs that will re-stabilize the disturbed behavior" (Habermas, 1968, p. 120).

When equilibrium is in some way "punctuated," it is not punctuated universally; instead, it is often simultaneously situated—marking fine-grained differences—and distributed—reflecting patterns, power relations, and anomalies. Consider the situated context of the Day of Remembrance incident featured in the Introduction. Despite national media attention to the suicides of queer youth and gatherings at flagpoles in schools across the country—something that might point to and "punctuate" a public controversy—many students local to Nate's high school did not recognize a concern even while some of their peers were regularly bullied and harassed in their school's classrooms and hallways. In this case, if bullying at this school—and at other schools across the country—is to stop, then people besides those who are bullied must come to see this as a concern they share. That many teachers, students, parents, and principals across the country did not—and still do not—recognize this as a concern points to the ways what occurred at Nate's high school reflects larger structural patterns, relations, power dynamics, and inequities. Thus, the public work Nate attempts is to call others to recognize and share a concern that is in some ways public and in some ways yet-to-be-public, in some ways situated in this particular time and place and in some ways more broadly distributed, producing and sustaining harmful rationalities, reasonabilities, and relations of power across otherwise isolated situations.

Consider a different example. In a writing class I taught, a young woman had recently experienced a death in the family:

> My cousin died from driving drunk. Yeah, she was affected but it goes deeper than that. She left behind two children, a now paralyzed husband, and an entire family. . . . I think it is only suitable to share the cause and effect of drinking and driving. Drinking and driving can change someone's life. . . . Understanding drunk driving in general can educate people on what is right and why not to drink and drive.

Her concern with drunk driving has been a more broadly public concern since the late '60s and early '70s when 29 states lowered their drinking age from 21 to 18 and saw an immediate increase in drunk driving crashes and alcohol-related deaths (MADD, 2015).

In response, in the 1980s the national drinking age was raised to 21 and organizations like Mothers Against Drunk Driving (MADD) began public awareness campaigns to aid victims and to prevent driving under the influence. More recently, schools have partnered with local police to facilitate two programs geared toward youth: one that stages an elaborate wreck and another that removes a student from a classroom every 15 minutes. Both aim at demonstrating the immediate and lasting consequences of drunk driving or of riding with someone who is under the influence of alcohol or drugs. In the U.S., it would be difficult to find a youth or adult who is not aware of drunk driving as a problem or who has no sense of the potential consequences of drunk driving. And yet, as the student in my class experienced firsthand, drunk driving persists. In this case, where a problem is generally recognized as a concern people either do or should share, the public work needed is quite different than when a concern is yet-to-be-public.

While this student frames the most pressing work as "educat[ing] people on what is right and why not to drink and drive," the difficulty, at least in her cousin's case, isn't primarily a lack of knowledge. What, then, is the difficulty? In this case, one kind of public work might involve engaging in dialogue with people who, despite knowing the dangers of drinking and driving, have decided at some point or another, even if they felt conflicted or worried about their choice, to drive while under the influence—*not*, however, talking together to "educate" them by advancing *a priori* claims, but rather to engage them in shared inquiry, to gain access to their own situated expertise and to facilitate collaborative problem-solving to construct possibilities that might be compelling to them in the moments when they or others are faced with the decision to drive drunk or not.

This example also reveals the iterative and ongoing nature of public life and public literacies. Public life is never once-and-for-all finished. Inevitably—as in the case of this student or of MADD (2015)—people find themselves navigating situations not of their making—venturing courses of action with consequences they can neither predict nor control. There is a constant need for invention and re-invention and no completely sure way of achieving what we aim for. Even our best efforts need to be responsive to new data, to alternative experiences, to the ongoing and unanticipated impacts of courses of action and democratic processes. Whether learning new information, encountering additional or changed constraints, or bumping against unpredictable results that refine the ever-shifting rhetorical situation, attending to situational "back talk" (hooks, 1989, p. 5) allows us to "connive with reality" (Atwill, 2010, p. 93) and chart alternative courses of action (Flower, 2008, p. 98) with others in public life.

4.1 Becoming Experienced

In my own classes, the kinds of grounded, well-tooled inquiries I've described so far move toward and help youth prepare for public dialogue. Either individually, in smaller groups, or as a whole class, depending on the kinds of concerns youth share and how they share them, I ask students to do their best to call a deliberative public into being and to scaffold a problem-solving dialogue with multiple stakeholders, using or creating available means. I ask that their materials reflect critical bifocality—focusing on specific situations and broader structures (If we talk about this one situation, we also need to talk about . . .)—and suggest or support specific tools and practices for dialogue across difference. One way I scaffold this work is with two practices: courting backtalk and user testing; these practices ask young people to regularly test and refine their thinking and writing with stakeholders, especially with those they are most likely to disagree with or misunderstand.

Courting Backtalk

As youth—any of us, really—attend to public and yet-to-be-public concerns, they inevitably face the limitations of their own perspectives. It is important, then, that young people have opportunities to test and revise the ways they are representing people and the situation necessitating dialogue and change. If they are going to be able to entice people who disagree to spend their time and energy addressing this concern, youth need to court backtalk—"the questions, qualms, concerns and conditions that need to be named and negotiated before people with their own interests, commitments and desires can venture next steps together" (Long, forthcoming).

User Testing

One productive way of courting backtalk is to have youth *user-test* writing or media that young people are hoping will be sufficient to frame a productive dialogue and to get people to the table. This is not simple peer review; instead, it is essentially an informal interview about usability and design, specifically about the representation of the issue at hand and the possibilities of supporting productive dialogue across difference:

- Does this describe a "shared problem" that each of the stakeholders might identify as a dilemma they care to deal with? How would you name the problem they are posing?
- Does it have clear "good guys" and "bad guys"?

  - Who gets cast as a "bad guy"? What part of the text leads you to think that?
  - Who gets cast as a "good guy"? What part of the text leads you to think that?

- Does it contain genuine conflicts within the problem (or does it imply a "right answer" or invite moralizing)?

  - How would you name the conflict?

- Does this mini-drama invite people to elaborate the story-behind-story in this incident? In other words, does it invite people to talk about "what's really going on"?
- Does it invite rivals—different ways of reading or interpreting what's going on, what the conflict is, what the problem is—and offer a springboard into dialogue?

  - If so, what are the specific places in the text that lead you to contribute?

- Does the explanation of the purpose of the dialogue signal an important reason for and a different way of participating with others who might disagree?
- How would you name the purpose of the dialogue?
- How would you describe ways people will need to participate together? What would make the dialogue productive? How might it go wrong?
- What specific places in the test might lead you to contribute differently? What do the prompts invite you to do differently?
- Does this page reflect a range of important conversations related to the critical incident?
- How would you name the broader context of the critical incident? What other situations or systems are connected to this incident: When we talk about ____, we also have to talk about ____?
- Does anything somehow skew the broader context of the critical incident?
- Are any important broader conversations left out?

Globalization, Wicked Problems, and Public Life

Determining the public work most needed is still more complicated as we take into account a world that is simultaneously local and global. Consider an extended scenario in which you and I may be implicated even if we've been unaware—a scenario that dramatizes a "wicked problem" (Rittel & Webber, 1973) and illustrates how tangled, hard hitting, and elusive contemporary dilemmas can be. Most of us in the U.S. give little thought to the many commodities, smart phones, computers, and ink cartridges we use, discard, and replace at regular intervals. And yet, when you and I start our cars, power our laptops, load our washing machines, or make our copies, we're using products that are made by flesh-and-blood people and with materials and parts that have likely traveled the globe as manufacturers search for low-cost materials and low-cost production. These processes have likely included someone like Miriam Delgado.

Miriam Delgado, a single mother of two, said she couldn't make ends meet working nine-and-a-half-hour shifts 6 days a week at Lexmark for $6 dollars a day. That's about 39 cents an hour. She picked up an additional night shift four days a week that earned her $9.80. On those days, she worked nearly 16 hours overnight, from 3:30 p.m. to 7:00 a.m. (Villagran, 2016). Delgado, who was fired after 5 years and 7 months at Lexmark packaging ink into printer cartridges, told the *Guardian*:

> They didn't provide face masks or gloves to protect us, many people have injured hands. They cut our salaries for being even slightly late, even if our children were sick and we had to take them to hospital, and we had to put up with harassment from supervisors.
>
> *(Lakhani & Thielman, 2015)*

As another worker, Gregoria Medina, explained, "Many years ago they stopped seeing us as people to instead see us as robots" (Alvarez, 2016). Like Delgado, Medina cannot stretch her meager wage to care for her family. As Ignacio Alvarez (2016) reports, Medina's house consists of a kitchen without tap water and another wider and colder room where she has only two beds. At night the room is shared by her elderly parents, an older brother who is mentally challenged, her 14-year-old daughter and two boys aged 17 and 8, along with her husband, who is a worker in another *maquila*.

In the fall of 2015, in the *maquiladora* sector of Ciudad Juárez—just a few miles from the U.S. border and the city of El Paso—workers who manufacture and package products for Kentucky-based corporation Lexmark expressed discontent about low pay and unsafe working conditions. The company, worth more than $2 billion at the end of 2015, refused to increase the daily wage for experienced employees from 114 pesos to 120 pesos—an increase of approximately 35 cents—despite earlier promises to raise the daily wage. When workers protested in December, Lexmark fired 120 workers.

Francisca Rivera, another of the workers fired by Lexmark, is 40 years old and has a severely injured right shoulder due to her work lowering boxes 1,200 times per day. She and her two teenage daughters have menacing coughs and lingering respiratory difficulties from the freezing cold that makes its way through the wooden walls of their small house. Now she must rely on the 150 pesos ($8) a week she receives from her 13-year-old son who works as an assistant bricklayer. She told Alvarez (2016): "They cut off the electricity more than a year ago and I am being honest when I tell you: I'm stealing it from the light pole because I have no way to pay for it. I also could not afford the water bill," she said. "The little that we get in money or food that is given to us is just enough to get by, just enough to keep alive." In Rivera's case, her broken rotator cuff and respiratory infection reveal the way the Mexican government relaxes worker protection laws in order to preserve Juárez's status as an exceptional industrial zone for transnational corporations, said Susana Prieto Terrazas, who took the defense of the workers fired by Lexmark as a personal cause. "The whole system is configured so that the workers burn out and get tired of claiming their rights," she explained. "It is a perfect marriage in which there are no scruples of any kind" (Alvarez, 2016).

It's not just Lexmark. Some 320 maquiladora assembly plants in this border city produce goods for homes, offices, and clinics around the world, including auto parts, refrigerators, televisions, medical scopes, printers, cables, plugs, air conditioners, computers, battery cases, and Christmas lights (Villagran, 2016). On average, goods imported to the United States from Mexico contain 40% U.S.-made content, according to Luis Torres, a research economist at Texas A&M University. On their way to market, products "crisscross the border multiple times as U.S. and Mexican suppliers and factories alternately add parts and value" (Villagran, 2016).

Years ago, the multinational corporations in Juárez implemented a system of bonuses in order to avoid raising real salaries. The "bonuses" can be exchanged for food, although they rarely exceed 100 pesos a week—about $7. Bonuses are also given out for punctuality and attendance records, which means that workers cannot miss even a single day to remain eligible (Alvarez, 2016). "Now you have a working class who have had all their human rights violated," said Prieto Terrazas.

> You have individuals who earn 600 pesos per week—about $33—when the [office of the Mexican census] sets a required 5,800 pesos—equivalent to $322 dollars monthly to ensure basic feeding for a family of four. That means workers cannot even afford to eat.
>
> *(Alvarez, 2016)*

Despite ongoing security concerns, American companies are drawn to the city by tax benefits offered through the North American Free Trade Agreement, low transport costs due to its proximity to the border, and low wages (Lakhani & Thielman, 2015). Just a few miles away, "[f]ew El Pasoans know about the paltry wages and substandard working conditions of their neighbors, despite buying products produced there by major global corporations with distant CEO annual earnings in the multi-million-dollar range and U.S.-based managers in the six-digit range" wrote Kathleen Staudt and Oscar Martinez (2016), two professors whose scholarship focuses on border justice issues, in an *El Paso Times* op-ed. Staudt and Martinez (2016) also implicated the Borderplex Alliance, an organization that cultivates bi-national business interests in the region in hopes of attracting more distant corporations to the area: "they advertise our region's 'global competitiveness.' To us, these seem like code words for low-cost labor."

In addition to Lexmark, workers at Mexican subsidiaries in Juárez have also protested working conditions and compensation at FoxConn, which manufactures products for Hewlett Packard, Dell, Cisco, and Scientific Atlanta; Eaton Cooper, which manufactures items such as fuses, auto parts, surge protectors, and electrical receptacles, and which has its major corporate office in Houston but is incorporated in Ireland where the company makes good on significant tax advantages; and North Carolina–based Commscope, a manufacturer of products for networking infrastructure like fiber optics.

In Foxconn's factories the labor force assembles electronic products—like computers, tablets, desktops, and laptops—on production lines with very little technology except the odd electronic device to check that the finished products actually work. Since tasks are dumbed down and no learning process is involved, workers are easy to replace. The manual and cognitive skills required may be elementary, but the level of intensity is exhausting. A worker told reporters: "It's not hard to do what they ask but it's very tiring standing all day on the assembly line doing the same task. Sometimes we have to work so fast we don't even have time to go to the bathroom" (Sacchetto & Cecchi, 2015).

The workers have the cost of food deducted from their pay, and they are only allowed to consume what the company sells, which is nothing more than chips and Coca-Cola. One of the workers explained:

> We have eight-hour shifts, and until a few years ago, we had chairs and stools to sit on. But the manager went on a trip to China, and there, they told him that if we worked standing up, we would be more productive. So now we work on our feet, without being able to move. My legs are now full of varicose veins, and a few days ago, I fell getting out of bed and got a huge bruise.

At one of the protest camps, a woman recounted, "They show us video after video of the working conditions in China, where workers' beds are meters away from their work stations, and they tell us, 'See how they work there? You're lucky—you should be thankful you are allowed to go home'" (Rangel, 2015).

Women also tell of sexual harassment at the factories and of working multiple shifts to make ends meet (Semuels, 2016). "There is a lot of sexual harassment in the industry. The most common one is that the assembly line chiefs and supervisors demand sexual favors for such basic things as overtime hours," a Lexmark worker told a reporter in Mexico City. "The base salary never makes ends meet, and [supervisors] condition overtime to what the women workers agree to give them" (Semuels, 2016).

Wanting to change these conditions, workers sought protection under a law that permits the formation of independent unions. But it wasn't possible. Besides better compensation—still under $10 a day—they wanted dignity (Alvarez, 2016). So they resorted to the means available to them: occupying protest encampments in front of the maquiladoras to make their plight visible to others. In response, a Fox-Conn representative said, "It is unfortunate that a small number of the company's employees have chosen to try to disrupt its operations to promote their personal agendas outside of the law and the approved and recognized company channels of communication" (Villagran, 2016). In April 2015, a settlement was reached under a nondisclosure agreement so that the workers could not make the terms of their settlement known. Later that month, Lexmark was bought by China's Apex Technology, a maker of inkjet cartridges, for a cash sum of $3.6 billion (Goliya, 2016).

In this complex, ongoing situation that extends across state and national boundaries, what is the public work most needed? It is in these most complex circumstances that traditional models of argument are perhaps least useful. It would be difficult, and insufficient if not also unproductive, for an individual to plot a singular course of action or advance a singular claim as a solution. After all, "messy, confusing problems defy technical solution" (Schön, 1987, p. 3). Messiness and confusion are markers of what Horst W. J. Rittel and Melvin M. Webber (1973), professors of design and urban planning, call "wicked problems." However, "[w]ickedness isn't a degree of difficulty. Wicked issues are different because traditional processes can't resolve them" (Camillus, 2008).

Many of the most pressing difficulties youth face today are "wicked problems" brought on or intensified by globalizing markets, media, and migration—contributing to changes material and intangible, rapid and unprecedented, irregular and unsettling. Many of us have some sense of how some of these changes impact our everyday lives, but there is also much that we cannot see and still more that seems out of our control. This lack of control creates a general sense of anxiety about jobs, about the future (remember the eighth grader worried about his future?), about our own limited capacity to anticipate, let alone shape, the changes most impacting our day-to-day lives (Dingo & Strickland, 2012).

Consider the tragic story of the Colorado rancher Hank in Eric Schlosser's (2012) *New York Times* best-seller *Fast Food Nation*. In the wake of losing his ranch, Hank committed suicide. As Schlosser writes:

> It would be wrong to say that Hank's death was caused by the consolidating and homogenizing influence of the fast food chains, by monopoly power in the meatpacking industry, by depressed prices in the cattle market, by the economic forces bankrupting independent ranches, by the tax laws that

favor wealthy ranchers, by the unrelenting push of Colorado's real estate developers. But it would not be entirely wrong.

(p. 146)

Wicked problems, like those Hank experienced or those the maquiladora workers recount, "ha[ve] innumerable causes, [are] tough to describe, and [don't] have a right answer" (Camillus, 2008).

And yet full citizenship today, or the pursuit of full citizenship, requires youth to develop the capacity to make strategic inquiries and gain strategic knowledge on a continual basis about those concerns that most affect their selves, their communities, and their futures (Appadurai, 2006). Without these capacities, it is difficult to know how a person's rights are being violated even if a person experiences quite keenly that he or she is being violated; this is especially significant as the idea of rights has been a central idea connecting ethics, arguments, and public life in democracies (Appadurai, 2007). However, as is evident in U.S. history, the language or concept of rights does not necessarily equate to or guarantee equity. Instead, we might consider the hopeful work of deliberative publics as the pursuit not of rights but of equity—of engaging and transforming the space between the *is* and the *ought to be* (Appadurai, 2007; Branch, 2007; Horton, 1961). This hope-filled project requires interrogating and deliberating over "the very conditions of bare life" (Appadurai, 2007, p. 32) that point to the deepest threats to equality and the biggest obstacles to democracy. Further, a hope-filled democracy does not take an instrumental tack, preparing youth for public life "someday"; instead, embracing equality as a central tenet, a hopeful approach to democracy engages youth in public literacies now—regardless of how we or others might perceive their current capacity and despite uncertainty due to the "lag between globalisation and knowledge of globalisation" (Appadurai, 2006, p. 172). Democratic public life, is, after all, a road we make by walking.

Addressing the Complexities of Wicked Problems With Youth

Working with youth to confront the issues that confront our communities (Paris, 2012, p. 9) sometimes involves confronting wicked problems. These are not simply more difficult or persistent problems. Unlike ordinary problems, wicked problems defy definition. How would you describe the problem of the maquiladoras? Writing a problem statement won't do justice to the acute predicaments, competing claims, and multiple systems that get tangled together—knotted in ways that are virtually impossible to navigate effectively (Long, forthcoming).

Wicked problems cannot be solved in any traditional sense. Instead, they can be addressed and, to some degree, limited or tamed. With wicked problems, there is a "no stopping rule" (Rittel & Webber, 1973, p. 162); the search for solutions never stops. Wicked problems often emerge in the face of constant change or unprecedented challenges. Numerous stakeholders—youth; mothers; schools; police; workers and trade unions; shareholders, investors, and creditors; suppliers; governments; consumers; non-governmental organizations; and so on—are involved and bring competing values, histories, perspectives, experiences, and priorities. The social complexity and the volatility of difference contribute to the "wickedness" of a problem.

Wicked problems are also technically difficult, requiring interdisciplinary approaches. Describing an inquiry about the fast food industry and how it affects our health, agriculture, values, laws, economy, and society, Harvey Daniels and Steven Zemelman (2004) note the range of content areas a cross-disciplinary team of senior teachers called on to design a sustained inquiry: science, social studies, English, special education, math, technology, and art. They read *Fast Food Nation* as well as Upton Sinclair's *The Jungle*; biology textbook chapters on nutrition, digestion, viruses, and bacteria; magazine articles, including a *Fortune* piece about lawsuits against fast food restaurants for causing obesity, a *Science* article taking an alternative perspective and arguing that fat may actually be good for you, and a *Harper's piece* about fast food companies intentionally targeting poor urban neighborhoods; six articles about animal cruelty from the PETA (People for the Ethical Treatment of Animals) website; a web-based press release "The Truth About *Fast Food Nation*," quoting negative reviews of the book and arguing against denying people freedom to enjoy food they love. Students also produced interdisciplinary data. They kept diet journals; took field notes of observations at local fast food restaurants; joined in two elaborate simulations, one about life as a teenage employee in a fast food restaurant and another that dramatized the unionization of a slaughterhouse; documented their own miserable school lunches, taking photos and collecting wrappers. The result: "80 kids with a lot of questions, concerns, and opinions" (Daniels & Zemelman, 2004, p. 4).

In a similar inquiry on the same topic, Eileen Schell (2012) includes chapters from Naomi Klein's *No Logo* "introduc[ing] students to debates over globalization, multinational corporate branding, and consumerism" (p. 48); visits to the online archive at the World Trade Organization History Project at the University of Washington to view and analyze protest materials from a 1999 protest in Seattle, Washington; excerpts from Naomi Klein's *Fences and* Windows, which include observations about fair trade, free trade, and global linkages to help students make sense of the food industrial complex that spans across the globe and also lands close to home; three films to help students visualize how the food industrial complex impacts workers, consumers, and the environment: *Fast Food Women*, an analysis of the lives and working conditions of Southern women working at three fast food outlets; *Super Size Me*, focusing on a man's declining health as he eats McDonald's fast food for a month; and *The Meatrix*, documenting the ways small family farms have been replaced by factory farms run by large agribusiness corporations.

The point here is that addressing wicked problems requires making sense of the complexities, including:

- Competing values, priorities, and experiences of multiple stakeholders
- Complex and tangled roots and practices

- Changes over time and in motion
- Interdisciplinary tools and perspectives
- Global linkages (Klein, 2002), structuring structures (Bourdieu, 2000), and networked arguments (Dingo, 2012)
- Uneven impacts on stakeholders' lived lives

In an era of neoliberalism and globalization, "wicked problems" (Rittel & Webber, 1973)—characterized by uncertainties and seemingly unresolvable difficulties—bear down on and are woven into people's lives in ways that threaten people's life chances for thriving, while also complicating the ways we find our lives interdependently intertwined. These concerns of equity and polity are at the heart of democratic public life—especially where what is shared, with whom, and how has gone terribly and unjustly awry.

Recognizing the prevalence of uncertainty, conflict, and difference troubles assumptions about the certainty and dominance prevalent in chess match models of argument. In complex situations, it is also perhaps more clear that our knowledge is perspectival and limited rather than impartial, universal, generalizable, let alone full and complete; that no particular discourse or expertise, data or claim is necessarily enough to come to a conclusion that is comforting and reassuring, that we all somehow experience as "right"; that relevant epistemological knowledge alone is insufficient.

Instead, engaging in the deliberative and pragmatic work of public life requires drawing on a range of knowledge (procedural, artistic, ethical, and propositional), data (scientific studies, artful renderings, narratives, observations, and so on), and ways of knowing (reasoning, perception, imagination, memory, emotion, and so on). As importantly, the *praxis* of deliberative publics involves *using* the sum of these wisely and well in practice with others. *Applying* multiple knowledges, ways of knowing, and data *in situ* is its own way of knowing and central to public literacies.

4.2 Moving Across Youth Literacies

In the same way that young people might call on a host of languages in a single repertoire (Alvarez, 2014; García & Wei, 2014; Lu & Horner, 2016), young people also have available to them—as a single repertoire—literacies that support their engagement in public life. A single youth might, for example, enact with varying degrees of insider expertise any combination of these situated literacies: *hip hop literacies*, like hush mode or battlin (Alim, 2004); *gaming literacies*, like those associated with Minecraft or World of Warcraft (Gee, 2003; Steinkuehler, 2008); *multilingual literacies* like language sharing (Paris, 2013), translanguaging (Alvarez, 2014; Lu & Horner, 2016), multimodal translation (Gonzales, 2015), and code-switching (Young et al., 2014); *rural literacies*, like understanding local food production, the "farm crisis," and Farm Aid (Azano, 2015; Donehower, Hogg, & Schell, 2007; Green & Corbett, 2013); *indigenous and mestizo literacies*, like performing the dances of each season, knowing the sacred values of certain animals, recognizing trickster characters, reading and writing pictographs and syllabaries, hiding in plain sight, knowing how to grow different varieties of corn or how to dig and maintain an acequia (Baca, 2008; Cushman, 2013; Long, Jarvis, & Deerheart Raymond, 2013; Powell, 2014); *urban literacies*, like recognizing impacts of gentrification (Kinloch, 2009), valuing "street survivors" (Kinloch, 2009), and producing multimodal identity texts (Kirkland, 2009; Morrell et al., 2013; Paris, 2010); *athlete literacies*, like how to read a playbook or a strength training workout or how to read a change in defense on the court; *Muslim literacies*, like when and how to wear a hijab, how to read the Koran, and which way to turn to face Mecca; *drama literacies*, like how to do improv or staged fighting; or *migrant literacies*, like keeping vaccination records and work papers or knowing migratory patterns that follow different harvest times and crop locations (Purcell-Gates, 2013).

Engaging youth in the work of deliberative publics invites them to move fluidly across these literacies to make real-time decisions about when and how to enact these practices with others. Taking a critical approach also scaffolds conversations about the ways others perceive those literacies and what is at stake in the situated decision-making youth do as they try to navigate and re-figure complex power dynamics and call together people who disagree to listen and learn from one another.

Inventing Alternative Literacies

Just as some models and practices of argument may limit what is possible with others, so, too, may some cultural literacies be limited in their capacity to reach across or transform moments when youth and other stakeholders most experience literacies, cultures, and identities in conflict. In these cases, alternative literacies (Higgins, Long, & Flower, 2006) are needed that offer new or hybrid practices to resist the ways some literacies are stigmatized, to create at least a temporary shared We-ness, to construct more just self–other relations, and to forge a way forward together.

This involves deliberately constructing practices together and ways of marking when those practices need to be adapted or revised or abandoned. This could include the co-construction of shared aims, worries, and ground rules, among other practices and stances. It might also include moving fluidly between or meshing institutional and legitimized literacies with vernacular literacies. It would also likely attempt to re-figure power relations through practices so that familiar ways of relating don't reduce deliberation to winning and losing.

However, none of these possibilities—a shared purpose, ground rules, alternative practices—*guarantee* productive dialogue or more just relations. Just as we are always doing, being, and becoming, so, too, are our literacies—our ways of dialoguing and using texts, our ways of being and doing together—always in process, always in need of inventing and re-inventing.

This is a significant departure from conceptualizing and teaching argument as text types or cognitive processes. After all, "[a]pplying relevant epistemological knowledge to a particular, highly uncertain dilemma . . . calls for a quite different kind of knowledge than that of episteme alone, *one that embraces the messiness of practice*" (Kinsella & Pitman, 2012, p. 6; emphasis added). Far from embracing the certainty and tidiness of universal truths or generalizable knowledge, public literacies recognize that we cannot escape uncertainty, conflict, and difference. Instead, public literacies acknowledge uncertainty, embrace difference, and value conflict as important sites of productive knowledge building and social action.

Novice practitioners—new teachers or medical residents, for example—know only too well "that generalizable knowledge is fragile in the face of practice" (Phelan, 2005, p. 353) as difficulties emerge in practice when they need to apply practical, situated judgment. Writing about medical residents, Montgomery (2006) writes that the "obstacle they encounter is the radical uncertainty of clinical practice: not just the incompleteness of medical knowledge but, more important, the imprecision of the application of even the most solid-seeming fact to a particular patient" (p. 37). Reading and discussing generalizable facts does not prepare a person to *do* something with those facts in real time with other people or to know how to act wisely and well in a world beyond her or his ability to fully understand or control.

An "expert" knower of generalizable facts is not necessarily a "virtuoso social actor" (Flyvbjerg, 2001) who can call on or "play on all the resources inherent in the ambiguities and uncertainties of behavior and situation" (Bourdieu, 1977, p. 8) in order to produce actions or invent alternative possibilities that may be useful, good, and wise. This is true of professions like teaching and medicine; it is also true of public life. If youth are to become "virtuoso social actors" in public life (Flyvbjerg, 2001), youth must engage in the situated acting–knowing of public literacies—(1) accessing and attending to public and yet-to-be-public concerns; (2) fostering inclusive public dialogue across difference; (3) embracing a productive rhetorical pragmatism; (4) becoming agile performers in contemporary public life; and (5) generating conditions, forums, tools, and practices for contemporary public life—which link individual and collective *praxis*, or practical acting–knowing, with individual and collective practical wisdom, what Aristotle called *phronesis*.

Practical Acting–Knowing and Practical Wisdom

Phronesis, or practical wisdom, "straddles cognition and emotion, as well as intellect and character" (Kinsella & Pitman, 2012, p. 7). It is a virtue-oriented, agile and artful athleticism that enables a person's entire self—a dialogical, embodied synthesizing self-in-systems (Hermans & Hermans-Konopka, 2010; Fecho & Clifton, 2017)—to judge what it is she should do in any given situation. It involves developing a sense of how we are particularly situated and cultivates "emergent self-awareness or self-revelation" (Sellman, 2012, p. 115) as well as an emerging awareness of particular people-in-systems and situations-in-systems. The development of practical wisdom is, thus, not founded in skills-based learning; instead, as a morally committed rhetorical expertise, *phronesis* is based on learning—over time and across situations and systems—to navigate tensions between moral wisdom and structuring structures (Bourdieu, 2000) that constrain and reproduce particular practices (Kemmis, 2012, p. 156).

Praxis, on the other hand, is a particular kind of action *"that is morally committed, oriented and informed by traditions in a field"* (Kemmis & Smith, 2008, p. 4). While Kemmis and Smith (2008) wrote of professional *praxis* and disciplinary fields, it is important to note that *praxis* in public life is oriented and informed differently. With regard to public life, pragmatic and relational considerations of the commons and polity are most often at stake, but a range of fields and other affiliations may orient and inform the ways people approach deliberations around a particular concern. After all, the dialogue of deliberative publics is "the language of everyday life" (Cicero, *De Oratore 1.3.12*) that often also needs to include private and technical discourse as part of public argument (Crick & Gabriel, 2010; Simmons & Grabill, 2007).

Many of us may be more familiar with this kind of interweaving in the *praxis* of deliberation in our more private spheres. Consider this, for example: My mother is currently in good health, but if she were in need of serious medical care, my stepfather with whom I have a troubled history, my younger sister who is a nutritionist, and I would need to determine a course of action. Certainly my mother's health would be foremost in our minds, but we would likely think about health differently. Our different kinds of expertise; the different constraints we might experience in terms of time, proximity, and money; our own histories with each other; our different understandings of our family relationships would all inform—perhaps differently at different times—what we each decide, how we each decide, *and* how we talk together to come to some relatively shared decision. Of course, the available ends-in-sight also matter. We will reason together differently if some treatment might save my mother's life, even if it's a slim possibility, than if we are told no treatment will. But our talk will not remain fully *in one field*, as Kemmis (2012) conceptualizes *praxis*.

Instead, in our deliberative *praxis,* we will also call on different knowledges, data, and ways of knowing as well as different rationalities and reasonabilities that *move across fields*. For example, the science of medicine may be informative, but it is not necessarily definitive. We would have to put what medical experts, including my sister, know in relation to what we think is best for my mother in terms of her spiritual health and emotional well-being, her body's ability to withstand and possibly benefit from treatment, her quality of life in the short-run and long-term, how long the treatment must last as well as its risks and costs (physical, relational, financial and otherwise), and so on.

One set of disciplinary practices or texts or talk would not be sufficient. Our *praxis* would be more expansive and might include talk, writing and reading (among other practices) related to hospital charts, WebMD blogs, doctor bills, scripture, journal articles, CaringBridge posts, emails, insurance claims, text messages, photographs, X-rays, cards, bank statements—with texts, tools, and talk sometimes arriving from elsewhere and necessitating, constraining, or co-opting local *praxis*, and local action sometimes resisting, inventing and re-purposing the significance or uses of texts, tools, and talk. Neither would our *deliberative* practices fit tidily within one field. Our *praxis* would take on a different shape—one that might construct interweaving practices of shared and individual inquiry, negotiate differing perspectives, listen seriously to others' experiences and expertise, weigh conflicting data and accounts, put multiple perspectives and values in dialogue with each other and with data, venture alternative possible explanations and options, construct a stance of wonder with others, attend to possible gains and losses for different stakeholders, build solidarity with those who disagree, construct new ideas and opportunities, play with humor, grieve limitations and uncertain decisions, imagine future possibilities and so on.

The point is that *praxis* that is not directly tied to professional performance or "expert" participants is oriented and informed differently. In more private deliberations like the one I've just described or in more public deliberations, deliberation involves constructing new knowledge, data, and ways of knowing as well as learning the situations and systems—including their rules, procedures, protocols, and values—that might inform and orient one differently to the difficulty at hand.

4.3 Constructing Alternative Rationalities and Reasonabilities

We may all sometimes be blind to the logics and impacts of our own language and thinking, which can sometimes fall into binary, this-or-that, terms. With youth, it can be helpful to talk about the binaries that show up in institutions, organizations, and neighborhood life. The list that follows (see Table 4.1; Cintron, 1998) can serve as a touch point for analyzing the value-laden logics particular systems may be trying to uphold.

TABLE 4.1 Value-Laden Binaries Informing System Logics (Cintron, 1998)

System	Shadow
Clean/Neat	Decaying
Precise Ordering	Ambiguity
Coherence	Disorder
Rules	Instability
Control	Emptiness
Mastery	Formlessness
Taming/Domesticating	Wildness
Confined/Framed	Unpredictable

Exploding Binaries

In deliberative publics problem-solving a shared concern, it can also be helpful to explode binaries by considering alternative options that resist oversimplified understandings and stock solutions. For example, rather than thinking _____ OR _____, which present mutually exclusive and diametrically opposed options, it can be helpful to consider _____ AND _____. This move opens up possibility, presenting an opportunity for a third, fourth, or fifth option. Significantly, part of the work of this move is that it may create a new problem, a new question. For example, how do we create restroom policies in schools that honor and protect transgender youth _as well as_ cisgender youth while treating them all equally? We may not have ready answers, but considering something other than a binary constructs an alternative reasonability among those who disagree and presents the possibility of alternative rationalities—rationalities that need to be co-constructed in light of possible new goals.

It can also be helpful to explore options in more careful and thorough ways. For a particular concern and particular options, exploring multiple causes and effects, multiple benefits and damages, and multiple implications can construct more nuanced, qualified options. Considering localized options and outcomes from multiple perspectives can further explode binaries. Here, some of the questions in _Engaging Youth in Public Literacies 3.2_ might be especially generative. Youth might seek to construct more nuanced understandings of possible options and outcomes by considering how actionable options and consequences might play out: for whom/to whom, to what extent, in what situations, under what conditions. After constructing some possibilities, youth might weigh the pragmatic aims and likelihood of accomplishing those aims with the principled gains or losses involved in order to construct relationships among rationalities and reasonabilities. This is often a productive sight of dissensus that does need not need to lead to consensus. Instead, in these dialogues across difference, youth are performing rationalities and reasonabilities of public life as their dialogues inform and condition subsequent individual and shared actions with their own rationalities and reasonabilities. Finally, situational constraints are yet another site of knowledge building and invention. In the face of important or urgent work and situational constraints—of resources, of relationships, of systems—we often need to get something done despite limitations and apparent difficulties. Youth might consider what they may need to call on, adapt, invent, or transform in order to achieve to-some-degree-shared ends-in-sight.

Alternatives to Binaries

Rather than thinking: _____ OR _____

1. Try these alternatives:

    a. _____ AND _____
    b. Multiple implications (What might this mean that's not being said?)

    c.   Multiple causes/effects
    d.   Multiple gains/losses

2.   And tease these alternatives out. Consider:

    a.   For whom
    b.   To what degree/extent
    c.   In what situations
    d.   Under what conditions

3.   Explore individual and collective actionable options.

    a.   What if X happened?
    b.   What if X did Y?
    c.   What if Y did Z?

4.   Consider areas of dissonance/tension. Weigh rationalities and reasonabilities in relation to each other.
5.   Consider probabilities, constraints, available means, and risk.
6.   Construct available means, available ends for individual and collection actions.

Argument as Dialogue Across Difference: The *Praxis* of Public Life

Of course, people who engage in *praxis*—whether this is professional, private, or public—may aim to be wise, but informed moral action is not necessarily the same thing as, and certainly does not guarantee, accrued wisdom. As Kemmis and Smith (2008) explain *praxis*:

> It is the kind of action people are engaged in when they think about what their action will mean *in the world. Praxis* is what people do when they take into account all the circumstances and exigencies that confront them at a particular moment and then, taking the broadest view they can of what it is *best* to do, they *act.*
>
> *(Kemmis & Smith, 2008, p. 4; emphasis in original)*

While Kemmis and Smith (2008) note the significance of anticipating consequences of action, Kemmis (2012) later theorizes a distinction that is subtle but significant, especially as it grooves with a recent allegation that discursive models of public engagement constitute "a grand compromise" because their focus on discourse means shying away from consequential action (Parks, 2013). Kemmis marks a distinction between *praxis* and the thinking that may precede action, or the practical deliberation before action. *Praxis*, he argues, "is the action itself, in all its materiality and with all its effects on and consequences for the cultural-discursive, material-economic, and social-political dimensions of our world in its being and becoming. *Praxis emerges in* 'sayings,' 'doings,' and 'relatings'" (Kemmis,

2012, p. 150; emphasis added). He argues, in other words, that deliberations— "sayings, doings, and relatings,"—are somehow distinct from, and also not quite, action.

However, in public life, practical deliberation constitutes significant action in and of itself. Further, if we consider that language and symbol systems are the primary ways in which we take perspectives and come to understand as well as re-shape the world around us, then our use of language in self-deliberation or public deliberation is a primary means by which we act on the world. Public literacies— "sayings, doings, and relatings," to call deliberative publics into being and to engage in dialogue across difference in order to coordinate still other "sayings, doings, and relatings," to address the concern at hand—are the primary actions of critically re-imagining and rhetorically inventing and re-inventing public life under ever-changing local and global conditions. After all, determining what is to be shared and how and with whom is the primary action of deliberative publics— action that is inherently discursive. Creating a deliberative public where none previously existed—the call and response of coming to share a concern with strangers—is itself a consequential act of deliberation. What's more, if rationalization of actions that have avoided or bypassed deliberation is a primary strategy in the exercise of power (Flyvbjerg, 1998), then cultivating and scaffolding deliberation is a significant act of public life, which aims to coordinate and distribute power and justice equitably.

Interrogating and inventing the argument practices of deliberative publics is also perhaps "the best site for making interventions into material spaces" (Rice, 2012, p. 7). The language we use together does more than just shape the places and systems we find ourselves part of; it shapes us as well, producing us as particular kinds of citizens in particular kinds of relationships with one another (Rice, 2012, p. 13). The ways we deliberate together and the language we use to talk about and "do" public life together conditions how we "see ourselves within a public scene of crisis" (Rice, 2012, p. 15) as well as what we think is possible, and indeed what is possible, in public life. For example, in a study about land preservation and environmental policies, Tarla Rai Peterson and C. C. Horton (1995) noted that despite caring a great deal about local land policies, many ranchers did not engage in public debate about a local controversy that would surely impact them. When asked why, they explained that they felt that "the broader culture no longer accommodates their interests" (p. 167). The ways we do argument together in public life, then, is significant in its own right, not in small part because "how one chooses to read one's self into [or out of] a rhetorical act . . . is of great consequence" (Armstrong, 2006, p. 66).

Far from being separate from *praxis* or preceding it, in public life, deliberation is a central act of citizenship. Robert Asen (2004) writes:

> In both scholarly and popular assessments discourse is too often regarded as prefatory to genuine action. According to this view, talk is . . . a

bargain only insofar as it leads to activities such as voting and volunteering. Citizenship should not be preserved for special occasions, however. Discourse practices present potentially accessible and powerful everyday enactments of citizenship.

(p. 207)

The flip side, sobering for those of us teaching ways with words, is that everyday talk and texts are also where poor and even harmful practices and habits of citizenship are cultivated (Rice, 2012, p. 17).

Schools, then, have a special and significant role in shaping public life and the everyday citizenship of young people through the ways youth learn to engage in dialogue across difference. Schools are, whether they want to be or not, often at the center of some of our most pressing public issues. Consider the talk around recent concerns about gender-neutral bathrooms in schools. Jayne Ellspermann, principal of a Florida high school, notes the significance of how schools handle these issues:

> One of the challenges that we have in working in schools is that we end up being that place where we confront social changes and we have to make those—we have to make sure that moving forward, when we make our policies, when we create the—what the future's going to look like in our country, that oftentimes begins in our schools. And that's where we are right now.
>
> *(Montagne & Ellspermann, 2016)*

Every day students, teachers, custodians, parents, and principals are enacting some version of citizenship and public talk. How, then, do we and the youth and communities we work with learn to do public life wisely and well? I contend that it is not by sealing youth off from these difficulties or making decisions and rationalizing them later; instead, our schools and universities, and especially ELA and FYC teachers, are the ones who are in the most immediate and worthwhile positions to engage youth in the *praxis* of public literacies and to invite youth to develop practical wisdom as they coordinate and scaffold the *praxis* of deliberative publics.

While character education and other initiatives in schools aim to teach a kind of moral wisdom that might, despite being detached from *praxis*, somehow filter into *praxis*, this is the wrong way around to *phronesis*. *Praxis* is a *prerequisite* for *phronesis*. It is through experience and action—through *praxis*—that we develop *phronesis* (Kemmis, 2012, p. 158). Therefore, if we hope to entice youth to develop wisdom in public life, we must cultivate and coordinate their involvement in the *praxis* of public life, and especially in deliberative publics.

4.4 Cultivating Participatory Publics: A Case Study

Engaging youth in public literacies requires youth to think differently about audiences. They must imagine and meet, listen to and engage with people they otherwise might not have a reason to talk with. They must also do more than circulate material to those folks; instead, to call a deliberative public into being and to invite them to argue differently (Kroll, 2005), youth must also design experiences that *cultivate participatory publics*. This puts youth in a space of thinking about the ways media, tools, texts, materials, spaces, places, etc., converge to cue particular ways of "saying, being, and relating" (Kemmis, 2012).

This work also means that there is a dynamic and dialectic relationship between the experiences of deliberation they aim to design and their inquiry to more fully understand and better represent people-in-systems and situations-in-systems. Consider an example in which a pair of students made an inquiry into bullying at a local middle school and high school. Because of their siblings' experiences, they were particularly concerned about what administrators do about bullying once they learn of it. As this pair of students set about the work of simultaneously better understanding these student experiences and producing a multimedia text that might create an exigency for dialogue capable of creating a deliberative public, they also learned more about what a productive dialogue would need to entail: not only procedural discussions, but more importantly, attunement to the complexities of multiple power dynamics and the ways people experience and reproduce those in real time.

The students interviewed several students, parents, and a school administrator. With permission, the students filmed these interviews in preparation for a mini-documentary they hoped might prompt a deeper collaborative inquiry into the limitations of current policies and practices. In an early interview, the principal of one of the schools noted that the administrators take bullying very seriously and follow a specific protocol outlined by the district. The principal told the students, "Every incident of bullying we come across, we deal with it. And we actually have records on it. We have to fill out an incident report. The district and the state have guidelines on how to handle bullying." Importantly, with regard to genre ecologies, these tools-in-use both document and coordinate much of the activity of a school's responses to bullying; as such, they might also point to potential sites for re-thinking particular institutional activities. The guidelines and incident reports point to processes that students learned about as they conducted interviews and made a documentary; they also inform the ways they designed deliberation as they realized they might need to ask students, parents, teachers, and administrators to describe their interactions around these texts.

The students looked up these guidelines, interviewed other students and parents about specific experiences of bullying, and in their film, referenced recent movies and documentaries about bullying in schools. They also conducted a survey of 80 students across the middle and high school about their experiences of bullying and took this to administrators to see how they might react to the survey. Seeing that 71% of the 80 students surveyed said that they had been bullied in the past, a principal was visibly surprised that the number was so high. Putting this in a broader context, the students referenced a UCLA study in which 20% of high school students reported being bullied. Subsequent interviews with middle and high school students described what happened, from a student perspective, when they reported bullying to administrators. A principal said he was sad to see that 22% of students who said they'd been bullied reported that the school did nothing at all to help their situation. Because they felt the school did little to protect their safety or improve their circumstances, many students reported that they stopped telling school officials about their own or others' experiences of bullying. One student said she felt like "they only care about their reputation."

The girl who makes the remark about the school's reputation seems to be making a Foucauldian analysis: that the school's commitment to its reputation, manifested in its practices to address bullying, produces some students as people who discipline and surveil themselves to stay quiet and thus, not tarnish the school's public reputability. Of course, this is one interpretation—perhaps astute even if not necessarily intended by any of the adults involved—but it indicates some of the significant work needed: to co-construct not only different practices and procedures, but also a different relationality together and more equitable power relations. The student filmmakers were also realizing the need for ongoing dialogue as the particular instances of bullying and addressing bullying are always different, requiring different judgments in each situation and different judgments or possible actions by different stakeholders—judgments that some of the reports and procedures in place stabilize, perhaps a bit too much.

In calling people together, they also needed to signal and construct the work at hand. Students who are bullied, their parents, and administrators already have a sense of how these conversations have gone in the past. To engage in a real problem-solving dialogue would require something different than what they've done previously, would call them to relate to each other and to data in new ways. Cultivating participatory audiences involves youth in considering what texts, materials, spaces, ways of talking together might be capable of coordinating new ways of participating publicly together.

The Need for Rough Ground: Experience, Uncertainty, and Consequences

Praxis in public life is a kind of embodied theorizing in the face of "some real-world need, some palpable contradiction" (Spellmeyer, 1993, p. 185). These difficulties make our questions and predictions, knowledge building and collaborations worth undertaking in the first place. At its best *our theory building* in the face of what doesn't work is *praxis*—opening up and negotiating possibilities, framing and re-framing deliberation and inventing and coordinating other paths and possible actions. As *praxis* is realized—as people take well-informed, morally committed action in the world—those actions initiate change in people, ideas, practices, materials, tools, activities, and systems. Of course, change of some sort occurs with all actions, praxis or not. This is, in part, why the nature of the change *praxis* introduces is not necessarily clear or stable or predictable. We act in ever-changing situations not of our making.

Even more daunting is the fact that we can neither fully know nor predict or control either the constraints or the results of our work. As Kemmis (2012) puts it, "the person who aims at *praxis* aims to be wise and prudent, but *as it happens, praxis* immediately begins to affect the uncertain world in uncertain and indeterminate ways. Consequences begin to flow, whether for good or for ill" (p. 158). And so, as we learn new information, are faced with additional or changed constraints, and bump up against unpredictable results, we find ourselves in a space of ongoing assessment and construction of an ever-shifting rhetorical situation (Clifton, 2013).

This space can be unsettling, to say the least. And so we sometimes lean toward the language of mastery and failure, sustainability and unsustainability in order to stabilize what is now out of our hands and to place our feet on more solid and more settled ground. Most often, we pit mastery against failure as ways of naming the goals and measuring the worth of our actions. However, to talk about our work in this way is to bracket or at least to render temporarily invisible a significant feature of the interaction between *praxis* and *phronesis*: that our embodied theorizing—our acting–knowing—is "responsive *in real time* to the test of outcomes" (Flower, 2008, p. 91, emphasis added). It is in this test of outcomes—waiting to see the actual existing consequences, intended or otherwise, of our actions—that "those who act begin to learn the measure of their wisdom and prudence" (Kemmis, 2012, p. 150).

Assessing the consequences of our actions is not simply a matter of attending to whether what we intended came about or not. Instead, we must see "the happening-ness of practice/praxis"—what our *praxis* brings about over time and "how it unfolds in history and society" in ways we could not control, predict, imagine, or anticipate (Kemmis, 2012, p. 157). Happening-ness suggests activity, energy, a buzz (*This is a happening place!*); uncertainty, not knowing, anticipation (*What's happening? What's going on?*); and events out of our hands (*Is this really happening? I can't believe this is happening!*). Facing the profound consequences of the happening-ness of practice/*praxis* orients us toward the energy and uncertainty and unfolding of the changes our actions have, intentionally or not, initiated.

In *praxis*, we are all submitted to the disciplining of reality and confronted with "the consequences of what happens as a consequence of our practice/praxis" (Kemmis, 2012, p. 158). We come to recognize through experience that our actions are always in relation to other people and also part of histories, systems, and ecologies in process and in flux. Further, we come to experience and, thus, see that our actions contribute to histories, systems, ecologies we share with near and distant others; in *praxis*, a person is "aware of acting in history, that it is history-making action, that it has, for the one acting, some world-historical significance (even the action is a small thing itself)" (Kemmis, 2012, p. 156).

Of course, *praxis* does not originate solely in a lone actor; people act within and upon a world ready-made with signs and systems, people and materials, histories and technologies already acting upon them. Nor does *praxis* always emerge from intentions or from rational thought (Hindess, 1977; Kemmis, 2012). Rather, rationalities and reasonabilities distributed across institutional and social practices shape and pre-figure the particular actions people can and will take. The recurrence of these practices and their recognizability cues and produces people "caught up" in a particular way, limiting and framing what can and should be done. The *praxis* of public literacies attends to these distributed arguments and their disruptions as sites for cultivating the "sayings, doings, and relatings," of deliberative publics in order to change ineffective or unjust practices, relationships, and systems and also to re-figure the ways those are socially, materially, and discursively constructed. So: *praxis* of individual and collective people-in-systems introduces "immediate effects and long-term consequences of . . . actions, and these effects become conditions" that, in turn, shape people, materials, tools, technologies, activities, and relations of power (Kemmis, 2012, p. 151).

In taking consequential action, *phronesis* involves weighing and interrogating values, interests, and power in localized contexts —"things that are good or bad for man" (Aristotle, 1355b12)—as a point of departure for *praxis* (Flyvbjerg, 2006, p. 372). Of course, what is ethical—good or bad—is always chosen in relation to particular values and interests in order for good and bad to have meaning. With regard to public literacies, then, *phronesis* is not only concerned with contemplating practical ethics to govern public deliberation, but also with accomplishing ends that fit a local public's values (Flower, 2008; Hauser, 1999) (Long, 2008). *Phronesis* aims at means and ends that are good and wise, but it cannot guarantee it.

Rhetorical action is, after all, an unpredictable art and does not always reliably achieve its outcome. We see the same phenomenon in medicine. A doctor might treat a patient conscientiously and expertly according to all the best research, and yet the patient's condition might deteriorate. Another patient might be treated rather carelessly by another doctor, yet the patient might regain full health. And so, in medicine as in other stochastic arts, masterful work does not necessarily guarantee a good outcome, and vice versa. It was this paradox that led the ancient Greeks to suggest that the aim of medicine should not be seen as the achievement of the desired end, but as doing everything possible to achieve that end.

In stochastic arts, mastery is not incompatible with failure. Here, an analogy from medicine is illuminating. When someone we care about has a disease that has no known cure, we do not hesitate to take our loved one to the most expert physicians, knowing that even their best efforts may not help. In fact, physicians who deal with the riskiest illnesses may be masterful even as they record high failure rates. As Aristotle writes, "It does not belong to medicine to produce health, only to promote it as much as possible" (1355b12). A doctor, or a person engaging in public life, cannot reliably bring about the goal she aims for.

4.5 Limitations as Sites of Knowledge Building: Generating and Theorizing Tools-in-Use

Youth learn the usefulness and wisdom of their words and actions over time "by experiencing the irreversibility of . . . actions and the consequences of . . . actions (and perhaps the actions of others, and the consequences of their actions)" (Kemmis, 2012, p. 154). Expertise and wisdom are *performed* "in the moment" but are *fostered* before and after a fleeting moment, and in anticipation of the next one.

Abby Knoblauch notes that even our most expansive models of argument are often little more than a re-tooling of traditional argument. I wonder if we don't teach argument differently because we don't often do argument differently. Public literacies aim to support youth in becoming experienced at dialogue across difference; the *argumentation toolbox* that follows constructs an opportunity for youth to engage in the iterative work of *conceptualizing* argument differently, while they also *tool* argument differently. Importantly, the argumentation toolbox asks youth to reflect on actual existing deliberation (Fraser, 1990) and especially on the places where argument stalled, for whatever reason. These situated sites of limitations point to places where it would be helpful to re-think our current concepts, stances, and tools for doing argument with deliberate publics. Importantly, not all conceptualizations, stances, and tools are equally useful at all times; thus, the argumentation toolbox pays particular attention to youth decision-making and the situated expertise they are developing as they call on and invent alternative models and practices of argument for deliberative publics.

Argumentation Toolbox

Create a brief handbook or field guide for yourself that can serve as an argumentation toolbox, useful to you in retrospect and also in real time during your next deliberation.

Conceptualizing Argument/Argumentation

* 3–4 guiding metaphors that express the complexities of the work and relationships involved in argument as dialogue across difference. Metaphors are limited, so you might consider ways of accounting for different aspects of productive argument (i.e., flint sparking a fire might account for tension, conflict, and the generation of something new; double dutch might account for a more collaborative, creative, athletic process).

- 2–3 goals and purposes of argument/ argumentation in deliberative publics
- A working list of what makes for productive relationships when others disagree
- A working list of some ways argument can go wrong or some things to be aware of and perhaps to guard against in argumentation

Productive Stances

3–5 stances

These should reflect productive, useful, generative ways of positioning yourself in relation to data, the concern at hand, others, relations of power, etc.
   For each stance:

> *Stance* [**Give it a name**]—Brief description.
> *Explanation*—What makes it necessary? Under what conditions is it useful? What are its limits/ at what point is it less useful? How do you enact this stance?

Useful/Generative Tools or Concepts

5+ Tools

Tools scaffold practices and generation of new ideas. They are flexible enough that they can be adapted for new situations (i.e., mapping genre ecologies or strong rivaling hypothesis; Flower, Long, & Higgins, 2000).
   For each tool:

> *Tool* [**Give it a name**]—Brief description
> *Explanation*—What makes it necessary/useful/generative? Under what conditions is it useful? How do you use this tool (there may be multiple ways)? What are its limits/at what point is it less useful? Or what do you have to keep in mind not to oversimplify the ways you use or think about this tool?

In his work about problem-solving, Matthew Crawford (2009) notes the intricate relationship between mastery and failure whenever we work under conditions not of our making:

> The mechanic or the doctor deals with failure every day, even if they are expert. This is because the things they fix are *not of their own making*, and are therefore never known in a comprehensive or absolute way. The experience of failure tempers the conceit of mastery; the doctor and the mechanic have daily intercourse with the world as something

independent. . . . In diagnosing and fixing things made by others, one is confronted with obscurities, and must remain constantly open to the signs by which they reveal themselves.

(p. 82)

Engaging youth in public literacies also requires entering worlds not of our making, or theirs. In determining what is wise and good in a given situation, practical wisdom "acknowledges the possibility of tragedy, of danger, of harm—possibility that is to be found deep within conflicts of values and interests, and conflicts of viewpoints, histories, and loyalties" (Kemmis, 2012, p. 157). These possibilities necessitate iterative and ongoing public deliberation around questions of values and power and action—the intersection of *phronesis* and *praxis*.

Praxis and *phronesis* together look to contemplate social action and take social action while continuing to contemplate the action just taken and its consequences along with other possible actions that could be taken (Kemmis, 2012). In public life, *praxis* involves questions of informed, morally committed action:

- What is the work that needs doing?
- What existing models can we call on?
- What is keeping the work from being done?
- What can we construct or invent to get the work done anyway?

(Clifton, 2013)

According to Brent Flyvbjerg (2001) in his study of contemporary social organizations and public policies, *phronesis* asks:

- Where are we going?
- Is this development desirable?
- What, if anything, should we do about it?
- Who gains and who loses, and by which mechanisms of power?
- What possibilities are available to change existing power relations, and is it desirable to do so?

(p. 33)

Phronesis interrogates values and power; *praxis* makes sure values remain valueable by doing something useful (Kemmis, 2012). Important to both *phronesis* and *praxis* is ongoing dialogue across difference about the *how* and the *why* of public life. Both *phronesis* and *praxis* in public life need others—a range of stakeholders who embody a range of I-positions in, out, and among systems (Fecho & Clifton, 2017; Hermans & Hermans-Konopka, 2010)—to make sense of complex experiences in an ever-changing world, to cultivate further dialogue when current systems are ineffective or unjust, and to join and create deliberative publics, offering and scaffolding co-constructed interpretations and judgments as well as wise and well-tooled action—that can then benefit from further dialogue and action.

4.6   A Framework for Public Literacies

The teaching and learning of argumentative writing is not monolithic, nor is the teaching of literacies needed for engaging youth in public life. Publics are rife with complexities, contradictions, and intersections in which multiple arguments emerge, implode, travel, flip, rotate, calcify, expand, multiply, and converge. Indeed, public life is in many ways precisely productive and hopeful, as well as volatile, because of the "grit and tumble" (Ackerman & Coogan, 2010) of agitation, assembly, and deliberation. So, too, in theorizing and enacting public literacies, we gain traction in the rough ground of inclusive democracy because of friction about what the shared project of public life is and ought to be. After all, as Ackerman and Coogan (2010) remind us, "We are not all building the same things for the same reasons with the same tools in the same public" (p. 8).

Any framework for public literacies, then, needs to be responsive to the conditions people find themselves navigating with others and tested in the here and now. And any argument, perhaps especially those that pertain to public life, needs to solicit backtalk and be open to further dialogue and revision. With that in mind, I offer a framework for public literacies as a *working theory.* Of course, the real test of a working theory is that it *works*: that "it is operational (a tool kit of conditions and strategies); it is situated (adapted to its particular time, place, and people); and it is always under revision (responding to the test of outcomes)" (Flower, 2008, p. 90).

Overall, I've articulated a framework for public literacies that instantiates five core commitments for rhetors engaging in public life: (1) accessing and attending to public and yet-to-be-public concerns; (2) fostering inclusive public dialogue across difference; (3) embracing a productive rhetorical pragmatism; (4) becoming agile performers in contemporary public life; and (5) generating conditions, forums, tools, and practices for contemporary public life. Engaging youth in this work requires cultivating public literacies that are:

Performative

Rather than theorizing, studying or teaching *about* performance, public literacies engage youth directly in theory-guided *rhetorical practices* of public life. Public literacies teach youth to "do" public life by joining and constructing forums for public deliberation, public inquiry, and public action in real time with real people for real purposes. Public literacies aim at developing "agile performers" (Coogan, 2006, p. 671) and "virtuoso social actors" (Flyvbjerg, 2001, p. 85) who, over time, become expert at acting quickly, wisely, and well with others in an instant and at utilizing spontaneously their experiences from similar prior situations (Flyvbjerg, 2001, p. 15–16).

Collaborative

Public literacies start with the premise that all youth must be welcomed and supported in their efforts to become active working partners in an intercultural collaboration toward inclusive public life. Public literacies envision a world none of us can build on our own with problems none of us can solve on our own. Engaging youth as working collaborative partners in public life involves teaching them to step outside of typical and familiar roles and relationships and to draw on diverse perspectives, experiences, and expertise to build new knowledge.

Rhetorical

Public literacies recognize *local publics* as rhetorically constructed polities. A polity consists, as Iris Marion Young (1997) explains, of "people who live together, who are stuck with one another" because of geographic proximity, shared resources, and economic interdependence (p. 126). Because one person's interests and pursuits affect other people's pursuits, they must deliberate together in some public way to determine how they will live together. This version of public is not merely about demographics, similar interests, or entertainment politics. Rather, the public of public literacies is called into being by a shared issue or concern; is sustained by dialogue, persuasion, and deliberation about values and actions; and is characterized by collective invention, discovery, and change.

Inclusive

Rather than seeing difference, however that shows up, as simply an obstacle to work around or work against, public literacies engage difference as a difficult and much needed part of sustaining more just, more creative, and more inclusive versions of public life. This inclusivity is not merely about allowing marginalized people into the powerful center where normative ideas, identities, practices, and values continue to hold sway; instead, it is about shifting and de-centralizing the center, even re-orienting to move away from the metaphor of a modernist center. Wary of normative ideals of inclusivity, public literacies recognize that relations are often characterized by uncertainty, conflict, difference, and power—conditions that produce and sustain valuable ties and tensions of democracy (Flyvbjerg, 1998, p. 6)—and that we negotiate these relations and make decisions together in "contexts [that] are unpredictable, dynamic, evolving, and nonlinear" (Fecho, 2014). Public literacies are, thus, inclusive in the spaces where we most need difference and where we are most resistant to difference; they scaffold an orientation toward people and ideas that is at once dialogic, inventive, artful, shrewd, and expansive.

Productive

Public literacies position a rhetor as someone up to something in the world, as someone in dialogue with others, and as someone who must *venture* some course of action, some positive endeavor to take up. Recognizing that critique and deconstruction only get us so far, public literacies take up the "what next?" in order to build a just, desirable world alongside others with whom we find ourselves in interdependent relationships.

Dialogic

More than simply "speaking our minds," public literacies are rooted in multi-voiced dialogue, dialogic consciousness-raising, and ongoing deliberation about desire, damage, values, and choices. Democratic deliberation invites participants to work together as securers of their own well-being and the well-being of the communities they find themselves part of. Within this context where citizens are concerned both with material outcomes and with each other's well-being, public literacies teach youth (1) to make public claims (2) to dialogue together with others who are also making (possibly conflicting) public claims, and (3) to make wise decisions under difficult circumstances with knowledge that is necessarily perspectival and, thus, inherently limited.

Pragmatic

Public literacies consider how particular cases, not general issues, can be dealt with effectively and justly. The invitation to dialogue emerges when some particular experience(s) disrupt a sense of stability to such a degree that we are compelled into inquiry and action or when change we want or need impacts others and requires more than we can marshal through our own private resources. Public literacies pay attention to the everyday, to what is actually done, and invoke a pragmatism that brings urgent and compassionate critique to bear on systems and institutions that dampen, diminish, and deaden creative democracy and social freedom. Public literacies also move beyond critique to take practical action, to get something done and, thus, involve a process of continual inquiry, venturing, testing, reflecting, and revising.

Deeply Aesthetic

As well-tooled and pragmatic as public literacies are, they are also profoundly artful and inventive (Long, forthcoming). They are deeply attentive to context and are both performative and precise in pursuit of some productive, purposeful, daring aim. Public literacies are artful in the contingent, "mak[ing] the most of contextually available materials and methods (including those that come from relative institutional privilege) to speak with and for others against damaging scripts" (Long, forthcoming). But public literacies do not invoke the artistry of the genius or the elite or the natural talent; instead, public literacies invoke a democratized vernacular artistry, do-able, teach-able, and revise-able. Public literacies are, therefore, not confined to a static system or the conventions of established norms; nor are they confined to a lone artist or a lone performance (Atwill, 2004, p. 167). Furthermore, the aesthetic of public literacies moves everyday cultural workers toward their "most original, most strikingly deviant" work (Walker, 1983, p. 4) in spaces of uncertainty, conflict, and difference, generating new knowledge and new paths for new possible futures. Public literacies embrace the unfamiliar and invoke a border-land aesthetic of the in-between and the both-and to destabilize exclusionary cultural practices and to re-imagine, re-invent alternative, hybridized inclusive cultural practices.

Complexly Situated

Public literacies attend not only to where personal, private knowledge needs to garner more public attention but also to the ways personal knowledge is con-textualized over time and across systems. These sensibilities and literate practices for attending to situated expertise recognize fine-grained details of people's lived lives as simultaneously personal, complex, relational, patterned, systemic, local, and transnational. Public literacies situate otherwise isolated interactions within broader contexts in, out, and among institutions and contextualize *this one person* and *this one area of concern* in relation to larger, networked social arrangements.

Unpredictable

In the realm of human affairs no two contexts are ever the same and we often must engage under conditions we cannot control. Public literacies embrace the practical, intellectual activity of clarifying the affordances, constraints, risks, and possibilities we face and value the work of grounded *theorizing* in uncertain contexts where we must articulate a working theory (Flower, 2008, pp. 90–91), put that theory to the test by venturing some course of action, and then attend to the "backtalk" of a situation where we may face outcomes we couldn't have predicted (Clifton, 2013, p. 227).

References

Ackerman, J. & Coogan, D. (2010). *The public work of rhetoric: Citizen-scholars and civic engagement.* Columbia, SC: University of South Carolina Press.

Alim, H. S. (2004). Hearing what's not said and missing what is: Black English in white public space. In C. Paulston & S. Keisling (Eds.), *Discourse and intercultural communication: The essential readings* (pp. 180–197). Malden, MA: Blackwell Publishers.

Alvarez, I. A. (2016). Fight for 50 cents: In Ciudad Juarez, workers rise up against the maquila system. *Aljazeera America*. Available online at http://projects.aljazeera.com/2016/02/lexmark-juarez/

Alvarez, S. (2014). Translanguaging tareas: Emergent bilingual youth as language brokers for homework in immigrant families. *Language Arts*, 91(5), 326–339.

Appadurai, A. (2006). The right to research. *Globalisation, Societies, and Education*, 4(2), 167–177.

Appadurai, A. (2007). Hope and democracy. *Public Culture*, 19(1), 29–34.

Armstrong, E. (2006). *A Ciceronian sunburn: A Tudo dialogue on humanistic rhetoric and civic poetics*. Columbia, SC: University of South Carolina Press.

Asen, R. (2004). A discourse theory of citizenship. *Quarterly Journal of Speech*, 90(2), 189–211.

Atwill, J. M. (2004). Art and disciplinarity. *Enculturation*, 5(2). Available online at http://enculturation.net/5_2/atwill.html

Atwill, J. M. (2010). *Rhetoric reclaimed: Aristotle and the liberal arts tradition*. Ithaca, NY: Cornell University Press.

Azano, A. P. (2015). Addressing the rural context in literacies research: A call to action. *Journal of Adolescent and Adult Literacy*, 59(3), 267–269.

Baca, D. (2008). *Mestiz@ scripts, digital migrations, and the territories of writing*. New York: Palgrave Macmillan.

Baumgartner, F. R. (2006). Punctuated equilibrium theory and environmental policy. In R. Repetto (Ed.), *Punctuated equilibrium and the dynamics of U.S. environmental policy* (pp. 24–46). New Haven, CT: Yale University Press.

Bitzer, L. (1969). The rhetorical situation. *Philosophy and Rhetoric*, 1, 1–14.

Bourdieu, P. (1977). *Outline of a theory of practice*. Cambridge, UK: Cambridge University Press.

Bourdieu, P. (2000). *Pascalian meditations*. Trans. Richard Nice. Stanford, CA: Stanford University Press.

Branch, K. (2007). *Eyes on the ought to be: What we teach when we teach about literacy*. New York: Hampton Press.

Brante, T. (1993). Reasons for studying scientific and science-based controversies. In T. Brante, S. Fuller, & W. Lynch (Eds.), *Controversial science: From content to contention* (pp. 177–191). Albany, NY: SUNY Press.

Camillus, J. (2008). Strategy as a wicked problem. *Harvard Business Review*, 86(5), 98–106.

Cintron, R. (1998). *Angels' town: Chero ways, gang life, and rhetorics of the everyday*. Boston: Beacon Press.

Clifton, J. (2013). Mastery, failure and community outreach as a stochastic art: Lessons learned with the Sudanese diaspora in Phoenix. In L. Cella & J. Restaino (Eds.), *Unsustainable: Owning our best, short-lived efforts at community writing work*. Cultural Studies/Pedagogy/Activism Series (pp. 227–252). Lanham, MD: Lexington Books.

Coogan, D. (2006). Service learning and social change: The case for materialist rhetoric. *College Composition and Communication*, 57(4), 667–693.

Crawford, M. (2009). *Shop class as soulcraft: An inquiry into the value of work*. New York: Penguin.

Crick, N. & Gabriel, J. (2010). The conduit between lifeworld and system: Habermas and the rhetoric of public scientific controversies. *Rhetoric Society Quarterly*, 40(3), 201–223.

Cushman, E. (2013). *Cherokee syllabary: Writing the people's perseverance*. Norman, OK: University of Oklahoma Press.

Daniels, H. & Zemelman, S. (2004). *Subjects matter: Every teacher's guide to content-area reading.* Portsmouth, NH: Heinemann.

Dingo, R. (2012). *Networking arguments: Rhetoric, transnational feminism, and public policy writing.* Pittsburgh, PA: University of Pittsburgh Press.

Dingo, R. & Strickland, D. (2012). Anxieties of globalization: Networked subjects in rhetoric and composition studies. In D. Payne & D. Desser (Eds.), *Teaching writing in globalization: Remapping disciplinary work* (pp. 79–94). Lanham, MD: Lexington Books.

Donehower, K., Hogg, C., & Schell, E. (2007). Rural Literacies (Studies in Writing and Rhetoric). Conference on College Composition and Communication.

Fecho, B. (2014). Proposal for The Ninth Annual International Dialogical Self Conference. The Hague, Netherlands.

Fecho, B. & Clifton, J. (2017). *Dialoguing across cultures, identities, and learning: Crosscurrents and complexities in literacy classrooms.* New York: Routledge.

Flower, L. (2008). *Community literacy and the rhetoric of public engagement.* Carbondale, IL: Southern Illinois University Press.

Flower, L., Long, E., & Higgins, L. (2000). *Learning to rival: A literate practice for intercultural inquiry.* New York: Routledge.

Flyvbjerg, B. (1998). *Rationality and power: Democracy in practice.* Chicago: University of Chicago Press.

Flyvbjerg, B. (2001). *Making social science matter: Why social inquiry fails and how it can succeed again.* Cambridge, UK: Cambridge University Press.

Flyvbjerg, B. (2006). Making organization research matter: Power, values, and phronesis. In S. R. Clegg, C. Hardy, T. B. Lawrence, & W. R. Nord (Eds.), *The sage handbook of organization studies* (2nd ed., pp. 370–387). Thousand Oaks, CA: Sage.

Fraser, N. (1990). Rethinking the public sphere: A contribution to the critique of actually existing democracy. *Social Text*, 25/26, 56–80.

García, O. & Li, Wei. (2014). *Translanguaging: Language, bilingualism, and education.* Basingstoke: Palgrave Macmillan.

Gee, J. P. (2003). *What video games have to teach us about learning and literacy.* New York: St. Martin's Press.

Goliya, K. (2016). Printer giant Lexmark fires Mexico factory workers demanding $0.35 raise. *The Guardian.* Available online at https://www.theguardian.com/business/2015/dec/15/printer-giant-lexmark-fires-juarez-factory-workers-demanding-raise

Green, B. & Corbett, M. (2013). *Rethinking rural literacies: Transnational perspectives.* New York: Palgrave.

Gonzales. L. (2015). Multimodality, translingualism, and rhetorical genres studies. *Composition Forum*, 31. Available online at http://compositionforum.com/issue/31/multimodality.php

Gross, A. (2006). *Starring the text: The place of rhetoric in science studies.* Carbondale, IL: Southern Illinois University Press.

Habermas, J. (1968). *Knowledge and human interests.* Trans. Jeremy Shapiro. Boston: Beacon Press.

Habermas, J. (1987). *Theory of communicative action,* volume 2: *Lifeworld and system: A critique of functionalist reason.* Trans. T. McCarthy. Boston: Beacon Press.

Habermas, J. (1996). *Between facts and norms.* Trans. W. Rehg. Cambridge, UK: Polity Press.

Hauser, G. (1999). *Vernacular voices: The rhetoric of publics and public spheres.* Columbia, SC: University of South Carolina Press.

Hermans, H. & Hermans-Konopka, A. (2010). *Dialogical self theory: Positioning and counter-positioning in a globalizing society.* Cambridge, UK: Cambridge University Press.

Higgins, L., Long, E., & Flower, L. (2006). Community literacy: A rhetorical model for personal and public inquiry. *Community Literacy Journal*, 1(1), 9–43.

Hindess, B. (1977). *Philosophy and methodology in the social sciences.* Hassocks, England: Harvester Press.

hooks, b. (1989). *Talking back: Thinking feminist, thinking black.* Brooklyn, NY: South End.

Horton, M. (1961). Myles Horton's Talk at Experimental Citizenship School Workshop, February 19–21. Highlander Archives, Box 40, folder 4, n.p. Monteagle, TN: Highlander Folk School.

Kemmis, S. (2012). Phronesis, experience, and the primacy of praxis. In E. A. Kinsella & A. Pitman (Eds.), *Phronesis as professional knowledge: Practical wisdom in the professions* (pp. 147–162). Rotterdam, Netherlands: Sense Publishers.

Kemmis, S. & Smith, T. (2008). Personal praxis: Learning from experience. In S. Kemmis & T. J. Smith (Eds.), *Enabling praxis: Challenges for education* (pp. 15–36). Rotterdam, Netherlands: Sense Publishers.

Kinloch, V. (2009). *Harlem on our minds: Place, race, and the literacies of urban youth.* New York: Teachers College Press.

Kinsella, E. A. & Pitman, A. (2012). *Phronesis as professional knowledge: Practical wisdom in the professions.* Rotterdam, Netherlands: Sense Publishers.

Kirkland, D. (2009). Researching and teaching literacy in the digital dimension. *Research in the Teaching of English*, 44(1), 8–22.

Klein, N. (2002). *Fences and windows: Dispatches from the frontlines of the anti-globalization debates.* New York: Picador.

Kroll, B. (2005). Arguing differently. *Pedagogy: Critical Approaches to Teaching Literature, Language, Composition, and Culture*, 5(1), 37–60.

Lakhani, L. & Thielman, S. (2015). Printer giant Lexmark fires Mexico factory workers demanding $0.35 raise. *The Guardian.* Available online at https://www.theguardian.com/business/2015/dec/15/printer-giant-lexmark-fires-juarez-factory-workers-demanding-raise

Long, E. (2008). Community Literacy and the Rhetoric of Local Publics. West Lafayette, IN: Parlor Press.

Long, E. (2009). Rhetorical techne, local knowledge, and challenges in contemporary activism. In Peter Goggin (Ed.), *Sustainability: Rhetorics, literacies, and narratives* (pp. 13–38). New York: Routledge/Taylor & Francis.

Long, E. (forthcoming). *A responsive rhetorical art for local public life.*

Long, E., Jarvis, J., & Deerheart Raymond, D. (2013). The Nipmuck people do exist: Imagining the what next—an experimental alternative to evidentiary legal discourse. In Christopher Wilkey & Nick Mauriello (Eds.), *Texts of consequence: Composing rhetorics of social activism for the writing classroom* (pp. 317–348). Cresskill: Hampton Press.

Lu, M. Z. & Horner, B. (2016). Introduction: Translingual work. *College English*, 78(3), 207–218.

MADD. (2015). History speaks for itself. Available online at http://www.madd.org/underage-drinking/why21/history.html

McGuire, J. E. & Tuchanska, B. (2000). *Science unfettered: A philosophical study in sociohistorical ontology.* Athens, OH: Ohio University Press.

Montgomery, K. (2006). *How doctors think: Clinical judgment and the practice of medicine.* Oxford: Oxford University Press.

Morrell, E., Dueñas, R., Garcia, V., & Lopez, J. (2013). *Critical media pedagogy: Teaching for achievement in city schools.* New York: Teachers College Press.

Montagne, R. (Interviewer) & Ellspermann, J. (Interviewee). (2016). [Interview transcript]. Oral principal weighs in on Obama directive on transgender bathrooms. Available online at http://www.npr.org/2016/05/13/477900485/principal-weights-in-on-obama-directive-on-transgender-bathrooms

Paris, D. (2010). Texting identities: Lessons for classrooms from multiethnic youth space. *English Education*, 42(3), 278–292.

Paris, D. (2012). Become history: Learning from identity texts and youth activism in the wake of Arizona SB 1070. *International Journal of Multicultural Education*, 14(2), 1–13.

Paris, D. (2013). *Language across difference: Ethnicity, communication, and youth identities in changing urban schools.* Cambridge, UK: Cambridge University Press.

Parks, S. (2013). Opportunity lost: Disciplinarity, community activism, and the grand compromise. *Trans-Scripts*, 3, 202–210.

Paroske, M. (2009). Deliberating international science policy controversies: Uncertainty and AIDS in South Africa. *Quarterly Journal of Speech*, 95(2), 148–170.

Peterson, T. R. & Horton, C. C. (1995). Rooted in the soil: How understanding the perspectives of landowners can enhance the management of environmental disputes. *Quarterly Journal of Speech*, 81, 139–166.

Phelan, A. (2005). A fall from (someone else's) certainty: Recovering practical wisdom in teacher education. *Canadian Journal of Education*, 28(3), 339–358.

Powell, M. (2014). A basket is a basket because. . .: Telling a Native rhetorics story. In J. H. Cox & D. H. Justice (Eds.), *Oxford handbook of indigenous American literature* (pp. 471–488). Oxford: Oxford University Press.

Purcell-Gates, V. (2013). Literacy worlds of children of migrant farmworker communities: Participating in a migrant head start program. *Research in the Teaching of English*, 48(1), 68–97.

Rangel, L. (2015). A wave of labor struggles in Ciudad Juárez. *Socialistworker.org*. Available online at https://socialistworker.org/2015/12/09/labor-struggles-in-ciudad-juarez

Rice, J. (2012). *Distant publics: Development rhetoric and the subject of crisis.* Pittsburgh, PA: University of Pittsburgh Press.

Rittel, H. W. J. & Webber, M. M. (1973). Dilemmas in a general theory of planning. *Policy Sciences*, 4, 155–169.

Sacchetto, D. & Cecchi, M. (2015). On the border: Foxconn in Mexico. *Open Democracy: Free Thinking for the World*. Available online at https://www.opendemocracy.net/devi-sacchetto-martìn-cecchi/on-border-foxconn-in-mexico

Schell, E. (2012). Think global, eat local: Teaching alternative agrarian literacy in a globalized age. In D. Payne & D. Desser (Eds.), *Teaching writing in globalization: Remapping disciplinary work* (pp. 39–56). Lanham, MD: Lexington Books.

Schlosser, E. (2012). *Fast food nation: The dark side of the all-American meal.* New York: Perennial.

Schön, D. (1987). *Educating the reflective practitioner.* San Francisco: Jossey-Bass.

Sellman, D. (2012). Reclaiming competence for professional phronesis. In E. A. Kinsella & A. Pitman (Eds.), *Phronesis as professional knowledge* (pp. 115–130). Rotterdam, Netherlands: Sense Publishers.

Semuels, A. (2016). Upheaval in the factories of Juarez. *The Atlantic*. Available online at http://www.theatlantic.com/business/archive/2016/01/upheaval-in-the-factories-of-juarez/424893/

Simmons, M. & Grabill, J. (2007). Toward a civic rhetoric for technologically and scientifically complex places: Invention, performance, and participation. *College Composition and Communication*, 58(3), 419–448.

Spellmeyer, K. (1993). *Common ground: Dialogue, understanding, and the teaching of composition.* Englewood Cliffs, NJ: Prentice-Hall.

Staudt, K. & Martinez, O. (2016). Staudt/Martinez: Raise Maquila wages. *Rio Grande Guardian: International News Service.* Available online at https://riograndeguardian.com/staudtmartinez-raise-maquila-wages/

Steinkuehler, C. (2008). Cognition and literacy in massively multiplayer online games. In J. Coiro, M. Knobel, C. Lankshear, & D. Leu (Eds.), *Handbook of research on new literacies* (pp. 611–634). New York: Taylor & Francis.

Villagran, L. (2016). Juárez maquiladoras see rumblings of a labor rebellion. *El Daily Post.* Available online at http://www.eldailypost.com/news/2016/01/juarez-maquiladoras-see-rumblings-of-labor-rebellion/

Walker, A. (1983). Saving the life that is your own: The importance of models in the artist's life. *In Search of Our Mothers' Gardens: Prose* (pp. 3–15). Orlando, FL: Harcourt Books.

Weart, S. R. (2008). *The discovery of global warming.* Cambridge, MA: Harvard University Press.

Young, I. M. (1997). *Intersecting voices: Dilemmas of gender, political philosophy, and policy.* Princeton, NJ: Princeton University Press.

Young, V. A., Barrett, R., Young-Rivera, Y., & Lovejoy, K. B. (2014). *Other people's English: Code-meshing, code-switching, and African-American literacy.* New York: Teachers College Press.

INDEX

CPSIA information can be obtained
at www.ICGtesting.com
Printed in the USA
FFHW012210091118
49329096-53601FF